THE COMPLETE BOOK OF
MEXICAN
COOKING

THE COMPLETE BOOK OF
MEXICAN
COOKING

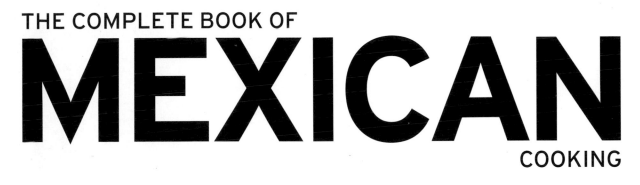

Explore the authentic taste of Mexico in over 150 fabulous recipes
shown step by step in more than 750 stunning photographs

Jane Milton

HERMES
HOUSE

This edition is published by Hermes House

Hermes House is an imprint of Anness Publishing Ltd
Hermes House, 88–89 Blackfriars Road, London SE1 8HA
tel. 020 7401 2077; fax 020 7633 9499

www.hermeshouse.com; www.annesspublishing.com

If you like the images in this book and would like to investigate using them for publishing, promotions or
advertising, please visit our website www.practicalpictures.com for more information.

© Anness Publishing Ltd 2000, 2007

Publisher: Joanna Lorenz
Executive Editor: Linda Fraser
Senior Editor: Joanne Rippin
Consultant Editor: Jenni Fleetwood
Designer: Nigel Partridge
Photography: Simon Smith (recipes) and Janine Hosegood (reference)
Food for Photography: Caroline Barty (recipes) and Annabel Ford (reference)

Front cover shows Tortilla Pie with Chorizo. For recipe see page 140.

Previously published as *Mexican*

ACKNOWLEDGEMENTS
Thanks to my Mum for typing my recipes and to Dad for proof-reading everything.
I would never have made my deadlines without your help.
Thanks too to Tom Estes of Cafe Pacifico, for sharing his knowledge of tequila
and much more, and for his enthusiasm for this project.
The publishers would like to thank South American Pictures for the use of their photographs in the book: 8bl, tr;
9tl, br; 10t; 11tl, br; 12tl, tr, bl; 13tl, m, br; 14tr, ml, bl; 15tl, br; 16tr, bl; 17tl, br; 18tr, mr, bl; 19tr, ml, bl.

ETHICAL TRADING POLICY
Because of our ongoing ecological investment programme, you, as our customer, can have the pleasure and
reassurance of knowing that a tree is being cultivated on your behalf to naturally replace the materials
used to make the book you are holding. For further information about this scheme, go to
www.annesspublishing.com/trees

NOTES
Standard spoon and cup measures are level.

Large eggs are used unless otherwise stated.

Electric oven temperatures in this book are for conventional ovens. When using a fan oven, the temperature
will probably need to be reduced by about 20–40°F. Since ovens vary, you should check with your
manufacturer's instruction book for guidance.

Contents

INTRODUCTION

Mexican food mirrors the culture of the country—it is colorful, rich, stimulating and festive. From the wild and barren north to the sultry heat of the south, this vast country offers the food lover a feast of flavors. The waters of the Gulf of Mexico and the Pacific Ocean teem with fish, while the sub-tropical regions that adjoin them yield abundant fruit, including pineapples and papayas. From the gardens of the high plateau come wonderful vegetables, while the north is cattle country. Chiles of every shape, color and size are everywhere, their flavors ranging from subtle to strident, providing the signature to one of the world's most exciting cuisines.

HISTORY OF COOKING IN MEXICO

Food is a very important aspect of the Mexican way of life. Producing and purchasing the raw materials, preparing food and eating it account for a large part of each day, and wonderful dishes are created to mark special occasions and celebrations.

Some Historical Influences on the Mexican Diet

In pre-Columbian Mexico there was already an established pattern of agriculture. Foods such as corn, beans, chiles and bell peppers were widely cultivated, along with avocados, tomatoes, sweet potatoes, guavas and pineapples. Vegetables such as *jicama*, *chayote* and *sapote* were also grown.

During the Mayan era, the priests, who were the ruling class, allocated land for the growing of crops. They also arranged for the storage of seed and the distribution of surplus food. The warlike Aztecs, who came to power in the 15th century, were less inclined to share. Their rulers appropriated food for themselves, including chocolate, which was made into a frothy drink believed to be an aphrodisiac.

The Aztecs inherited a rich culinary tradition. The central market in Tenochtitlan was famous for its fabulous array of foods, and it is reported that

Montezuma often required of his servants that they prepare more than two dozen dishes daily for his delectation. The emperor would then stroll among the groaning tables, discussing the ingredients with his chefs, before making his selection. During the subsequent meal, young women, chosen for their beauty, would bring him hot tortillas and gold cups filled with frothy chocolate.

Columbus Comes to Mexico

When the Spaniards first arrived in Mexico in 1492, they had few cooks with them, and so local people were hired to prepare food. Dishes made with corn, chiles, beans, tomatoes and chocolate were prepared, and the Spaniards became particularly fond of chiles, chocolate and vanilla. With the Spanish came livestock, which was warmly welcomed. Until this time, the native turkeys and the occasional wild boar were the only source of meat.

The introduction of the domestic pig was significant not merely for its meat, but also for the lard, which was used for frying and became a staple ingredient in Mexican kitchens. Frying had not been possible before, due to the absence of

Below: A modern mural by Diego Rivera showing pre-Columbian corn sellers.

Above: Corn cultivation in Mexico's pre-Columbian era. Mural by Diego Rivera.

animal fats and oils. The Spaniards began to adapt their own recipes to the local ingredients, and the local people in turn adapted their cooking to include meat, which had been such a rarity in the past. The fusion began.

In 1519 the Spanish adventurer Hernando Cortés landed near the site of present day Veracruz. Within three years he had conquered Mexico, and the country was ruled as a viceroyalty of Spain for the next three hundred years. Cortés portrayed himself as the liberator of the tribes oppressed by the Aztecs and used his fanatical missionary zeal to justify his own exploitation of the Mexicans. Monks and nuns were sent from Spain to convert the pagan Mexicans to Catholicism. When they reached the New World, these religious missionaries had more than missals in their luggage; they also brought seeds, and soon citrus fruit, wheat, rice and onions augmented the supplies that served the Mexican kitchen.

Texas is Lost to the United States

Mexican independence from Spain was finally gained in 1821, after a lengthy war. Three years later, on the death of General Iturbide, a new republic was established. At that time Mexico possessed large tracts of land in what is

Above: Hernando Cortés, the Spanish conqueror of Mexico.

now the United States, including Texas. In 1836 Texas formed an independent republic, joining the United States some nine years later. This triggered the Mexican Civil War, as a result of which Mexico ceded to the United States all territories north of the Rio Grande. From a culinary perspective, this is significant, as it helps to explain the historic links between Mexico and the "Lone Star" State, and the origin of the Tex-Mex style of cooking. It also accounts for the popularity of the Mexican style of cooking in California and New Mexico.

French Occupation of Mexico

The Civil War proved costly in financial terms, and put the country greatly in debt to France, England and Spain. When they could no longer repay the debt to France, that country seized the opportunity to take control of Mexico. Austrian-born Maximilian Hapsburg, a relative of Napoleon, was put in charge of the French occupation. The French met with considerable resistance and the *Cinco de Mayo* (May 5th) holiday commemorates a famous Mexican victory over their forces. However, this success was short-lived, and France installed Maximilian as the Emperor of Mexico in 1864. The French occupation lasted only three years, but left a lasting

legacy in the beautiful breads and pastries for which Mexican cooking is now renowned. Following Maximilian's execution in 1867, Mexico experienced another period of unrest, but since 1920 has been more stable.

Other Influences

The Mexican culture is often described as "*mestizo.*" The word means "a mixture" and was originally applied only to the offspring of ethnic peoples and Spanish invaders. Today it reflects many culinary influences from beyond its borders, such as the introduction of brewing by German settlers. The Germans also introduced a cheese, now called *queso de Chihuahua,* after the town in northern Mexico where the settlers lived. The presence of many sweet-and-sour

Below: Mayas in traditional dress perform the dance of the Mestizos.

dishes in the Mexican cuisine reflects an Asian influence, as does the Mexican classification of foods as "hot" or "cold." This has nothing to do with the temperature at which these foods are served, but relates instead to the effect they have on the body. "Hot" foods are considered to be easily digested and warming, whereas foods designated as "cold" are considered difficult to digest and likely to lower body heat. Examples of hot foods are coffee, honey and rice, while fish, limes and boiled eggs are all regarded as cold. A proper balance between hot and cold foods is believed to be vital for good health.

Mexican cuisine is sure to continue to evolve, adapt and embrace foreign influences. It is also likely to become more homogenous, as regional recipes are absorbed in the national repertoire. Like its language, the food and eating habits of a country are never static.

REGIONAL COOKING IN MEXICO

Mexico has not one single cuisine, but many. It is a vast country, the third largest in Latin America, with a wide diversity of landscapes, from snow-capped mountains to citrus groves, and a distinct range of climatic zones. These geographical factors have helped to shape a variety of different styles of cooking within the same country. The extremely mountainous nature of the landscape led, in the days before the Spanish Conquest, to the development of a large number of isolated and completely distinct Indian communities, each with its own style of cooking. When the Spanish invaded, they certainly had a considerable impact on the cuisine in the areas where they were most active, but parts of the country remained impervious to their influence, and the people there continued to cook in much the same

Above: Bananas and mangoes on sale in a street market in Chihuahua.

way as their parents and grandparents had done before them.

Even today, when tourism has introduced new ingredients and ideas, there remain pockets of Mexico where contact with the outside world is limited, and where old dishes, some of which hark back to Aztec times, are preserved.

The altitude, rather than the latitude, determines the climate in Mexico. The coastal region below 3000 feet is *tierra caliente*—the hot zone. Here the climate is sub-tropical, and mangoes, pineapples and avocados flourish. Next comes *tierra templada,* the temperate zone, which rises to 6000 feet.

Culinary Regions

Even in present-day Mexico, regional foods are still very important. This is due in some measure to the different climates, which mean certain things cannot grow in every area, or to favorable geographic locations: in Vera Cruz, a coastal area, fish dishes are prevalent. In the coming years this is likely to change as improved transportation allows products from the different regions to be transported more easily and quickly between areas.

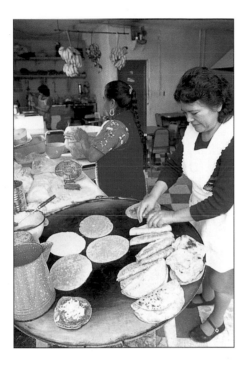

Above: Cooking tortillas in a Mexican street-cafe.

Many familiar vegetables and fruits are grown in Mexico, including green beans, bell peppers, tomatoes, cabbages, cauliflowers, onions, eggplant and zucchini. At the greatest altitude lies the cold zone (*tierra fria*).

These areas of Mexico are all very different from each other, and when it is considered that the rainfall varies from as little as 2 inches a year in the north-west to over 120 inches in parts of the southwest, it is easy to comprehend how so many diverse styles of cooking came to evolve. Better infrastructure may mean that the regionality of the cuisine will be eroded in time, but at the moment each region has a strong individual identity.

The North

The northern area of Mexico, stretching from Sonora, near the Gulf of California, to Monterrey in Nuevo León, has some striking contrasts. The mountain areas are sparsely populated, and life here is very tough. Sonora and Chihuahua are the cattle rearing parts of Mexico. Good grazing encouraged the Spanish to establish herds of their hardy longhorns here, and specialties of the region

include a beef stew called *Caldiddo* and the famous dried beef, or *carne seca*. This is produced by first salting the beef, then drying it and finally treating it with lemon juice and pepper.

The ubiquitous beans are as popular in the north as they are elsewhere. A favorite dish of the local *charros* or cowboys is *frijoles* (beans), cooked with scraps of meat, chiles, herbs and spices over an open fire. So well loved is the dish that it is often served in homes and restaurants.

Monterrey is the industrial heart of the region. Brewing employs a large percentage of the population, and this is the home of *frijoles borrachos,* a dish that consists of beans cooked in beer with onion, spices and garlic. The flavor of the beer permeates the beans, earning them their name, which translates as "drunken beans."

The north of Mexico is also the main cheese-producing region. Cheese was introduced by monks who traveled with the Spanish conquerors. Chihuahua is known for *chiles con queso*—melted cheese with chile strips.The greatest treasure of the north is the soft flour tortilla, produced here because this is the only part of Mexico where wheat is grown. Burritos, portable parcels of meat, beans and rice wrapped in wheat flour tortillas, are typical of this region.

Baja California is a peninsula in the northwestern corner of the country, bordering the Pacific and the Gulf of California. It is the oldest continuously producing wine-making region of Mexico. In recent years the region's wines, particularly the whites, have won international acclaim.

The Coastal Regions

The northern Pacific coast has some magnificent beaches. The sea is well stocked with fish, especially bass, tuna and swordfish. *Ceviche*, that delicious dish made of raw fish "cooked" by the action of lime juice, is very popular in the region. It is often made from shrimp or other local shellfish.

This area generally has good soil, and grains of various types are widely cultivated, as well as chiles and other vegetables. So famous are the tomatoes produced in this region that the state basketball team is called *Tomateros* (the tomato growers). There are a number of coconut plantations along the coast, and dishes such as coconut soup are popular. Further south is the state of Jalisco, the home of tequila. Red snapper are caught on this part of the coast and cooked over open fires.

Below: Maguey, *growing here in the Oaxaca valley, is used in tequila.*

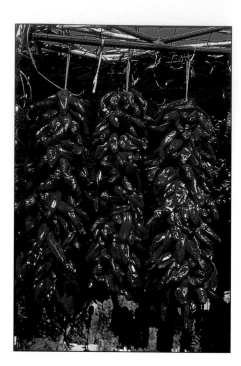

Above: Strings of chiles drying in the sun on the Pacific coast of Mexico.

Inland is the colonial town of Guadalajara, famous for *pozole*, a pork stew thickened with hominy—yellow or white corn which has been dried and has had the husk and germ removed, and which has been eaten by the Indians in Mexico for centuries. Another specialty is *birria*, a stew made from lamb or kid.

Down the coast is Acapulco, a very cosmopolitan city with Latin, Asian and indigenous Indian influences. The cuisine of this area—Oaxaca—has strong Spanish influences, but is also home to some of the most traditional Mexican dishes, such as the *moles*— gloriously rich meat stews that incorporate nuts and chocolate. This is orange country, too, and citrus fruit features strongly in the recipes of the region. *Asadero*, a supple cheese similar to the Italian cheese *Provolone*, originated in Oaxaca.

Chiapas, the southernmost state bordering Guatemala, exhibits some influences from that country. Chiles are commonly served alongside dishes, as accompaniments, rather than as integral ingredients.

The eastern seaboard, lapped by the Caribbean Sea, is known as the Gulf Coast. The climate here is tropical, and this is reflected in the food. Bananas, vanilla, avocados, coffee and coconuts grow on the coast, mangoes and pineapples in the south, and to the north are orchards of apples and pears.

The Gulf Coast has abundant fish stocks. The southern state of Tabasco, on the isthmus of Tehuantepec, is

Below: A palm tree in Chetumal with coconuts ready for harvesting.

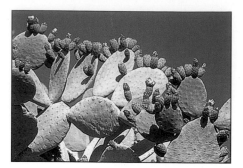

Above: Prickly pear cactus growing at Santa Bulalia.

particularly famous for its fish. The catch includes sea bass, striped bass, crabs, lobsters and shrimp. The port of Veracruz has a famous fish market, with red snapper the local specialty. The cuisine in this area is rich, and many of the towns have lent their names to dishes or ingredients.

In this part of Mexico, *tamales* (little filled parcels) are rolled in banana leaves, rather than the corn husks that are used elsewhere. Another local specialty is *jicama*, a crisp vegetable, which is served raw with a sprinkling of lime juice and ground chiles.

The Bajio, Central Mexico and Mexico City

To the north of Mexico City is the Bajio, a fertile area bordered by mountains. This is sometimes referred to as Colonial Mexico, and many of the local specialties are distinctly Spanish in origin, such as stuffed tongues and rich beef stews. Traditional Mexican foods are to be found here too, especially *nopales* (cactus paddles) and prickly pears (cactus fruit). *Pulque*—the drink made from the juice of the agave (or century) plant—is popular in this area. Pork is the favourite meat, often served as *Carnitas*. These are pieces of pork that are cooked in lard flavored with orange, until the outside of each piece is crisp, while the inside is beautifully tender and succulent.

Central Mexico, a land-locked area, lies to the south of Mexico City, and includes the towns of Puebla and Tlaxcala. Puebla is the home of the classic dish, *Chiles en Nogada*, which consists of stuffed chiles dipped in batter, then fried and served with a walnut sauce. Puebla is also associated with the famous *Mole Poblano*, which was said to have been invented by nuns in a local convent. *Mole Poblano* is a wonderfully complex dish in which turkey or chicken is cooked in a paste made by mixing crushed dried chiles, cinnamon and cloves, with sesame seeds and ground nuts, as well as onion, garlic and sometimes tomatillos.

Tlaxcala, which means "the place of many tortillas," is a town renowned for its food. Chicken stuffed with fruit and nuts is one popular dish, while another consists of lamb cooked in agave leaves. Both are usually washed down with the local *pulque*.

Vast, sprawling and vibrant, Mexico City is one of the most cosmopolitan places on earth, a fact that is reflected in its food. It is often said that Mexicans love to eat and would eat all day if they could, and in Mexico City there is nothing to stop them. The streets are filled with vendors selling all sorts of snacks. Some offer tortas and tortillas filled with various meats (including the chorizo for which nearby Toluca is famous), cheeses, beans and chiles. Others sell *tamales*, *sopes* and tacos to the commuters who rush past on their way to work. Another item available on

Above: Dried chiles and other fruit for sale on the streets of Mexico City.

Below: Thick tortillas are served here with cooked meats, chiles and beans.

market stalls is *cuitlacoche*, a corn fungus that tastes like a flavorful mushroom. This has been regarded as a delicacy since pre-Columban times. *Cuitlacoche* is cooked and used to fill *crepas* (crêpes), which the Mexicans adopted into their cuisine after the French occupation in the 19th century.

The South

Although there are differences between all the regions of Mexico, it is in the Yucatán that these are most marked. This is partly due to the isolation of the area, which was for centuries cut off from the rest of the country by dense

rainforest and swampland. The Maya lived here before the conquistadors came to Mexico, and their influence on the cooking can still be seen, particularly in *pibil*-style dishes, which got their name from the *pib* or pit in which they were steamed in Mayan times.

Although the poor soil does not readily support agriculture, corn is grown in areas where the vegetation has been cut and burned, and is ground to make meal, *masa harina*, which is used for corn tortillas and a host of other Mexican dishes. The pungent herb *epazote* is used in the cooking of this region, imparting a distinctive flavor.

Good fish, squid and shellfish, including the large shrimp for which the area is well known, are available all along the coast. *Ceviche* is a popular dish, and is made from several different types of fish and shellfish, either singly or in combination.

Huevos Motuleños, a dish of eggs with refried beans and tomato sauce, is a well known Yucatec dish. Also typical of the area are dry spice pastes, called *recados*. These are mixtures of dried spices and vinegar or citrus juice, which are rubbed onto meat before it is cooked. *Recados* are made throughout the country, but they are particularly popular in the Yucatán. Some include ground achiote seed (annatto powder), which is valued for the earthy flavor and bright yellow color it imparts. Another hallmark of Yucatec cooking is the habañero, a fiery chile that is grown exclusively in the region.

Below: A field of corn drying on the plants.

MEXICAN MEAL PATTERNS

Many of the traditional Mexican dishes are very labor-intensive, reflecting the old society where the women worked all day long collecting the food required and then preparing it. Today, despite industrialization, the traditional meal patterns are still observed, especially in rural areas. Most Mexicans still eat their main meal in the middle of the day, and follow it by a siesta. Even in the cities, where meals are beginning to conform to the international pattern of breakfast, lunch and dinner, the biggest meal of the day is still eaten at lunchtime.

Desayuno

This is a light meal eaten first thing in the morning, soon after waking. It usually consists of a cup of coffee and a bread or pastry—perhaps *churros* or *pan dulce* (sweetened bread).

Almuerzo

Having started work very early in the morning, most Mexicans are ready for something fairly substantial by about 11 AM. Almuerzo is more brunch than

Above: Prickly chayote, *used in Mexican salads and vegetable dishes.*

Below: Green chiles for sale in a Mexican market.

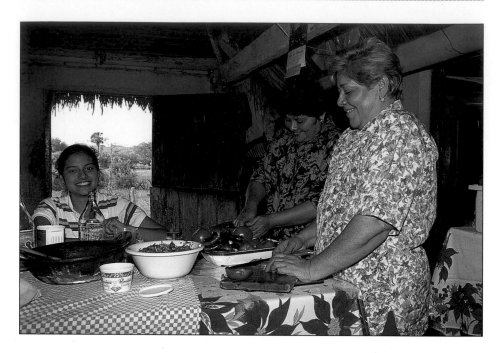

breakfast, and usually includes an egg dish such as *Huevos Rancheros* or scrambled eggs with salsa and cheese. Tortillas are served, and coffee, milk or fruit juice washes everything down.

Comida

This is the main meal of the day, generally eaten at a leisurely pace from about 3 PM. The meal is made up of several courses. Soup is almost always served, and this is followed by a rice or pasta dish. The aptly named *platillo fuerte*—the phrase means "heavy dish"—is the main attraction. This dish is accompanied by tortillas, salad and pot beans or Refried Beans. The clay pot used to cook the pot beans—*Frijoles de Olla*—adds flavor to them. Garlic, cilantro, onion and stock with chiles are additional ingredients, and cream or cheese is stirred in just before serving. The meal closes with *postre* (dessert) and an after-dinner coffee.

Merienda

A light supper, this is often made up from the leftovers of the lunchtime *comida* dishes, which are wrapped in a tortilla to make a burrito. If a more substantial meal is required, a stew or *mole* might be served, with *Cafe con Leche* or hot chocolate to follow the food. *Merienda* is usually eaten between 8 and 9 PM.

Above: Women prepare the main family meal in a rural Mexican kitchen.

Cena

This more elaborate meal—dinner—is served when entertaining guests in the evening or on special occasions. It replaces the *merienda* and is made up of two or three courses served any time between 8 PM and midnight.

The Main Event

Comida—the main meal of the day—provides the perfect opportunity for relaxing with family or friends. Here are some suggestions of suitable dishes to serve at this time:

Sopa

A hearty soup would not be appropriate, as this is the prelude to a large meal. *Thalpeno*, a thin soup with chicken and avocado, would be ideal, as would a cold coconut soup.

Sopa Seca

Translating as "dry soup," this is actually a rice or pasta dish, served after the conventional soup and before the main course. Rice or vermicelli is cooked in a little oil and then simmered in a broth with onions, garlic, tomatoes and other vegetables. Most of the liquid used is absorbed by the rice or pasta, hence the name. The rice dishes vary—peas are sometimes added to the basic recipe, and cilantro and chiles are used to make the popular "Green Rice." In another variation, yellow rice is flavored and colored with achiote (annatto), a golden coloring made from the ground seeds of a flowering tree.

Pescado y Legumbres

Sometimes a fish course is served before the main dish. Typically this would be *Ceviche*—raw fish "cooked" by the action of lime juice. Alternatively, a vegetable dish might be offered; perhaps a native vegetable such as *jicama*, served as a salad with a chili and lime dressing. Plantains are also popular, and either these or zucchini might be fried along with cheese and green chiles.

Platillo Fuerto

The "heavy dish" is typically a stew, served with corn tortillas and a salad. Meatballs in a tomato and chili sauce is one option; pork with green cactus sauce another. A fisherman's stew of mussels, scallops, shrimp and cod would also be suitable. For the accompaniment, a cactus or *chayote* salad would be ideal, or a fresh-tasting salsa of *rajas con limon*—strips of chile and lime.

Above: A family eating their main meal in an open-air restaurant in Mexico City.

Frijoles

Cooked dried beans are an inevitable and important—part of the main meal. Traditionally, they formed a very big part of the staple diet of the indigenous people, so the number and variety of bean dishes is exhaustive. Most people, if asked to name a Mexican bean dish, suggest Refried Beans, which is all too often a flavorless mush of badly seasoned pinto beans. The home-cooked equivalent couldn't be more different: tender beans deliciously flavored with bay leaves, garlic and chiles. Equally delicious are pot beans, *Frijoles de Olla*—dry pinto beans put into a pot and cooked very slowly with water and a little lard until they are tender. These are traditionally served with Guacamole, salsa, sour cream and crumbled cheese.

Postre y Cafe

After such a heavy meal, the dessert often consists of a fruit platter or a simple, refreshing *Flan*—similar to a crème caramel. A cake made from ground pecans and honey is another favorite. *Comida* traditionally concludes with a drink of coarsely ground coffee sweetened with *piloncillo* (the unrefined dark brown cane sugar typical of Mexico) and stirred with a cinnamon stick. A delicious alternative, which packs more punch, is coffee with a shot of Kahlúa or tequila.

Snack Foods

Mexicans love to snack. Street food is very popular throughout the country. In towns, stalls equipped with steamers sell *tamales*—little corn husk parcels filled with spiced meat or cheese—from first thing in the morning, so that shift workers can still have their *almuerzo* even if they cannot get home. Later in the day, the stalls sell corn soup or *menudo*, a soup made with tripe. Still more stalls are set up at lunchtime by women who serve homemade food to the workforce. The food is very similar to what would be eaten at home: soup, rice or pasta dishes, stews with tortillas or bread, and desserts. In the evening, the stalls sell *quesadillas*, enchiladas and *antojitos* ("little whims"). On the coast, traders sell shrimp on skewers, *Ceviche* (marinated raw fish) threaded on sticks or *elotes*—tender ears of cooked corn dipped in cream and sprinkled generously with well-flavored crumbly cheese.

Below: Corn on the cob is cooked and sold as a snack at street stalls.

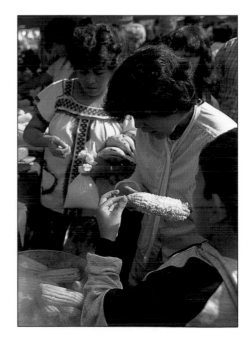

FEASTS AND FESTIVALS

Long before Christianity came to Mexico, the indigenous peoples worshipped gods whom they believed provided their food. The Aztecs were convinced that the world would come to an end unless the gods were constantly propitiated with prayers, sacrifices and rituals. Corn was regarded as a divine gift—a miraculous staple food which grew in all climates and soils.

Feast days, when people cooked particular dishes or brought specific foods as offerings to the gods, were frequent events. When Christianity spread through Mexico many of these days were appropriated by the Church and either assigned as saints' days or linked to celebrations marking important days in the religious calendar.

January 6th—*Día de los Santos Reyes*

As the culmination of two weeks of Christmas festivities, January 6th marks the meeting between the Magi—the Three Kings—and the infant Jesus. Mexicans commemorate that exchange of gifts with ceremonies of their own, and this is the day on which Christmas presents are given and received. Central to the celebration is King's Day Bread, a yeasted sweet bread ring filled with crystallized fruit, covered with icing and decorated with candied fruit jewels.

Right: Mayas in traditional dress perform a bottle dance.

Below: A Mexican dancer wearing a Spanish-influenced traditional dress.

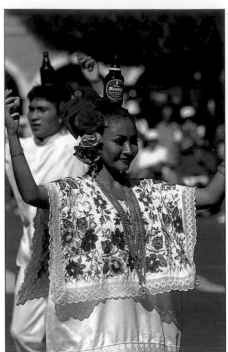

February—Carnival

The weekend before the beginning of Lent sees the beginning of a five-day carnival, a final fling before the period of self-denial. Processions of brightly colored floats, dancing in the street and feasting are all characteristic of this celebration.

April—*Semana Santa*

Holy week—the period leading up to Easter Day—is an important time in the Mexican calendar, particularly for the many Catholics in the country. One custom peculiar to Mexico is the breaking of confetti-filled eggs over the heads of friends and family.

May 5th—*Cinco de Mayo*

This day commemorates the defeat of the French army at the Battle of Puebla in 1862. After the defeat Napoleon sent 30,000 soldiers into the country, and after a year the French had taken power. *Cinco de Mayo* is of particular importance in the state of Puebla, but is celebrated in other parts of the country and in some American states with large Mexican populations such as southern central California and Texas. Nowadays the holiday is a celebration of Mexican culture, drink and music.

Above: Sugar skulls on sale for the celebration of one of Mexico's most important festivals, The Day of the Dead.

September 16th—Mexican Independence Day

A holiday to mark the day in 1810 when the revolt against Spanish rule began. Outside Mexico, the festival is often promoted by commercial outlets, such as Mexican restaurants and bars.

November 1 & 2—*Los Días de los Muertes*

Commonly called The Day of the Dead, this is in fact a two-day festival that combines in one both the ancient Aztec tradition of worship of the dead and the Christian festival of All Saints' Day.

The festival originally came about because of a widely held belief that the souls of the dead are permitted to spend a brief period on earth every year—like a vacation—to give their families a chance to spend time with them. Family members gather at the graveside, bringing the favorite foods of the deceased person, as well as other symbolic dishes that are traditionally eaten on this day. The foods include a sweet pumpkin dessert and *tamales*. At the grave candles are lit, incense is burned, special prayers are said and the food and drink are eaten in a party atmosphere. Although the festival

commemorates the dead, it is seen by everyone as a joyous occasion. The Mexican attitude is that life is to be lived to the full, and death is simply a part of the cycle.

December 25th—*Navidad*/Christmas Day

For 12 days before Christmas Day, the festival is heralded by processions—called "*posadas*"—depicting Joseph, with Mary on the donkey, searching for a room at the inn. Christmas Day sees

Below: A shop window advertises "bread of the dead" for the festival.

the start of a two-week family holiday for most Mexicans. On the afternoon of the day itself families share a special meal. This traditionally starts with the sharing of the *rosca*—a sweet ring-shaped loaf with a small ceramic doll representing the infant Jesus baked inside it. Whoever finds the doll in their slice of cake must host a party on February 2nd, *Día de Candelaria* (Candlemas). The high point of the Christmas feast is the main course, when *Mole Poblano*, a rich turkey dish made with chiles, nuts, tomatoes, garlic, cinnamon and chocolate is served. It is accompanied by *tamales blancos*—corn husk parcels filled with a flavored mixture that is based on white cornmeal.

Mexican Weddings

These almost always take place in church. It is traditional for the bride and groom to be united during the ceremony with a *lazo*—a large rosary that is wrapped around them both. Gold or silver coins, a Bible and a rosary are given to the couple during the service by the "*padrinos*," a man and woman especially chosen by the bride and groom for this task. The coins symbolize prosperity. Mexican wedding cookies are served at the subsequent feast. Made from almonds and butter, baked and then sprinkled with confectioners' sugar, these have a shortbread-like texture.

MEXICAN COOKING OUTSIDE MEXICO

In the United States, there has been a tremendous growth in the number of Mexican restaurants and establishments serving what has come to be known as Tex-Mex food—Mexican food with a Texan influence. Sadly, these restaurants are not always very representative of the wonderful and varied cuisine Mexico has to offer, but what they have done is to stimulate interest in Mexican food and therefore a demand for more authentic Mexican ingredients and equipment. The growing popularity of Mexico among tourists has created even more of an interest in the country's varied cuisine.

United States

Mexicans who have emigrated to the United States for political, economic or personal reasons have created their own communities within that country. Parts of the United States, such as southern California and Texas, which have strong historical links to Mexico as well as sharing a common border, have large communities of Mexicans and offer some of the best Mexican food. The Mexican cuisine in these areas has evolved over time to please the palates

Below: Mexican chiles, when dried, are exported all over the world.

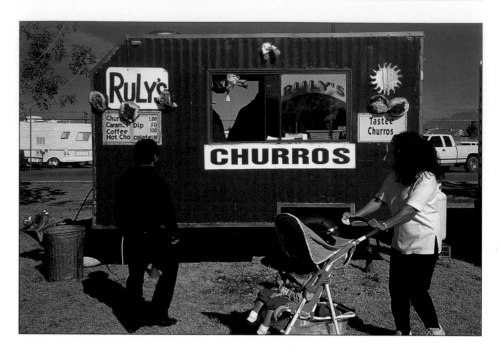

of local residents. Authentic Mexican ingredients are used, but American products are as well. This style of cooking is often referred to as "fusion," the combining of ingredients and flavors from several cultures in one dish, a practice that carries with it the real danger of diluting each country's contribution and distorting the diners' perceptions of each cuisine. In southern California and Texas, however, authentic Mexican ingredients tend to be readily available, thanks to demand and to the proximity to the border, and improved transportation links across Mexico and into the United States ensure that products arrive fresh and undamaged.

The same cannot be said for the rest of the United States. Availability of authentic Mexican ingredients varies from state to state, and some fruits and types of chile are difficult, if not quite impossible, to obtain.

Other items, such as pinto beans, squash, avocados and chocolate, have become such an integral part of the American diet that few people would consider them to be Mexican foods.

Europe

With the growing number of European people vacationing in Mexico, the trend for new culinary flavors or experiences

Above and below: Fast-food stalls serving Mexican or Tex-Mex food are a common sight all over the United States, especially in the South. These two stalls are in New Mexico.

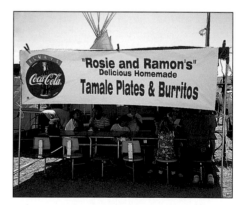

and the increasing market for travel features on television and in magazines, interest in Mexican cuisine has escalated. Nowhere is this more apparent than in Scandinavia, where Mexican food is enormously popular.

Increased demand has led to more varieties of fresh and dried chiles becoming available at both major supermarkets and specialty stores, and this in turn has persuaded more people to experiment with cooking Mexican food at home. The most significant advance in recent years has been the introduction of ready-made corn and flour tortillas at supermarkets and in heat-sealed packages that can be kept in the refrigerator until needed, when they are heated very briefly in the microwave. These have made many dishes much more accessible to the average home cook. People for whom Mexican food meant serving chile in a taco shell—and who were put off by the sheer messiness of this awkward dish—

Above: Tequila husks. Tequila has grown in popularity around the world.

Below: An American fast-food stall selling Mexican-inspired roasted corn.

discovered ready-made tortillas and were soon experimenting with making fajitas and enchiladas, at first using prepared sauces and ready meals, but then becoming more adventurous. Supermarkets sell ready-made Guacamole, but in order to give it a shelf life, add extra ingredients such as mayonnaise that dull the fresh, clean taste of the original dish. More discerning cooks still prefer to make their own.

Burritos, nachos and chimichangas are becoming well known, with cooks beginning now to differentiate between Mexico's regional cuisines. Just as the more regional Indian restaurants have persuaded the public that all of India cannot be represented by "chicken curry," so people are becoming familiar with the variety and depth of Mexican cuisine and are beginning to seek out more authentic Mexican dishes.

Good quality, reasonably priced Mexican ingredients are available by mail order from a number of specialty suppliers, and this has made it much easier for the enthusiast to recreate genuine dishes at home. Traditional Mexican cooking equipment such as *metates* (used for grinding *masa harina*) and the *molcajete* and *tejolote* (the

Above: Chocolate is now so widespread that people don't necessarily link it with its country of origin, Mexico.

Mexican mortar and pestle) are also available by mail order, but many of the functions for which these utensils are intended are either not necessary or can be carried out just as quickly and efficiently in a food processor.

Restaurants

In America and to a lesser extent in Europe, a number of restaurant chains specializing in Mexican and Tex-Mex food have been established. Tex-Mex restaurants tend to offer burgers and steaks alongside predominantly tortilla-based dishes, so it is not surprising that many people perceive these as being all that Mexico has to offer. Even some restaurants purporting to serve authentic Mexican food perpetuate the myth that Mexicans eat plates piled high with indistinguishable mounds of food, all fairly bland, covered with melted cheese, dollops of sour cream, Guacamole and salsa. In the United States there is an increasing number of small restaurants serving authentic dishes from all over Mexico. A welcome trend indeed.

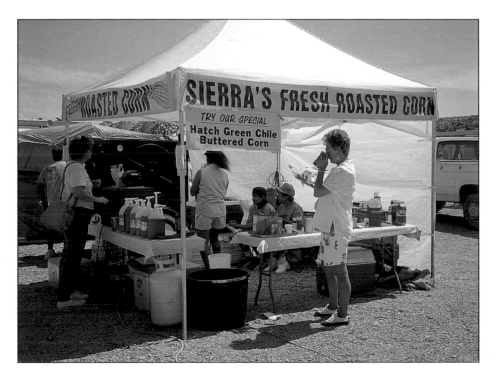

EQUIPMENT

You need very little by way of specialty equipment in order to cook Mexican food. Most modern Mexican kitchens today have a food processor to do much of the chopping and grinding. However, the items listed below will make many of the tasks easier and are worth investing in if you make a lot of Mexican food.

Tortilla Press

Traditionally, tortillas were always shaped by hand. Skilled women were able to make an astonishing number of perfectly shaped tortillas in a very short time, but this is something of a dying art today. Most people now use metal tortilla presses. Cast iron presses are the most effective, but they must be seasoned (oiled) before use and carefully cared for, so many people today prefer steel presses. These come in various sizes and are heavy, in order to limit the leverage needed to work them. Cover the plates with plastic bags or waxed paper and it will be easier to lift the tortillas once they are pressed. Tortilla presses are available at good specialty kitchenware stores and by mail order.

Comal

This is a thin, circular griddle, traditionally used over an open fire to cook tortillas. A cast iron griddle or large frying pan will do this job equally well.

Right: Tortilla press

Above: Metate

Below: Comal

Metate

A *metate* is a grinding stone used to grind corn to make *masa*. It is also used to grind cocoa and *piloncillo* (unrefined cane sugar). The design has not changed for centuries. Made from a sloping piece of volcanic rock, it has three short legs. Before a new *metate* can be used, it must be tempered. A mixture of dry rice and salt is placed on the grinding surface and the *muller*—the implement that does the actual grinding—is used to press the mixture into the surface and remove any loose pieces of sand or grit. The *muller* is made of the same stone as the *metate* and is called a *mano* or *metlapil*. These are quite difficult to locate outside Mexico, but are available by mail order.

Molcajete and Tejolote

The mortar and pestle of Mexico, the *molcajete* and *tejolote* are made from porous volcanic rock and must be tempered in the same way as the *metate* before being used. They are ideal for grinding spices such as achiote (annatto) or for grinding nuts and seeds when making *Mole Poblano*.

Tortilla Warmer

Ideal for keeping tortillas warm at the table, this is a small round basket or clay dish with a lid. The size most readily available outside Mexico is suitable for 6-inch tortillas. Look for them at specialty kitchenware stores.

Below:
Molinollo and wire whisk

Right: Molcajete *and* Tejolote

Left: Dishes

Ollas

These are the clay pots traditionally used for cooking stews and sauces. They give food a unique flavor, but are seldom found outside Mexico, as they are quite fragile. Sadly, they are becoming relatively rare in Mexico too. Flat earthenware dishes decorated around the edge are used for serving and are more easily found than *ollas*.

Molinollo

A carved wooden implement used for whisking drinking chocolate. Some of these are beautiful and are popular with tourists. A wire whisk can also be used.

Above: Ollas

INGREDIENTS

Across Mexico, the very different types of terrain and variations in climate provide a remarkable range of ingredients. Mexicans are very resourceful, and have made good use of their native foods, as well as adapting many of the ingredients and recipes brought by successive settlers. Some of their favorite foods will be familiar, others will be unusual, still more may seldom be seen outside their country of origin, but as the popularity of Mexican food continues to soar, ingredients that were once rare will become increasingly commonplace. This chapter is a guide to key ingredients, and offers advice on purchasing, preparing and storing, as well as cooking tips.

CORN

The native Indians of Mexico regarded corn as a gift from the gods. How else would they have come by such a versatile food, so hardy and adaptable and able to flourish in all the different climates and soils of their country? They offered up gifts to the god of corn, celebrated him on feast days and even added tiny grains of corn pollen to their traditional sand paintings to give the artworks healing powers. A popular myth held was that corn was in fact the very stuff from which the gods created people. Even now, corn accounts for almost 20 percent of the world's calories taken from food.

In the traditional Navajo Indian wedding ceremony, the bride's

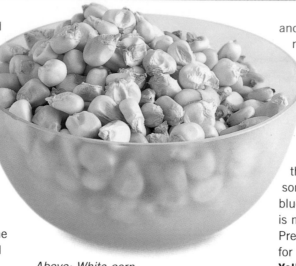

Above: White corn

grandmother presents the couple with a basket of cornmeal and the couple exchanges a small handful with each other—such is the significance of corn in their culture.

Every part of an ear of corn is used in Mexican culture: the husks for wrapping *tamales*, the silk in medicines, the kernels for food and the stalks for animal feed. The husks from corn are most commonly used for *tamales*, but are also used for wrapping some other foods before cooking. When they are ready, the husks can be peeled off from the filling. The husks are not eaten, but are discarded once the *tamales* are cooked. In Oaxaca, *tamales* are wrapped in banana leaves, which impart a distinctively different flavor.

Varieties and Uses

Corn is the common name for a cereal grass. With wheat and rice, it is one of the world's key grain crops. A native of the Americas, it was introduced into Europe by Columbus, who brought it to Spain. A wide variety of products are produced from corn, including corn syrup, bourbon and starch.

Hybrid varieties of corn can be produced very easily, as corn mutates and adapts to different surroundings readily. There are a few main types of corn used for food, each with several different varieties.

Flint corn This is also known as Indian corn and is described as "flint" because of the hard texture of the kernel. This can be red, blue, brown or purple, which has made this type of corn a popular choice for some of the more novel foods such as blue or red corn tortilla chips. Popcorn is made from a type of flint corn. Predominantly, however, flint corn is used for industrial purposes and animal feed.

Yellow corn A type of "dent" corn, so called because the sides of the kernel are composed of a hard starch and the crown of a softer starch, which shrinks to form the characteristic depression or dent. Yellow corn has large, full-flavored kernels and is used for making many processed foods. It is also the basic ingredient used in corn syrup, cornstarch and corn oil.

White corn is used to make *masa*, a type of dough that is widely used in Mexican cooking. It may seem odd to call it white corn, when the resulting *masa* is actually quite yellow, but the kernels are noticeably whiter than those of yellow corn varieties.

Flour corn is composed largely of soft starch and can readily be ground to make flour for use in baked goods.

Below: Red corn

Above: Blue corn

Below: Corn husks; fresh and dried

Preparing Dried Corn Husks

If you are able to buy dried corn husks you will need to make them soft and pliable before using.

Soak the corn husks in a bowl of cold water for several hours. When they are soft, remove them from the bowl and pat dry.

Place the husks flat on a dry surface. Pile on the filling, then tie in neat parcels before steaming.

Grinding produces the very white cornstarch with which we are familiar, and which is the main constituent of custard powder.

Sweet corn contains more natural sugar than other types of corn. The kernels can be eaten right off the cooked ear, and in Mexico a favorite snack is *elotes con crema*, where ears of corn are dipped in cream and sprinkled with fresh cheese before being served. The kernels can also be stripped from the cobs and used in soups and vegetable dishes. As soon as the corn is picked, the sugar in the kernels starts to convert to starch. This reduces the natural sweetness, so it is important that the corn is eaten as soon as possible after being picked. Strip off the husks and remove the silks (the thread-like stigmas that catch the pollen) before boiling or steaming the corn, or baking it. Corn can also be cooked on a broiler or grill, which gives the crisp kernels a delicious smoky taste. This is how the Mexicans cook corn on the street as a fast food snack.

Masa/Masa Harina

Masa is the Mexican word for dough, and specifically refers to the fresh corn dough used to make corn tortillas and other corn dishes. The flour—or *masa harina* is traditionally made with sun-dried or fire-dried white corn kernels which have been cooked in water mixed with lime (calcium oxide, not the fruit). They are then soaked in the lime water overnight. The lime helps to swell the kernels and brings about a chemical change that greatly improves the flavor of the *masa*. The wet corn is subsequently ground, using a *metate*—a traditional grinding stone that no self-respecting Mexican kitchen would be without. The resulting *masa* can be used for making corn tortillas—for *tamales*, other ingredients, such as chicken stock and lard, need to be added.

In America it is possible to buy fresh *masa* at the factories producing tortillas, but it is not available elsewhere. You can make your own *masa*, but it is a lengthy process and the essential lime is not easy to come by. If you do decide try, it is well worth making a large batch of it and freezing the surplus. *Masa* freezes well, although it will only keep in the refrigerator for a few days.

Right: Two types of Masa harina

Above: Wet corn being ground on the traditional metate.

In some parts of Mexico they serve blue corn *masa* dishes, using the same dough-making process, but a less common corn type.

Corn Tortillas

Have ready a tortilla press and two clean plastic bags, slit if necessary so that they will lie flat. Tortillas are more traditionally cooked on a special griddle called a *comal*, but a cast-iron griddle or large heavy frying pan will work just as well.

MAKES 12 × 6-INCH TORTILLAS

INGREDIENTS
    2 cups *masa harina*
    pinch of salt
    1 cup warm water

1 Place the *masa harina*, salt and water in a large bowl and combine using a wooden spoon until it forms a dough.

2 Turn out the dough onto a lightly floured surface and knead well for 3–4 minutes, until firm, smooth and no longer sticky. Cover the bowl with plastic wrap and let the dough stand at room temperature for 1 hour.

3 Pinch off 12 pieces of dough of equal size and roll each piece into a ball. Work with one piece of dough at a time, keeping the rest of the pieces of dough covered with plastic wrap so that they do not dry out.

4 Open the tortilla press and place a plastic bag on the bottom. Put a dough ball on top and press with the palm of your hand to flatten slightly.

5 Lay a second plastic bag on top of the round of dough and close the press. Press down firmly several times to flatten the dough into a thin round.

6 Place a large frying pan or griddle over medium heat. Open the press and lift out the tortilla, keeping it sandwiched between the plastic bags. Carefully peel off the first bag, then gently turn the tortilla over onto the palm of your hand. Carefully peel off the second plastic bag.

7 Flip the tortilla onto the hot frying pan or griddle and cook for about 1 minute or until the lower surface is blistered and is just beginning to turn golden brown. Turn over using a spatula and keep warm until ready to serve.

8 Place a clean dish towel in a large ovenproof dish. Transfer the cooked tortilla to the dish, wrap the dish towel over the top and cover with a lid. Keep warm while you cook the remaining tortillas in the same way.

COOK'S TIP
If you do not have a tortilla press, you can improvise by placing the dough between two clean plastic bags and rolling it out with a rolling pin.

Basic *Masa*
Traditionally, tortillas are made with *masa*. *Masa* is made by mixing dried white corn with food grade calcium oxide, although this is difficult to locate in small quantities. For making tortillas, most cooks, even in Mexico, find it easier to use *masa harina*, which is the flour made when *masa* is dried and ground. *Masa harina* should not be confused with cornmeal or polenta, which are made from corn that has not been soaked or cooked with lime. The taste of tortillas made with *masa harina* is slightly different from that of tortillas made from fresh *masa*, but the flour is much easier to cook with and eliminates the need for a *metate*.

Flour Tortillas

Flour tortillas are more common than corn tortillas in the north of Mexico, especially in the areas around Sonora and Chihuahua, where wheat is grown. Flour tortillas differ from corn tortillas in that they include lard, which gives them more pliability and elasticity. For best results, make sure you use good quality all-purpose flour.

MAKES ABOUT 12 × 10-INCH TORTILLAS

INGREDIENTS
    5 cups all-purpose flour,
      sifted
    ½ teaspoon baking powder
    pinch of salt
    scant ½ cup lard
    ½ cup warm water

1 Mix the flour, baking powder and salt in a large bowl. Rub in the lard, then gradually add enough water to draw the flour together into a stiff dough.

2 Turn out the dough onto a lightly floured work surface and knead it for 10–15 minutes, until it is elastic.

3 Divide the dough into 12 even-size pieces and roll into balls using the palms of your hand. Cover the pieces with plastic wrap while you are working to keep them from drying out.

4 Roll out each ball on a lightly floured surface. Give the dough a quarter turn after each roll to keep the round even. Keep rolling until the round is about 12 inches.

5 Warm a large heavy frying pan or griddle over medium heat. Cook one tortilla at a time, placing each one in the ungreased pan or on the griddle and cooking it for 45 seconds–1 minute or until the lower surface begins to blister and brown. Turn over and cook the other side for about 1 minute.

6 Wrap the cooked tortillas in a clean, dry dish towel to keep them soft and warm while you make the rest.

COOK'S TIPS
• If the corn tortillas crack when they are pressed, remove the dough from the press, return it to the bowl and add a little extra water.
• To reheat cold tortillas, sprinkle them with a few drops of water, wrap them in foil and place in an oven preheated to 275°F for 10 minutes. Alternatively, wrap them in plastic wrap and microwave on maximum power for about 20 seconds.

Quick and Easy Tortilla Fillings
• Cut a skinned chicken breast into thin slices and stir-fry with slices of red and yellow bell pepper. When the chicken is cooked, add the juice of a lime and some fresh oregano, add salt and pepper to taste then use the mixture to fill freshly warmed tortillas. Add some grated cheese, if desired, and a spoonful of sour cream.
• If you have some rice and refried beans left from the previous day, combine them and reheat in a frying pan with a little oil. When the mixture is thoroughly heated, spoon it into the tortillas with some grated cheese, slices of tomato and chopped scallions.
• Stir-fry some mushrooms with plenty of black pepper. Add a dash of soy sauce and a little heavy cream, season to taste, then spoon into the tortillas.

FOLDING AND COOKING TORTILLAS

Many Mexican dishes are made with tortillas. The difference lies in the filling, folding and cooking.

Burritos

These are flour tortilla envelopes enclosing various fillings and then folded into the classic shape and sealed with flour and water.

Chimichangas

A chimichanga is a burrito that has been folded, chilled to let the edges seal and then deep fried in hot oil until crisp and golden.

Chalupas

Chalupas are pieces of *masa* shaped to resemble canoes or boats and fried until opaque and golden. They are topped with beans, salsa and cheese.

Enchiladas

These can be made from either corn or wheat tortillas. A little filling is laid down the center of a tortilla, which is then rolled to make a tube, much like cannelloni. Filled tortillas are laid side by side in a baking dish before being topped with a sauce and baked or finished under the broiler.

Fajitas

These are ideal for informal dinner parties, as various fillings are placed on the table with the hot tortillas, and guests fill and roll their own. The tortilla is then folded to form a pocket around the filling.

Flautas

Corn tortillas are filled with a pork or chicken mixture, rolled tightly into flute shapes, then fried until crisp.

Quesadillas

These tasty treats are made by placing a corn or flour tortilla in a warm frying pan and spreading one half lightly with salsa. A little chicken or a few shrimp are sometimes added, and fresh cheese is sprinkled on top. The other half of the tortilla is then folded over, and the quesadilla is cooked for 1–2 minutes, during which time it is turned once.

Tacos

The crisp tortilla shells that are often sold in supermarkets as tacos are in fact a Tex-Mex invention. True Mexican tacos are corn tortillas that have been filled and folded in half; they still remain soft. *Taquitos* are miniature tacos—ideal for picnics or parties.

Tostadas

These are individual corn tortillas fried until crisp and then topped with shredded meat, Refried Beans, salsa, Guacamole, sour cream and a little fresh cheese. The finger-food versions are called *tostaditas*.

Totopos

Triangles of corn tortilla, fried until crisp, are called *totopos*. Serve them with salsa—they are delicious served while still warm.

READY-MADE TORTILLAS

Making Mexican meals is much easier than it once was, thanks to the availability of ready-made tortillas and tortilla chips.

Corn Tortillas

Many supermarkets stock 6-inch fresh corn tortillas. Look for them in the bread section. They are ideal for making tacos, tostadas, *totopos* and enchiladas. They do not have a very long shelf life, but they do freeze well. Follow the manufacturer's instructions for warming them, as methods vary.

Flour Tortillas

These are available in 6-inch, 8-inch and 10-inch rounds, and the packaging is usually marked in inches rather than centimeters. The smallest ones are perfect for fajitas or flour tortilla quesadillas, while the 8-inch tortillas are a good size for large quesadillas (to share). Use the largest tortillas for burritos and chimichangas, as they allow more room for the filling. Like corn tortillas, fresh flour tortillas are sold in the bread section of supermarkets or in vacuum packages in the ethnic food section. The longer-life products tend to be a bit drier and less pliable than the fresh variety, which can be frozen. Flour tortillas sold at stores often contain lard, which makes them softer than the ones that use vegetable oil or fat.

Above: Corn tortillas

Below: Wheat flour tortillas

Taco Shells

A Tex-Mex invention, these are so awkward to eat that they are responsible for turning many people off Mexican food. They are, however, an excellent substitute for *chalupas*, if making your own seems too much like hard work. Fill them with salsa, beans and fresh, crumbly cheese.

Tortilla Chips

The quality and authenticity of these vary greatly. The best are often to be found in the ethnic food sections of supermarkets rather than with the chips and snacks. Many of the ones sold in the snack food section have added flavorings, some of which are not remotely Mexican. Plain, lightly salted chips are best for dipping with salsa. Many specialty food stores and health food stores sell organic corn chips and naturally colored red and blue corn chips (made from colored corn kernels). These look especially good mixed with yellow corn chips in a dish. Warm them in a low oven or microwave before serving.

Above: Blue and yellow tortilla chips. Plain, lightly salted chips are best for dipping with salsa.

Below: Taco shells are difficult to eat but do have their uses.

BEANS AND RICE

The importance of beans in the Mexican diet cannot really be overestimated. Indigenous to the country, they were cultivated by the Indians along with corn, and the two staple crops coexisted in a remarkable fashion. Successive plantings of corn soon deplete the soil; beans enrich it by introducing nitrogen. The early inhabitants of Mexico knew this, and planted both together. They ate them together too, and benefited from the fact that beans supplied nutrients corn lacked and, unlike corn, were also an excellent source of protein. Rice was first introduced to Mexico by the Spanish and is also an important staple ingredient.

BEANS

Beans continue to be a staple food in Mexico, and there is a pot of dried beans simmering daily on the stove in many homes. Fresh beans are eaten, too, of course, but it is the dried beans, with their better keeping properties, that are most widely used. They make a colorful display on market stalls, and there are many different varieties to choose from.

Popular Varieties

Pinto beans and black beans are the most commonly used dried beans in Mexico, although lima beans, which are sold both fresh and dried, are used in a number of dishes and side dishes.

Chickpeas, which in Mexico are called garbanzos, are not native to the country but were brought in from the Middle East. They have become popular, however, and feature in several dishes.

Pinto beans Pinto is Spanish for "painted" and refers to the speckles of red-brown on the pale pink skins. These beans are native to Latin America and are now widely used in most Spanish-speaking countries. A rich source of protein and iron, they are only available dried. Mexicans use them for all sorts of dishes, but it is as *Frijoles de Olla*, the simple bean dish that is eaten daily in most homes, that they are most familiar. The cooked beans are also the basis of *Refritos* (Refried Beans), and are used in salsas.

Black beans Small, with black skin and cream-colored flesh, these beans have a wonderfully sweet flavor. Do not confuse them with black-eyed peas, which are white, with a small black eye. The glossy skins look particularly attractive after cooking. They are used in soups and salsas, and are often substituted for pinto beans in *Frijoles de Olla*. Despite their small size, black beans can take quite a long time to

Above: Pinto beans

soften when cooked, so always test before draining to ensure that they are perfectly tender.

Buying and Storing

Dried beans keep very well, but not indefinitely, so it is best to buy them in relatively small quantities, at a store with rapid turnover. That way, they are likely to be tender and full of flavor when soaked and cooked, unlike beans that have been kept for too long, which become dry and so hard that they are only fit for use as weights in pie crusts. Store beans in tightly closed containers in a cool, dry place.

Preparation

Before you use dried beans, put them in a colander or sieve and pick them over, removing any foreign bodies, then rinse them thoroughly under cold running water. Drain, transfer to a large bowl and pour in plenty of cold water.

Above: Black beans

Let soak for several hours and preferably overnight. Alternatively, you can boil the beans in plenty of water for 3–4 minutes, then cover the pan and set it aside for an hour before cooking. This is very useful when you have forgotten to soak beans for a particular dish, although the long cold soak is preferable.

Main Uses and Cooking Tips

In Mexico, beans are widely used in soups, as fillings for tortillas, in many meat dishes and on their own, either freshly cooked or refried.

To cook pre-soaked dried beans, simply drain them thoroughly, then put them in a clean pan with plenty of water. Do not add salt, as this would cause the skins on the beans to toughen. Bring the water to a boil and then cook for the time recommended in the individual recipes, usually 1–1¼ hours.

Right: Long-grain (top) and ground rice

Cooking times can vary considerably, so always taste for tenderness before finally draining and serving the beans.

RICE

Mexicans have been using rice since it was introduced to the country by the Spanish in the 16th century. It was originally brought to Mexico from the Philippines and was also shipped on to Spain itself.

Description and Varieties

The rice grown and used in Mexico is long-grain— this means that each grain is four times longer than its width. White long-grain rice that has had the husk removed is most common, although it is often not as refined as the white rice most widely sold in the West.

Buying and Storing

Most rice for sale in the West comes in packages. It keeps extremely well in a cool, dry place, but once packages are opened, any unused rice should be transferred to an airtight container and used as soon as possible. For Mexican food, it is important to use rice that absorbs the flavors of other ingredients well. It is customary to use ordinary long-grain rice, but you may want to experiment with other types.

Main Uses and Cooking Tips

Rice is used in a variety of Mexican dishes, from *sopa seca* (dry soup), which is served as a separate course in the *comida* or main meal, to rice pudding. When served as an accompaniment, rice is usually mixed with other ingredients, as in the popular Green Rice, which includes chiles, and Yellow Rice, which owes its color to achiote (annatto). Ground rice is used as a flour (*harina de arroz*) in cakes and cookies. *Horchata* is a drink made with rice that has been soaked and then finely ground. Most Mexicans tend to soak their rice in boiled water for a minimum of 10 minutes before they cook it. This reduces the cooking time and also encourages the rice to absorb other flavors. After soaking, it should be drained thoroughly before being cooked.

CHOCOLATE, NUTS AND SEEDS

Candy, cookies, cakes and pastries are much loved by the Mexicans, but the sweet ingredients that go into these are also used in savory dishes, and chocolate, along with various types of nuts and seeds, is a very important element of Mexican cooking.

CHOCOLATE

When the Spanish reached Mexico, they discovered a wealth of unfamiliar ingredients, including potatoes, vanilla, avocados and squash. One of their greatest finds, however, was chocolate. The Aztecs were very partial to a drink made from the beans of the cacao tree, which they flavored in many different ways, and the Spanish, like the rest of the world after them, embraced this wonderful new taste with enthusiasm,

developing a fondness for a variation that included corn, honey and spices.

The conquistadors took chocolate back to Spain, and it was not long before all the most fashionable resorts and cities in Europe boasted cocoa houses. Initially it was served as a drink, but Spanish women also prepared it as candy, mixing it with sugar, cinnamon, eggs and almonds. Europeans started producing chocolate in slabs some two hundred years later, but women in Guatemala began pressing chocolate powder into bars for storage some time before this. When slabs of chocolate were finally produced in Mexico, the chocolate was sweetened and spiced in Spanish style.

Mexican Chocolate

This is made using dark and bitter chocolate mixed with sugar, ground nuts and cinnamon, and pressed into disks. The chocolate has a grainy quality, thanks to the sugar and almonds, and is crumbly when broken. One of the most popular brands is *Ibarra*, which comes in a distinctive yellow hexagonal box. Some specialty suppliers outside Mexico stock this product.

Buying and Storing

Mexican chocolate comes in packages, each containing five or six disks that are wrapped individually in waxed paper. Check the package for a use-by date. Store in a cool, dry place.

Left: Ibarra chocolate

Making Mexican Chocolate

If you cannot buy Mexican chocolate, you can still make an acceptable substitute, using dark bitter chocolate with a minimum of 70 percent cocoa solids.

Break 4 ounces dark chocolate into pieces and put it in a food processor. Add ¼ cup ground almonds, ¼ cup sugar and 2 teaspoons ground cinnamon. Process into a fine powder, then transfer into an airtight container, close the lid tightly and store in the refrigerator for up to 2 weeks, using as needed.

Main Uses and Cooking Tips

The main use for chocolate in Mexico is still as a beverage. Mexicans are very partial to *Champurrada*, a chocolate corn drink, and the classic Mexican Hot Chocolate, which is whisked into a froth with a special whisk called a *molinollo*. Mexican Hot Chocolate is served with *Churros*, long fritters that are dunked in the drink, or *Pan Dulce*, the sweet bread that Mexicans eat for breakfast or as a snack late in the day. The extra ingredients make Mexican chocolate unsuitable for *moles*, the rich stews to which chocolate is traditionally added, so bitter chocolate or cocoa is used.

NUTS AND SEEDS

The three types of nut that are most widely used in Mexican cooking are the pecan, walnut and almond. Pine nuts are used in some desserts and pastries, and coconuts are valued both for their flesh and the cooling liquid they contain. Pecans grow in Northern Mexico. Walnuts, which were introduced from Europe, are cultivated in the colder, central highlands. The Spanish introduced almonds into Mexican cooking during the colonial era, but ensured that the trade with Spain was not disrupted by making it illegal for Mexicans themselves to cultivate them on a large scale.

Seeds from various types of pumpkin and squash have been important ingredients in Mexican cooking for centuries. At one time, pumpkins were grown mainly for their seeds; the flesh was discarded. Sesame seeds are also used, both in pastes and as a garnish on dishes such as *Mole Poblano*.

Buying and Storing

All types of nuts have a limited shelf life once they have been shelled. The oil in them quickly turns rancid, so they should only be bought as needed, and stored in a cool, dry place for as short a time as possible. Nuts can, however, be frozen.

Main Uses and Cooking Tips

Salted or coated with sugar, pecans are eaten as a snack food, but their primary use is in desserts such as Pecan Cake. Almonds are used extensively, either whole, chopped or ground, and in sweet and savory dishes, including soups. Mexicans use ground almonds to thicken sauces, and substitute ground almonds for flour in some cakes and cookies. Walnuts are also used in cookies, including *Polvorones de Nuez*, which are traditionally eaten at Christmas time (Christmas Cookies with Walnuts). They also feature in savory dishes such as Stuffed Chiles in a Walnut Sauce (*Chiles en Nogada*). Roasted salted pumpkin seeds are often served as snacks, while ground pumpkin seeds are used in sauces such as *Pepián* (Pumpkin Seed Sauce). Pine nuts, known as *piñon* seeds in Mexico, are added to dishes like *Picadillo* and are also ground for use in desserts and cakes.

Above: Pecans, almonds and walnuts

PILONCILLO—MEXICAN SUGAR

Mexico produces an unrefined brown cane sugar called *piloncillo*. It comes in small cones and adds a distinctive flavor and color to any dish to which it is added. Unfortunately, *piloncillo* is still not readily available outside Mexico, but brown sugar can be used in recipes as a substitute.

Left: clockwise from top left: pumpkin seeds, sesame seeds and pine nuts

Roasting Seeds

When dry-roasting or toasting pumpkin or sesame seeds, watch them carefully so that they do not burn. Use a heavy pan placed over low heat, and stir or shake the pan frequently to keep the seeds on the move at all times. If they are allowed to burn, they will taste bitter and will spoil the flavor of any dish to which they are added.

FRUITS

Visit any Mexican market and what will strike you first are the colorful displays of fruit of every size, shape and color. Some, such as mangoes, papayas and limes, will be familiar, but others may not look or taste like anything you have ever seen before. Fruit is an important part of the Mexican diet, providing the vitamins to balance the corn and beans that are the staple foods. Most of the fruit consumed in Mexico is grown in the country, and some of the surplus is exported to Europe.

CITRUS FRUIT

All types of citrus grow well in Mexico, and because the fruit is allowed to ripen naturally on the trees, it tends to have a very good flavor.

Description and Varieties

Limes have very thin skins, which would eventually turn yellow if they were left on the tree long enough. The pulp is green and juicy. Mexican limes—limones—are smaller than other varieties. Almost round in shape, they taste very

Below: Lemons and limes

aromatic. **Lemons** are more oval, and have thicker skins with a dense layer of white pith just below the surface. Their pulp is yellow and acidic, but tastes markedly different than that of lime. **Oranges** grow well in Mexico and freshly squeezed orange juice is widely available, especially in the south. The fruits tend to look much paler than their brightly colored counterparts in American markets, but are very sweet and juicy.

Buying and Storing

Mexican limes are seldom available outside the country, but any other type of lime can be substituted in recipes. Select limes with smooth, dark green skins, and avoid any that look wizened. The fruit should be heavy for its size. Small brown patches on the skin are harmless and will not affect the flavor or the juiciness of the fruit. Store uncut limes in a plastic bag in the refrigerator or a cool room. They will keep for up to 10 days in their peak condition. Lemons should be plump, with unblemished bright yellow skins. Avoid any whose skins are tinged with green, as this would indicate that the fruit is under-ripe. Oranges should feel heavy for their size. Avoid any that are damaged, shriveled or have moldy skins. Oranges keep well at room temperature.

Above: Oranges

Preparation

The zest on citrus fruit is often thinly pared or grated and used for decoration or flavoring. When paring the zest, take care to remove only the colored outer layer, leaving the bitter white pith behind. The pith must be removed before the fruit is sliced or segmented.

Main Uses and Cooking Tips

Limes, lemons and oranges are used extensively in cooking. Both lime and lemon juice are used to preserve vegetables, as in Onion Relish (*Cebollas en Escabeche*) and are added to casseroles, fruit platters and fresh vegetable dishes to heighten the natural flavors. The most famous use of limes—other than with tequila—is in *Ceviche*. Raw fish or shellfish is marinated in the juice until the texture of the flesh changes, becoming as firm and white as if it had been cooked. Citrus juices are also used to prevent vegetables or fruits, such as avocados, from discoloring on contact with the air. The skins of oranges, lemons or limes are often ground, and the oil is used as a flavoring.

GRANADILLAS

These fruits are the largest members of the passion fruit family. Native to South America, they are round, with a small stem attached at one end, so that they resemble Christmas tree ornaments. The tough, shell-like outer skin is bright orange, while the pulp inside is green and very seedy. It smells and tastes like citrus fruit and is not as fragrant as the pulp of the smaller, purplish-black passion fruit.

Buying and Storing

Unlike passion fruit, which are wrinkled and dimpled when ripe, granadillas should be smooth, with no marks. They can be stored at room temperature for up to 1 week. When ripe, the pulp is moist and juicy, but it dries out if they are stored for too long.

Preparation

Cut the fruit in half and scoop out the pulp with a teaspoon. The seeds are edible, but sieve the pulp if you prefer.

Main Uses and Cooking Tips

Granadilla pulp can be used in desserts, either with the seeds, or sieved. It is often poured over ice cream or fruit salad, either on its own or in a dessert sauce. It also makes a superb fruit drink, and the sieved pulp is often mixed with fresh orange juice.

Right: Granadillas

GUAVAS

These fruits—known as *guayabas* in Mexico—are native to the tropical areas of South America and grow in the warmer parts of Mexico. The guava tree grows to a height of about 30 feet and has smooth bark and fragrant white flowers. Guavas are an extremely good source of vitamin C. Purées or pastes made from the fruit have been popular in Mexico for centuries, and are still eaten today. They are either served alone or as accompaniments to fresh, soft cheeses.

Description

Guavas vary considerably in color, shape and size. The variety most popular in Mexico is the yellow guava. When it is ripe the yellow guava has a slightly musky, not particularly pleasant smell. The skin is quite thick, and is referred to as the shell. Inside is a creamy pulp, which is full of edible seeds. The flesh has a clean, sweet, slightly acidic flavor.

Buying and Storing

Guavas should be bought when they are still firm and unblemished. You will find that under-ripe fruit will ripen quite quickly at room temperature. Ripe fruit, however, should be kept in a cool, dark place—or in the refrigerator—as guavas readily ferment and will soon become inedible.

Left: Guavas

Preparation

Cut the fruit in half and scrape out the flesh with a spoon. The seeds can be eaten, or the pulp can be pressed through a sieve, if preferred.

Main Uses and Cooking Tips

Guavas are usually used in desserts, but their flavor is such that they are equally good in savory dishes. Sweet guava sauces are served with cakes; savory ones are excellent with fish.

In Mexico, guava flesh is often boiled with sugar, lemon juice, cinnamon and other spices to make a thick fruit purée. The purée is then poured into a shallow dish and left to cool, then cut into pieces to eat either on its own or with cheese. The fruit is also made into a preserve or relish.

Preparing a Mango

1 Place the mango narrow side down on a cutting board. Cut off a thick lengthwise slice, keeping the knife as close to the pit as possible. Turn the mango around and repeat on the other side. Cut off the flesh adhering to the pit.

2 Score the flesh on each thick slice with criss-cross lines at ½-inch intervals, taking care not to cut through the skin.

3 Fold the mango halves inside out. The flesh will stand proud, in neat cubes. Slice these off, or, for a "hedgehog," leave attached and serve.

MANGOES

Perhaps the most popular of all tropical fruits, mangoes have a wonderful perfume when ripe. The buttery flesh can be absolutely delicious, although some Mexican mangoes have a slightly resinous flavor.

Description and Varieties

There are thousands of varieties of mango. All start off green, but most will change to yellow, golden or red when they are ripe.

Buying and Storing

The best way of telling whether a mango is ripe is to sniff it. It should have a highly perfumed aroma. Next, press it lightly. If it is ripe, the fruit will just yield under your fingertips. Mangoes will ripen at home if placed in a paper bag with a banana. Eat them as soon as they are ripe.

Preparation

It has been said that the best way to eat a mango is in the bath. Failing that, use a sharp knife to take a lengthwise slice off either side of the fruit, as close to the pit as possible. Scoop out the flesh from each slice, then cut the rest of the flesh off the pit so that none is wasted.

Main Uses and Cooking Tips

Mexicans eat mangoes just as they are, but also use them in a range of desserts and drinks, with or without alcohol. A wonderful way to enjoy mango is in a Mango and Peach Margarita.

PINEAPPLES

Pineapples originated in South America and were introduced to other tropical areas by the Spanish and Portuguese. Historians have found records that prove that pineapples were cultivated by the indigenous peoples of Mexico long before the Spanish conquest.

Description and Varieties

Pineapples have hard, scaly skin and a crown of green leaves on top. The color of the skin varies. Although most ripe pineapples are yellow or orange, some, such as the Sugar Loaf that grows in Mexico, are green when fully ripe. The flesh is yellow and very juicy, with a sweet flavor that can be tangy or even slightly tart.

Above: Mangoes

Main Uses and Cooking Tips

Mexican pineapples are deliciously sweet, and are usually served quite simply, as dessert. Pineapple is often combined with rice, in savory dishes as well as sweet, and is used in desserts and candies. Pineapple juice is very popular, and is widely used in *agua frescas*, the fresh fruit drinks made at home and sold by street vendors.

Buying and Storing

Choose a pineapple that is slightly soft to touch, with a strong color and crisp, green leaves.
Pineapples must be picked ripe, as the starch doesn't convert to sugar after it has been picked.
Store in the refrigerator for up to 3 days.

Above: Pineapple

Preparing a Pineapple

1 Use a sharp knife to cut off the green leaves that form the crown and discard it.

2 With a sharp knife, remove the skin from the pineapple cutting deeply enough to remove most of the "eyes."

3 Use a small knife to take out carefully any "eyes" that remain in the pineapple flesh.

4 Cut the pineapple lengthwise into quarters and remove the core section from the center of each piece. Chop the pineapple flesh or cut it into slices and use as needed.

PRICKLY PEARS

Prickly pears are the fruits of several different types of cactus. Popular all over South America, they grow wild and are also cultivated, and serve as a staple food in some of the poorer rural areas of Mexico. The fleshy leaves of prickly pears—*nopales*—are treated as a vegetable, and you will find more information about them under the heading of Fruit Vegetables in the latter part of this introduction.

Description

Prickly pears are shaped like grenades and range in color from deep red to greenish orange. Their name is well earned, for the tough outer skin has tiny tufts of hairs or prickles, which can be very sharp. The fruit is valued for its pulp, which has a sweet aromatic flavor, much like that of melons, but even more subtle. The pulp contains small brown seeds, which are edible raw, but which become hard when cooked.

Right: Prickly pears

Buying and Storing

To tell whether a prickly pear is ripe, squeeze it carefully (avoiding the prickles!). Do not buy soft fruit or under-ripe fruit, which is dark green in color and very hard. Fruit that is slightly firm will ripen if left at room temperature for a few days.

Preparation

The prickles on these fruit are usually removed before they are sold, but if not, they can be scrubbed off with a stiff brush before the fruit is peeled. It is essential to wear kitchen gloves while carrying out this operation.

Main Uses and Cooking Tips

The peeled fruit should be halved and the flesh scooped out with a teaspoon. It can be strained and used as a sauce, or the fruit can be served as part of a fruit platter. Lime juice and chili powder are sometimes added to enliven the flavor. Prickly pears can also be made into jelly or jam.

Peeling Prickly Pears

1 Having scrubbed off the prickles, put on a pair of kitchen gloves and hold the fruit down with one hand while you cut off the skin.

2 Alternatively, hold down the prickly pear with a fork and cut a thin slice from the top and bottom of the fruit, then slit the fruit from top to bottom on either side. Peel off the skin, then cut the flesh and arrange on a plate, or simply eat the pear whole.

3 If you prefer, cut the pear in half without removing the skin and scoop out the flesh with a teaspoon. You can eat the flesh in this way as you scoop, or transfer the pulp to a bowl and serve with lime juice.

Above: Coconut

Other Tropical Fruit Treats

Other fruits popular in Mexico include **papayas**, which are valued for the tenderizing qualities of their skins, as well as that delicious flesh. These pear-shaped fruits, with vivid yellow skins, are also used in drinks sold by street vendors to quench commuters' thirsts on hot afternoons. Mexicans eat fruit with ground chiles and lime juice as a snack, or part of a meal and slices of papaya are often included. The peppery, round black seeds are edible but are seldom used in dishes. **Pomegranates**, which are used in sauces including the famous dish of Stuffed Chiles in a Walnut

Sauce called *Chiles en Nagada*, which is often prepared for special occasions. Pomegranates are also used in refreshing drinks called *Agua Frescas* sold by street vendors. Be careful only to use the seeds and not the bitter-tasting white pith. **Sapodillas** have luscious honey-colored flesh and taste like vanilla-flavored banana custard. **Coconuts** are grown in parts of Mexico and pieces are often sold from bowls, cooled with ice water on street corners in busy towns. A chilled coconut soup is often made in the northern Pacific areas. One of the most popular fruits in Mexico is the **sapote**, which has dark salmon-pink flesh. It is very sweet and rather cloying, but makes excellent marmalade, which accounts for its alternative name of marmalade plum.

Above: Papayas

Preparing a Pomegranate

1 Cut off a thin slice from one end.

2 Stand the fruit upright. Cut downward through the skin at intervals, using a small sharp knife.

3 Bend back the segments and use your fingers to push the seeds into a bowl.

4 Remove all the bitter pith and membrane and use as needed.

FRUIT VEGETABLES

There are some fruits that are used so often in savory dishes that we tend to think of them as vegetables. Tomatoes are the obvious example, but avocados, bell peppers and chiles also are in this category. Mexico seems to have more than its fair share of these fruit vegetables, including the tomatillo, which is often called the Mexican green tomato, although it is actually related to the cape gooseberry.

AVOCADOS

It is believed that the Aztecs introduced avocado seedlings to Mexico during the 13th and 14th centuries, calling them *ahuacatl*, a name whose Spanish version was first corrupted to alligator pear and then to the name by which the fruit vegetable is known today.

Description and Varieties

There are several varieties of avocado. Most are pear-shaped and contain a central pit. The flesh ranges in color from creamy yellow to bright green and has a buttery texture and mild but distinctive flavor.

The indigenous Mexican avocado has fragrant green flesh around a large pit. The thin skin can be eaten, which is unusual, since most avocados have skins that are tough and inedible, and some, like the Hass variety, have

Left: Avocado

knobbly black skins that are almost shell-like. Hass avocados have creamy flesh and a very good flavor. Another variety is the fuerte avocado, which has glossy green skin and yellow-green flesh.

Buying and Storing

To confirm that an avocado is ripe, press the top end of the fruit gently. It should just yield. If it is soft, the fruit is over-ripe, will prove messy to peel and will have flesh that is soft and mushy. Avocados that are bruised will have blackened flesh.

Finding the perfect avocado is partly a matter of luck, however. Even if you have chosen carefully and have taken great care not to let the fruit get bruised on the journey from the store to your home, the flesh may still be flecked with brownish spots when you finally cut it open.

Store ripe avocados in the refrigerator; under-ripe fruit will ripen if left for a few days in a warm room. Cut avocados discolor quickly. Although this process can be delayed slightly, it is advisable not to prepare the fruit until you are ready to serve it.

Main Uses and Cooking Tips

Avocados are used extensively in Mexican cookingy, most famously in Guacamole, the mashed avocado dip. They are also used in soups—both hot and cold—or to make a hot sauce for meat. Fresh avocado tastes wonderful in salads and with seafood. It is often used in tortilla dishes and is also a favorite ingredient in a range of *tortas*—Mexican sandwiches.

As soon as an avocado is cut, the flesh begins to blacken. Sprinkling the slices or chunks with lemon or lime juice delays the process somewhat, and Mexicans swear that burying the avocado pit in the mashed avocado flesh has the same effect.

Avocado Leaves

In Mexico and other countries where the fruit flourishes, fresh or dried avocado leaves are used for their flavoring properties, much as bay leaves are used elsewhere. They can either be crushed and added to dishes or put in whole and then removed just before the dish is served. Dried avocado leaves are usually toasted before being added to dishes such as Refried Beans, stews and marinades or used for meat that is going to be broiled or grilled.

Guacamole

Guacamole originated in Mexico, but has become one of the world's most popular dishes. Mashed avocado is the main ingredient, but other items, such as onion, garlic, diced tomato, chopped chiles, lime or lemon juice as well as seasonings are added. The smooth, buttery taste of the avocado gives this dip a creamy texture, yet it contains no saturated fat. Guacamole is often served with tortilla chips as a simple dip. It is an essential accompaniment to fajitas, is used in *tortas*, and is served alongside meat and fish dishes.

Simple Guacamole

1 Cut two avocados in half. Remove the pits and scoop the flesh out of the shells. Place it in a blender and process until almost smooth. Transfer into a bowl and add the juice of half a lime.

2 Add one-quarter of a small onion, chopped finely, a crushed garlic clove and a handful of cilantro, also chopped finely.

3 Add salt and other seasoning to taste and serve immediately, with tortilla chips for dipping. The Guacamole will keep in the refrigerator for 2–3 days if it is kept in an airtight container.

VARIATION

Try adding chopped fresh tomatoes and fresh chile to give your Guacamole added flavor, texture and fire.

Preparing Avocado

1 If a recipe calls for avocado halves or mashed avocado, run a small, sharp knife all the way around the fruit, starting at the top and cutting right in until the knife touches the pit.

2 Gently prise the two halves apart with the knife.

3 Push the knife blade into the pit, then lift it away. If any of the brown skin from the pit remains on the avocado flesh, remove it. The avocado halves can be served with vinaigrette, filled with shrimp or topped with thin slices of ham. Alternatively, the flesh can be scooped into a bowl and mashed.

1 For avocado slices, cut the fruit in half, remove the pit, then nick the skin at the top of each half and ease it away until you can peel off the skin completely; if the avocado is ripe, it will come off cleanly and easily.

2 Cut the peeled avocado halves into slices, leaving them attached at one end if you want to fan them on the plate. Sprinkle them with lemon or lime juice to stop them from discoloring too quickly.

1 For cubes of avocado, score the half of avocado and then with the tip of the knife gently lift each cube out one by one.

Left: Tomatoes

TOMATOES

Tomatoes are native to western South America and were cultivated by the Aztecs long before the Spanish invasion. Hernando Cortés is credited with introducing the first tomatoes—yellow ones—to Europe. They were initially treated with suspicion, but after a pair of Jesuit priests introduced red tomatoes to Italy in the 18th century, they steadily become more and more popular.

Description and Varieties

There are numerous varieties of tomato, ranging from tiny cherry tomatoes to ridged beefsteak tomatoes that measure as much as 4 inches across. Great piles of plum tomatoes are a common sight at Mexican markets. Richly flavored, with fewer seeds than most other varieties, they are a popular choice for salads and salsas.

Buying and Storing

Tomatoes sold in Mexican markets will have ripened naturally, and will be full of flavor, so use ripe home-grown tomatoes or vine tomatoes when cooking Mexican dishes. Over-ripe tomatoes can be used for soups or purées, but avoid any tomatoes that show signs of mold. Avoid buying tomatoes that are still green, but pale ones that have begun to redden can be ripened in a brown paper bag, especially if you add a slice of apple. Try to either store fresh tomatoes at room temperature, or bring them to room temperature before use, as chilling dulls the flavor.

Preparation

If a recipe requires that a tomato be seeded, just cut it in half and squeeze gently, or scoop out the seeds with a teaspoon. To peel, cut a cross in the bottom of the tomato, immerse it in boiling water for 3 minutes, then plunge into cold water. Drain well. The skins will have begun to peel back from the crosses and will be easy to remove. Chop or slice the tomatoes, as needed for individual recipes. If sliced tomatoes are called for, it is better to slice them across, rather than downward.

Main Uses and Cooking Tips

Mexicans use tomatoes in so many of their recipes that it would be impossible to list them all. They feature in both hot and cold soups, salsas, salads and meat and fish dishes. Chopped tomatoes are added to beans to make *frijoles*, are mixed with avocados in Guacamole and are used in Sangrita, a popular drink that is sipped alternately with tequila.

Quick Fresh Tomato Salsa

A quick and easy tomato salsa, which can be prepared in minutes. Serve as a side dish with meat or fish, or as a simple appetizer with a pile of tortilla chips.

INGREDIENTS

3 fresh tomatoes, chopped
1 red onion, finely chopped
1 clove of garlic, crushed
½ green bell pepper, finely chopped
1 tablespoon chopped jalapeño or fresno chile, finely chopped
2 tablespoons chopped cilantro
3 tablespoons fresh lime juice
salt and ground black pepper to taste

1 Place the tomatoes, onion, garlic, green pepper and chile in a large bowl and combine.

2 Add the chopped cilantro and fresh lime juice, then taste and season with salt and ground black pepper to taste. Serve immediately or transfer to an airtight container and store in the refrigerator.

TOMATILLOS/TOMATE VERDE

Despite the name by which we know them—and the fact that they are sometimes referred to as Mexican green tomatoes—tomatillos are not members of the tomato family. Instead, they are related to cape gooseberries, those pretty little orange fruit surrounded by papery lanterns, which are so popular for garnishing. They have been grown in Mexico since Aztec times, when they were known as *miltomatl*. Mexicans seldom use the term "tomatillo," preferring to call these fruit by one of their many local names, which include *fresadilla* and *tomate milpero*.

Description

Ranging in color from yellowish green to lime, tomatillos are firm, round fruit, about the size of a small tomato, but lighter in weight, as they are not juicy. Fresh ones usually have the brown

*Left: Tomatillos
with husks*

papery husk attached to them at the stem end. The flavor resembles that of tart apples with a hint of lemon, and is enhanced by cooking, although a *salsa cruda* of raw tomatillos has a very pleasant, clean taste.

Buying and Storing

Fresh tomatillos are difficult to come by outside Mexico, but some specialty stores sell them, and they are also available by mail order in season. They can also be grown from seed, a most worthwhile enterprise for anyone who loves their clean, slightly acidic flavor. If you do locate a supply of fresh tomatillos, look for firm fruit with tight-fitting husks, and store them in the refrigerator for up to 1 week.

In the same way that canned carrots bear little resemblance to fresh ones, canned tomatillos are softer and not as tasty as fresh, but they are more readily available and preferable to missing out on this great flavor completely. When buying canned tomatillos, be sure to take account of the loss of weight when the liquid is drained off—it can be as much as a third of the total.

Main Uses and Cooking Tips

Tomatillos are used in table salsas and in the sauce (*tomate verde salsa*), which is poured over enchiladas before they are cooked. They can also be used instead of tomatoes in Guacamole, giving a piquant flavor to the sauce. To cook fresh tomatillos, remove the husks and dry-fry them in a heavy frying pan until the skins have begun to char and the flesh has softened. Alternatively, put them in a pan with water to cover, bring to a boil, then simmer them until they soften and begin to break down. If the dish in which they are used requires stock, use the cooking liquid.

*Above:
Canned tomatillos*

Salsa Cruda de Tomatillo

1 To make a rough textured salsa with tomatillos, process 1 pound fresh tomatillos in a food processor or chop them finely, then mix with one chopped small onion and one crushed garlic clove. Add two seeded and chopped jalapeño chiles and salt to taste.

2 Finely chop a small bunch of cilantro and add it to the tomatillo mixture.

3 Stir well, spoon into a clean bowl and serve immediately with freshly made corn tortilla chips.

Right: Plantains

PLANTAINS

Native to Southeast Asia, plantains are popular in many Latin American countries, and particularly those that have a coastline on the Caribbean.

Description and Varieties

Plantains are a type of banana, larger than the sweet bananas and with a harder skin. There are several varieties, all initially green, but some ripening to yellow, then black, while others become dark pink or red when ripe. The flesh is fibrous and starchy and must be cooked before being eaten. The flavor can be quite mild, resembling that of a squash, but when plantains are fried, the flesh tastes sweeter and has a more obvious banana flavor.

Buying and Storing

Both green and ripe plantains are used in cooking. Look for them at markets specializing in West Indian or African foods. Ripe plantains are slightly soft to the touch. If a recipe calls for ripe plantains, and you can only get green or yellow ones, they will ripen if left in a warm room for a couple of days. Unlike sweet bananas, ripe plantains can be stored in the refrigerator for a day or two.

Preparation

Plantains can't simply be peeled, like bananas. Removing the flesh can be quite tricky, unless they are very ripe. The best way to do it is to cut the plantains into short lengths, then slit the skin along one of the natural ridges so that it can be eased apart and removed. Unless you are going to use the peeled plantains immediately, put them in a bowl of acidulated water (water to which lime juice has been added) to prevent them from discoloring. When slicing plantains for chips, don't remove the skins first. Put the slices into a bowl of salted water for about half an hour, then drain them. It will be quite easy to press the slices of plantain out of their skins.

Main Uses and Cooking Tips

Plantains are used in both sweet and savory dishes. Fried plantain slices are delicious with a chili dip or simply a squeeze of lime and a sprinkling of chili powder. Slices can be cooked in butter and served as a vegetable, the sweet creaminess making them a good partner for a hot, spicy dish. They are good in meat dishes, but make a delectable dessert. Just cook them in butter and cinnamon, with a little sugar and a good amount of rum.

Banana Leaves

In parts of Mexico, banana leaves are used instead of corn husks for wrapping food before cooking. Before use, the leaves should be soaked in water until soft, then dried on paper towels. They will impart a unique, slightly lemony flavor to food cooked in them.

SWEET BELL PEPPERS

Sometimes known as capsicums, these are native to Mexico and Central America, and were also a staple food for the Incas in Peru.

Description

Sweet peppers range in color from green through yellow and orange to deep red, depending on ripeness, and there is even a purplish-black variety. They have a mild, sweet flavor and crisp, juicy flesh. Peppers can be eaten raw or cooked.

Buying and Storing

When buying peppers, try to look for specimens with bright, glossy skins. Avoid any that are limp or wrinkled, or that have "blistered" areas on the skin. Store them in a cool place or in the refrigerator for up to 1 week.

Preparation

Inside each pepper is a core that is surrounded by seeds, which must be removed. If the peppers are to be used whole, this can be lifted out if a neat slice is taken off the top, around the stem. If the peppers are halved or quartered, removing the core and seeds is even easier. Many Mexican recipes call for peppers to be roasted over a gas

Right: Sweet bell peppers

Right: Nopales

flame or in a dry frying pan, then sealed in a plastic bag until the steam loosens the skin, which is removed before the peppers are sliced or chopped.

Main Uses and Cooking Tips

Peppers are used extensively in Mexican cuisine, contributing color and flavor to salsas, stews and meat fillings, as well as fish dishes, vegetable medleys and salads. For salads, they are usually just cored, seeded and chopped, but for cooked dishes, it is more common for them to be roasted and skinned first.

NOPALES

Nopales are the edible leaves of several varieties of prickly pear cactus. Fat and fleshy, they are often called cactus paddles. Mexicans have been cooking and eating them for thousands of years.

Description

The leaves—or paddles—are oval in shape, with sharp spines. They range in color from pale to dark green, depending on variety and age. The flavor is similar to that of a green bean, but with a slightly acidic tang.

Buying and Storing

Fresh *nopales* are quite difficult to locate outside Mexico and the adjoining American states. If you do find them, choose the thinnest, smallest leaves with the palest color, as older leaves can be very woody, even when cooked. Store fresh *nopales* in the refrigerator for up to 1 week. Bottled *nopales*—called *nopalitos*—have had the spines removed and are sliced before being preserved in brine or vinegar. They are available at specialty food stores.

Preparing Peppers

1 For peppers to be served whole, use a sharp knife to cut a ring around the stem at the top of each pepper. Lift out the core and surrounding seeds. If the peppers can be cut into halves or quarters, do this taking care not to cut into the core, then cut around it and remove.

2 For roasted peppers, roast over a gas flame or in a dry frying pan or griddle.

3 Place them in a strong plastic bag and seal the bag. Leave until the steam loosens the skin. Remove the skin and slice or chop the peppers.

Preparing *Nopales*

1 Wearing gloves or holding each paddle in turn with kitchen tongs, cut off the bumps that contain the thorns with a sharp knife. Try not to remove the whole of the green outer surface; just the parts containing spines.

2 Cut off and discard the thick base of each paddle. Rinse the paddles well and either chop them or cut them into strips.

Main Uses

Nopales are used in stews and soups, particularly in the Tlaxcala area of Mexico, and are pickled for use in salsas and salad dishes. They are even added to scrambled eggs.

Cooking Nopales

Cactus can be slimy when cooked. Mexican cooks often add onion and garlic at the start of cooking, removing them after the sliminess has gone. You can also boil *nopales* in water, drain them, then rinse under cold water. Cover with a damp dish towel and leave for 30 minutes, by which time the gumminess will have disappeared.

CHILES

Chiles have been grown in South America for thousands of years. Over 150 indigenous varieties are found in Mexico alone. In 1492 Columbus brought chiles to Europe, and from there they spread around the world.

Mexican food is often perceived as being very hot, and some of the dishes certainly live up to their reputation, but it is possible to find many dishes that are only mildly flavored with chiles. The heat level of a chile is determined by the amount of capsaicin it contains. This compound is concentrated mainly in the ribs and seeds, so you can reduce the fieriness considerably by removing these parts. Chiles that have been pickled, or that are used raw, tend to have more heat than cooked chiles.

Left: Poblana chiles

The heat level of a chile is measured in Scoville units, on a scale where 0 is the heat level of a sweet pepper and 300,000 is the hottest chile, the habañero. In many instances, the ratings have been simplified to a scale of 1–10, to make them easier to remember.

The heat level of a particular chile will vary according to where it was grown, when it was picked, the irrigation, the weather during the growing season and a host of other factors, so Scoville units can only be a guide. Each crop from the same plant will be different.

Fresh Chiles

The following are the most commonly used fresh chiles:

Serrano Heat level 8. This is a small chile, about 1½–2 inches long and ½ inch wide, with a pointed tip. Serrano chiles change from green to red when ripe, and are sold at both stages of their development. The flavor is clean and biting. Serranos are used in cooked dishes, Guacamole and salsas.

Jalapeño Heat level 6. One of the most common—and most popular—types of chile, this is about the same length as a serrano, but plumper. Jalapeños are sold at all stages of ripeness, so you are as likely to find red as green. Green jalapeños are often pickled. One method of preparing jalapeños is to stuff with fresh cheese, coat in a light batter and deep-fry.

Poblano Heat level 3. Like many chiles, poblanos are initially green, and ripen to a dark red. They are large chiles, being roughly 3½ inches long

Below: Jalapeño and serrano chiles

Roasting and Peeling Chiles

1 Dry-fry the chiles in a frying pan or griddle until the skins are scorched. Alternatively, spear them on a long-handled metal skewer and roast them over the flame of a gas burner until the skins blister and darken. Do not let the flesh burn.

2 Place the roasted chiles in a strong plastic bag and tie the top to keep the steam in. Set aside for 20 minutes.

3 Remove the chiles from the bag and peel off the skins. Cut off the stems, then slit the chiles and scrape out the seeds.

Above: Fresno chiles

and 2¼ inches wide, and are sometimes said to be heart-shaped. Although not very hot, poblanos have a rich, earthy flavor which is intensified when the chiles are roasted and peeled. They are widely used in Mexican cooking, notably in Stuffed Chiles (*Chiles Rellenos*). Anaheim chiles, which are widely available in the United States and sometimes in the United Kingdom, can be substituted for poblanos.

Fresno Heat level 8. Looking much like elongated sweet peppers, fresnos are about 2½ inches long and ¾ inch wide. They have a hot, sweet flavor and are used in salsas, as well as in meat, fish and vegetable dishes. They are particularly good in Black Bean Salsa and Guacamole.

Buying and Storing Fresh Chiles

Look for firm fresh chiles, with shiny skins. Try to avoid any specimens that are dull or limp, as they will be past their prime. Fresh chiles can be successfully stored in a plastic bag in the refrigerator for up to 3 weeks. If they are to be chopped and added to cooked dishes, they can be seeded, chopped and then frozen, ready for use until needed.

COOK'S TIP

If you bite into a chile that is uncomfortably hot, swallow a spoonful of sugar. Don't be tempted to gulp down a glass of water or beer; this will only spread the heat further.

Preparing Fresh Chiles

Be very careful when handling fresh chiles, as the capsaicin that they contain can cause severe irritation to sensitive skin, especially on the face. Either wear gloves when working with them, or wash your hands thoroughly with soap after handling them. If you touch your skin by mistake, wash your hands quickly and then splash the affected area with plenty of fresh cold water. Avoid scratching or rubbing enflamed skin, as this could aggravate the problem.

1 Holding the chile firmly at the stem end, cut it in half lengthwise with a sharp knife.

2 Cut off the stem from both halves of the chile, removing a thin slice of the top of the chile as you do so. This will help to free the white membrane and make it easier to scrape out.

3 Carefully scrape out all of the seeds and remove the core with a small sharp knife.

4 Cut out any white membrane from the inside of the chiles. Keep the knife close to the flesh so that all the membrane is removed.

5 At this point make sure you carefully discard all of the seeds and membrane that are now lying on the board. Then take each half chile and cut as required. To chop finely first cut the chile half into thin strips. Then bunch the strips together and cut across them to produce tiny pieces. If the chile is being added to a dish that will be cooked for some time you can chop it less finely.

DRIED CHILES

Dried chiles are nothing new. The convenience of a product that could be stored and rehydrated when needed was realized centuries ago. Chiles were originally sun-dried, but today are more likely to be dried in an oven. Either way, they are a valuable ingredient, and are extensively used in this book because they are so much easier to obtain than fresh chiles.

Below: Cascabel chiles

In many cases, drying intensifies the flavor of chiles. Depending on the process used, drying can also impart extra flavor, as when jalapeños are dried and smoked. Not only does the flavor deepen to a rich smokiness, but the name of the chile changes, and it becomes a chipotle. The fact that the same chile can have two names, depending on whether it is fresh or dried, can be confusing, and it may be simpler to think of dried chiles as separate varieties. The heat rating given for the dried chiles in the list that follows is based on the same scale as that used for the fresh chiles on the previous pages.

Drying seems to spread the capsaicin through the chiles, so removing the seeds and membrane will do little to alter their heat. The seeds of a dried chile add very little to the flavor, however, so if they are loose, discard them. Dried chiles can be ground into a powder or cut into strips before being used. Unless the chiles are to be added to a dish with a high proportion of liquid, they are usually soaked in water before use.

Buying and Storing Dried Chiles

Good quality dried chiles should be flexible, not brittle. Store them in an airtight jar in a cool, dry place. For short term storage, the refrigerator is ideal, although they can also be frozen. Do not keep dried chiles for more than a year or the flavor may fade.

The following is a list of some of the more common dried chiles, all of which feature in this book.

Ancho Heat scale 3. The most common dried chile in Mexico, the ancho is a dried red poblano chile, and has a fruity, slightly sharp flavor. When rehydrated, anchos can be used to make Stuffed Chiles (*Chiles Rellenos*), but should not be peeled first.

Cascabel Heat scale 4. The name means "little rattle" and refers to the noise that the seeds make inside the chile. This chile has a chocolate brown skin, and

Above: Chile powder

Above: Ancho chiles

Right: Chipotle chiles

Grinding Chiles

This method gives a distinctive and smoky taste to the resulting powdered chile.

1 Soak the chiles, pat dry and then dry-fry in a heavy pan until crisp.

2 Transfer to a mortar and grind into a fine powder with a pestle. Store in an airtight container.

remains dark, even after soaking. Cascabels have a slightly nutty flavor and are often added to salsas such as *tomate verde*.

Chipotle Heat scale 6. These are smoked jalapeños. They add a stews. It is about 5 inches long and 1 inch wide, and has a burgundy-colored skin. A paste made from guajillos is often used for spreading on meat before cooking.

Habañero Heat scale 10. This is the grandaddy of them all, a chile so hot that when it is puréed, even the fumes from the blender can scorch the skin. Lantern-shaped, it is about 1¾ inches long and 1¼ inches wide, and is also called Scotch Bonnet. Habañeros are often used to make bottled hot chili sauces.

Pasada Heat scale 3. This chile is crisply dried, and has citrus and apple flavors. It is used in soups and in sauces used for cooking meat or fish.

Pasilla Heat scale 4. Pasilla means "little raisin." This is the dried version of a fresh chile called the chilaca. It is 6 inches long and 1 inch wide, with dark brown skin, and is suitable for stuffing. The rich flavor suggests herbs and licorice. When ground and transformed to a paste, the chile is used in a variety of dishes, including *moles*. The *pasilla de Oaxaca* is a smoked version of this chile, peculiar to the Oaxaca region.

Above: Habañero chiles

Above: Guajillo chiles

wonderfully rich smoky flavor to all sorts of dishes, from barbecue sauces to chicken, and are great in cowboy-style beans with pork. One of the simplest ways of using chipotles is to purée the soaked chiles, then stir them into cream to make a rich dipping sauce.

Guajillo Heat scale 3. Another popular dried chile in Mexican cuisine, the guajillo is used in sauces or

Above: Pasilla chiles

Right: Pasada chiles

Soaking Dried Chiles
In order to appreciate their full flavor, it is recommended that dried chiles that are not being ground should be soaked before being used. The amount of time chiles need to rehydrate depends on the type, the thickness of the skin and how dry they are. The longer they soak the better, so if there is time, leave them in the water for 1 hour before cooking.

1 Wipe them to remove any dirt, and brush away any seeds that are accessible.

2 Soak the dried chiles in a bowl of hot water for about 10 minutes (longer if possible) until the color is restored and the chile has swelled and softened.

3 Drain, cut off the stems, then slit the chiles and scrape out the seeds with a small sharp knife. Slice or chop the flesh. If the chiles are to be puréed, put them in a blender or food processor with a little of the soaking water and process them until smooth.

VEGETABLES

Mexico's indigenous peoples were very good agriculturists, and when the Spanish invaded they found a country blessed with abundant vegetables, including corn, sweet potatoes, *jicama*, pumpkins and zucchini. The Spanish in turn introduced onions, garlic, green beans, cabbage and cauliflower, all of which were integrated into the Mexican cuisine.

CORN

The vegetable we know as corn has been grown in the Americas for over five thousand years. It was brought to Europe by the Spanish in the late 15th century, but long before that it was a staple food of the indigenous peoples of Mexico, who used every part of the corn, including the husks and silks.

Description

An ear of corn consists of yellow, plump kernels on a firm cob, sheathed in long green leaves or husks. Between the leaves and the kernels are long thin threads called silks. Mexicans traditionally use these for tying *tamales*, but elsewhere they are usually discarded.

Buying and Storing

Look for ears whose outer leaves are a fresh, tender green. They should not be limp or faded. One way of testing whether the corn is fresh is to squeeze one of the kernels gently. A milky liquid should ooze out. Corn should be cooked within 24 hours of being purchased, because the sugar starts turning to starch the moment it is cut. The older the corn, the less sweet it will be.

Preparation

Peel off the husks, then pull off the silks. (If necessary, scrub the ears with a vegetable brush to remove any remaining silks.) If the corn is to be cooked on the grill, the husks can be pulled back, then replaced after removing the silks.

Main Uses and Cooking Tips

Corn can be cooked in boiling water, but do not add salt or the kernels will toughen. They can also be cooked in the oven or on a grill. In Mexico, corn is a popular street food. The cooked ears are dipped in cream, then sprinkled with

Above: Beans

cheese. A similar dish involves removing the kernels from the ears and cooking them in cream with pickled jalapeños and cheese.

GREEN BEANS

Green beans have been growing in the Americas for hundreds of years. In Mexico, lima beans, sometimes mistakenly called fava beans, are widely used, as are string beans.

Buying and Storing

Pods should be bright and crisp. Use on the day bought if possible.

Preparation

Trim the beans (cut off both ends) and remove any strings on the sides of the pods. Lima beans and fava beans must be removed from their pods before use, and are sometimes blanched.

Main Uses and Cooking Tips

Mexicans use beans in salads and vegetable dishes. A favorite dish is lima beans with a tomato sauce. Beans are best cooked briefly in boiling water or steamed until they are tender. Both these methods ensure that the beans retain maximum color, texture and flavor.

Above: Corn

Right: Sweet potatoes

SWEET POTATOES

One of the staple foods of the indigenous peoples of Mexico in pre-Columbian times, sweet potatoes are still a very important food.

Description and Varieties

Sweet potatoes are starchy tubers, and need to be cooked before being eaten. There are many different varieties, ranging from pale-skinned sweet potatoes with pale crumbly flesh to darker tubers with thick skins and moist flesh. The skin color can range from pink to deep purple, and the flesh can range from creamy white to the more familiar vivid orange. As their name suggests, they have a sweet flavor, but with a hint of spice.

Buying and Storing

Sweet potatoes have smooth skins and should not be damaged or soft. Smaller specimens often have finer flavor than large ones. They can be stored in a cool, dark place for up to 1 week.

Preparation

Cook sweet potatoes in their skins or, if you prefer, peel them just before boiling and mashing them.

Main Uses and Cooking Tips

Sweet potatoes are used in both sweet and savory dishes, either cooked slowly in their skins or peeled and boiled. Try them boiled and mashed with a little butter and cream, and some nutmeg, salt and black pepper. Mashed potatoes, with tomatoes and chiles, are a wonderful accompaniment to grilled food. Roasted sweet potatoes are excellent with roast pork. They are also used in stews and casseroles.

Below: Jicamas

JICAMAS

The *jicama*—or yam bean—is a native of Central America. It was introduced to the Philippines by the Spanish, and from there it spread to China, where it is still popular today. In fact, Chinese supermarkets are a good source of *jicama*. The Chinese name for it is *saa got*, but you may also find it labeled Chinese turnip.

Description

Jicama is the root of a climbing bean plant. The young beans are edible, but older ones are poisonous. It looks like a turnip or beet, but has a conical base. The skin is light brown and quite thin. The moist, creamy-colored flesh tastes slightly fruity, and the texture resembles that of a crisp green apple or a water chestnut. *Jicama* can be eaten raw or cooked.

Buying and Storing

Look for firm *jicamas* that are about the size of a large turnip; larger ones may be a bit woody. To keep the crisp texture, store them in the refrigerator for up to 1 week.

Preparation

Peel off the thin, papery skin by hand or with a sharp knife, then slice the *jicama* thinly.

Main Uses and Cooking Tips

Raw *jicama* makes a refreshing snack when it is sprinkled with freshly squeezed orange juice and served with chili powder and salt. It is also delicious added to salads and used in salsas. *Jicama* retains its pleasingly crisp texture when boiled, as long as it is not overcooked. Mexicans sometimes like to use grated *jicama* in desserts.

SQUASH

Pumpkins and other types of squash, cucumbers and *chayotes* all belong to the same family, and have been cultivated since ancient times. Pumpkin seeds dating back as far as 7000 B.C. have been found in Mexico. The word "squash" comes from an Indian word, "askutasquash," meaning raw or uncooked, which may seem odd to those of us accustomed to eating squash cooked. However, there are numerous types of squash, and some are indeed delicious eaten raw.

Description

There are two main classifications of squash—summer and winter. Many of the summer squash are now available all year round, but it can still be useful to differentiate between the two distinct groups.

Summer squash grow on bushes and have thin, edible skins and soft seeds. Examples include zucchini, patty pans and yellow squash. The flesh is soft,

Above: Summer squash

generally pale in color and has a high water content. It only needs a little cooking, and has a mild flavor. The seeds are dispersed through the flesh, and are usually eaten with it. Zucchini can be eaten raw, in salads. Winter squash have harder, thicker skins and tough seeds. They may grow on bushes, but are often the fruit of vine plants. The skin is usually cut off and discarded, although if the squash is roasted, its skin may be soft enough to eat. Acorn, butternut, spaghetti, onion squash and pumpkin are some of the better known varieties. The flesh is often yellow or deep orange, is firmer and requires longer cooking than that of summer squash. The seeds are generally removed and discarded before cooking, although some,

Above: Pumpkin

such as pumpkin seeds, are a valuable food in their own right.

The blossoms or flowers from both winter and summer squash are edible, and there are a number of Mexican recipes for cooking squash blossoms. In Mexico you can buy the blossoms separately, and they are sold at some specialty food stores elsewhere, but most cooks who want to try them will have to harvest them from home-grown vegetables. They are delicious coated in light batter and fried.

Buying and Storing

Summer squash, and zucchini in particular, are best when they are small, slim and still tender. They should have bright, smooth, unblemished skins with no bruising. They should be stored in the refrigerator, and will only keep for 3–4 days. The thicker skins of winter squash make them much better for long term keeping. They can be stored in a cool room for up to 1 month, depending on how mature they were when picked and on how old they were when sold. When buying winter squash, choose specimens that are heavy for their size and that have unmarked skins.

Main Uses and Cooking Tips

Summer squash can be steamed, stir-fried, boiled, baked or even coated in batter and deep-fried. As the flesh is soft, it will need to be cooked for only a few minutes and should still retain some bite. Popular Mexican recipes include Zucchini Torte and Zucchini with Cheese and Green Chiles.

Winter squash are often cut into pieces, seeded and baked, steamed or boiled. They need to be cooked for longer than summer squash because the flesh is firmer. The skin is usually discarded, and this can be done either before cooking or after.

Mexicans often roast pumpkins in large chunks. They also cook pumpkin in water and sugar, as a dessert, or bake it with sugar and spices. Other types of squash are used in similar ways, and cooked squash often features as a filling in both sweet and savory *empanadas*.

CHAYOTES

The *chayote* is native to Mexico. A member of the squash family, it grows on a vine, and goes under several names, including vegetable pear, *chocho* or *chow-chow*, *mirliton* and *choko*. In France it is called a *christophene*.

Chayotes are pale green and pear-shaped, with smooth and leathery skins, which are often furrowed and may be covered with short spines. Inside is a large, flat seed, similar in appearance to that found in a mango. *Chayote* seeds are, however, edible. The flesh is pale and crisp, like that of a tart green apple or a water chestnut.

Buying and Storing

Choose a firm *chayote* with a smooth, unwrinkled skin that is free from blemishes or bruising. Smaller *chayotes* will be more flavorful than large ones. They keep well in the refrigerator and can be stored for up to 1 month.

Left: Chayote

Main Uses and Cooking Tips

Chayotes have a fairly mild flavor and are best peeled and served simply in salads or salsas, with a squeeze of lime or orange juice and some chiles. If they are cooked, they should be seasoned well. The mild flavor makes them ideal for combining with other, more strongly flavored ingredients. To cook *chayotes*, either peel and cook them in the same way as summer squash, or bake them.

Above: Winter squash

Baked Chayote

Cut them in half, brush the cut sides with oil, then either fill them with a vegetable stuffing or simply sprinkle them with salt, pepper and a little spice, if desired. Bake in a pre-heated oven at 375°F for 25 minutes or until tender all the way through when pierced with a skewer.

CHORIZO, DRIED MEAT AND SALT FISH

In hot countries dried and preserved foods are an important part of the diet. Mexico's traditional dried ingredients are very popular and are used to flavor many dishes.

CHORIZO

Chorizo is a highly seasoned pork sausage made from coarsely ground pork, garlic and spices. It is widely used in Mexican cooking in dishes as varied as Eggs with Chorizo (*Huevos con Chorizo*), soups, stews and casseroles. Mexican chorizo is made from fresh pork, unlike the Spanish chorizo, which is based upon smoked pork. The sausage mixture can be made as needed and cooked immediately, just as it is, or packed into sausage skins. It can then be hung in a cool place and kept until needed.

DRIED MEATS

Machaca is meat, usually beef, that has been salted and sun-dried before being shredded. This way of preparing meat is typical of northern Mexico, from Sonora in the west to Monterrey in the east. *Machaca* is often mixed with scrambled eggs, beans and cheese and wrapped in a flour tortilla. *Carne seca* (the term simply translates as "dried meat") is cut into chunks and served as an appetizer with fresh lime juice. It is one of the most popular dishes of the northern part of Mexico.

Below: Chorizo

Making Fresh Chorizo

As is so often the case, bought sausages can be good, but there is little comparison to the homemade product. Chorizo is easy to make, and you can prepare it in bulk, then freeze the surplus. Air-drying is best left to the experts.

MAKES ABOUT 2 POUNDS

INGREDIENTS

2 pounds ground pork
2 teaspoons each salt and
  ground black pepper
½ teaspoon freshly grated nutmeg
1 teaspoon dried thyme
½ teaspoon ground anise
½ teaspoon ground bay leaf
3 garlic cloves, crushed
½ cup sherry
  or brandy
juice of 2 limes

1 Place the meat in a large bowl and mix in all the other ingredients. Cover and chill in the refrigerator for at least 4 hours or overnight, so that all the flavors blend together.

2 Fill sausage skins with the meat mixture to make individual sausages. Use the sausages immediately or freeze until needed.

3 Cook by pricking the skins in several places, then immersing the sausages in a saucepan of boiling water. Continue to boil for 10 minutes or until the meat is thoroughly cooked.

4 If you prefer, you can shape the sausagemeat into small patties and fry them in a little fat, turning them once to ensure even cooking. Serve the sausages hot, with a spicy tomato-based sauce.

SALTED MEAT AND FISH

Salting was a useful way of preserving meat for long periods in the days before people had refrigerators. If a family slaughtered a pig or cow, every piece of the animal was utilized; by drying surplus meat or making it into sausages, it would have been possible to make it last for several months. Fish was salted for much the same reason, but what began as a necessity is now a delicacy, as Mexicans became very fond of fish prepared in this manner. Today, when the need for preserving fish is not as pressing, salt fish, particularly cod, is still popular in Mexican, Spanish, Caribbean and even French cooking.

Soaking Salted Fish

To make it edible, salted fish should be soaked for several hours, preferably overnight. The fish will also have picked up grit and dirt, and is hard and stiff, and needs to be cleaned and softened before it is cooked. Place the fish in a large bowl of fresh water. Change the water frequently. After the fish has soaked for some time, test the water to see how salty it is. As it soaks, the fish will become soft and pliable.

SALT COD

Buying and Storing

Salt cod is available at ethnic food stores and some supermarkets, and can be kept in a cupboard for several months before use. The pieces on display look incredibly unappetizing and are rock hard. They are also usually unwrapped and might have a slightly grimy appearance. Don't let this turn you off, when it has been cleaned and rehydrated, salt fish is perfectly safe to cook with and consume.

Main Uses and Cooking Tips

Before cooking, salt cod must be soaked in water for several hours, or overnight if possible. Change the water frequently to get rid of any dirt and to reduce the salt content. *Bacalao a la Vizcalna* is a salt cod stew that originated in Spain, but is now the traditional dish for Christmas Eve dinner in Mexico. Salt cod can also be cooked and served with a chili sauce or a classic fresh tomato or citrus salsa.

Right: Salt cod

Making *Machaca* at Home

This might seem an unusual technique for preparing beef, but the results make for a totally authentic experience of Mexican food.

INGREDIENTS
  2 pounds sirloin steak, about
    ¼ inch thick
  3 tablespoons medium ground
    sea salt

1 Trim off any gristle from the meat and then sprinkle both sides with the sea salt.

2 Make a hole in each piece of meat and thread string through, or hang the meat from a butcher's hook.

3 Hang the meat for about 3 days in a cool dry place so it can dry out. Alternatively, place the meat on a raised broiler pan or suspend it from a rotisserie bar, so that the air can circulate around it, and dry it out in an oven heated to the lowest setting.

4 When the meat is completely dry, place it in a bowl and pour on water to cover. Let it rehydrate for about 30 minutes.

5 Drain the meat, and shred it with two forks.

6 Spread it out to dry again. When it has dried, store it in a covered box in the refrigerator until needed.

CHEESE

As it is a complete protein, cheese was an important addition to the Mexican diet. Until its arrival, Mexicans' main sources of protein were beans and corn, both of which are incomplete. Cheese is widely used in Mexican cooking. The type for each dish is carefully chosen, and the properties—crumbling, melting, grating—are as important as the flavor.

In terms of the history of Mexican cuisine, cheese arrived on the scene fairly late. Before the Conquest in 1521, the main source of meat was the pig, and there was therefore no milk. The Spanish invaders established vast estates and introduced dairy cattle to the country. Milk, cream and butter were produced, and the monks who traveled with the conquerors taught the local people how to make cheeses. At first these were based on traditional Spanish cheeses such as Manchego, but the Mexicans soon developed several cheeses of their own. Today, the range includes cheeses made from goat's and sheep's milk, and also includes varieties that were introduced to Mexico by later immigrants.

There are many different cheeses available in Mexico, but there are a few types that deserve special mention. Unfortunately, Mexican cheeses are seldom sold outside

Below: Feta and ricotta can be used as substitutes for Mexican cheeses.

the country, so acceptable substitutes are suggested for cooks who are unable to access the authentic ingredient.

Below: Mozzarella can be used as a substitute for Asadero.

QUESO FRESCO

As the name suggests, *queso fresco* (fresh cheese) is young and unripened. *Queso fresco* is actually the generic name for a number of different cheeses, of all which share some common characteristics, being moist and creamy in color, with a very mild flavor and a crumbly texture. The cheese is often used for crumbling on dishes such as scrambled eggs, cooked *nopales* (cactus leaves) or other vegetables. It is also used in tacos and other snacks based on tortillas.

Queso fresco has a clean, sharp taste and is a good melting cheese. If you can't locate it, substitute a good quality ricotta or mozzarella, preferably bought at a specialty Italian food store.

ASADERO

The name means "roasting cheese," and this is a mild curd cheese that is beautifully supple. *Asadero* is best when it is melted, and is ideal for stuffing chiles or other vegetables or meats, as it is unlikely to leak out. The closest equivalent is mozzarella.

Left: Queso Anejo

QUESO ANEJO

Anejo means "aged." This is an aged, hard, dry cheese. Sharp and salty, it can be grated easily. *Anejo* is often used for sprinkling on top of enchiladas. Parmesan cheese makes a good substitute.

QUESO CHIHUAHUA

This cheese resembles *anejo*, but is less salty. Substitute medium Cheddar cheese for it in recipes.

QUESO DE OAXACA

This is another stringy cheese that is ideal for cooking, as it has good melting properties. It tastes slightly tart. Monterey Jack is recommended as a substitute in recipes.

Monterey Jack

Monterey Jack is a Californian cheese that originated as *queso del pais* ("country cheese"). Spanish missionaries taught the people of California to make it in the early part of the 18th century. The recipe, which is still being used today, was actually refined in Monterey, California, about 200 years ago. The "Jack" part of the name is reputed to owe its origin to David Jacks, who made the cheese in his dairy; the "s" was dropped when it was felt that the name Monterey Jack was more catchy.

The cheese has a mild flavor and creamy texture and is good to eat on its own, as well as being a useful cooking cheese. It ages well, developing a sweet, nutty flavor over time. Monterey Jack can be substituted in any recipe calling for *Queso de Oaxaca*, *asadero* or *Chihuahua* cheese. Monterey Jack is very popular all over North America, and is now available in other countries too. If you can't locate Monterey Jack, a mild Cheddar cheese can be used.

Minguichi

Chiles and cheese make an excellent partnership, and the pairing is especially celebrated in dishes called *minguichi* in Michoacán and *chiles con queso* (chiles with cheese) in other areas. There are innumerable variations on the basic theme, using whatever ingredients are to hand. Serve *chiles con queso* on its own with corn tortillas or tortilla chips, or stir in some *Frijoles de Olla* to add more body to the dip. This dish is also very good if chipotle chiles (smoked jalapeños) are used instead of anchos.

In Mexico, this would be made with *crema*, a thick cream with a slightly acidic flavor. *Crema* is not readily available outside Mexico, so crème fraîche has been used instead.

MAKES ABOUT 3 CUPS

INGREDIENTS
1 cup crème fraîche
2 cups grated medium Cheddar cheese
2 ancho chiles, seeded and toasted until crisp

1 Spoon the crème fraîche into a heavy saucepan and cook over low heat until warmed.

2 Add the cheese and stir until it melts. Crumble in the chiles and mix well, then pour into a bowl and serve immediately.

HERBS, SEASONINGS AND SPICES

Mexican cooking makes use of a wide range of flavorings. Chiles are clearly at the top of the list. There are so many different varieties that fresh and dried chiles, chili powders and pastes can create a wide range of flavors, from fiery or merely spicy to supremely subtle. Chiles are by no means the only flavorings used in Mexico, however. Spices like cinnamon and allspice are popular, and herbs also play an important role. Some, such as epazote, are native to the country, while others were first introduced by Spanish and other immigrant groups.

Achiote

This is the hard red-orange seed of the annatto tree, which is native to the warmer parts of South America, including some areas of Mexico. The seed is ground and added to food to give color and flavor. Good quality, fresh achiote seeds give food a distinctive, earthy flavor. Achiote is used a lot in the Yucatán, where it is included in pastes that are spread on meats before cooking.

Allspice

This tree is native to Jamaica, although it may also have grown naturally in the coastal area of Mexico around Tabasco. Columbus is reputed to have brought it to Europe from Jamaica, having mistaken the berries for peppercorns—the Spanish call the spice *pimienta*, which means pepper. Allspice berries are picked, dried and ground or used whole. They are used in various types of *Escabeche* to add flavor to vegetables or fish which is being pickled, and are also added to meat dishes. They even feature in desserts and drinks.

Cinnamon

Sri Lankan cinnamon is used quite extensively in Mexican cooking in both sweet and savory dishes. It was introduced during the colonial era, and is a favorite spice in chorizo sausages. It is also used in rice pudding and is added to such drinks as *Rompope*. Mexican chocolate, which is used to make hot drinks, contains cinnamon. Both ground cinnamon and sticks are used in Mexican cooking.

Cloves

Cloves were brought to Mexico from Asia, via Spain. They are used in the complex spice mixes that are so important in making *moles* and *pepiáns* for cooking with meat and poultry.

Coriander

Fresh coriander leaves, called cilantro, are used in a number of savory dishes and salsas. The herb is native to

Above: Allspice, top, cinnamon sticks and ground cinnamon, and achiote, bottom.

Below: Cumin, right, coriander, left and cloves, bottom right.

Right: Oregano

Cumin Seeds

Cumin seeds are ground with other spices in some savory dishes, but are neither used alone nor used in large amounts, as their taste would overpower other, more delicate flavors. Native to Egypt, cumin was introduced in Mexican cuisine during colonial times.

Tamarind

The dark brown, bean-shaped pod comes from the tamarind tree, which has grown in India for centuries. The Spanish introduced it to the West Indies in the 17th century, and it has been growing there ever since. Tamarind is usually marketed as a pressed block of pods and pulp—much like a block of pressed pitted dates—and is often sold at Indian food stores. The taste is a refreshing mixture of sweet and sour.

Vanilla

Records depicting Aztec life reveal that they were familiar with vanilla, and there is also evidence that it was used

Europe, but is grown in South America too. It has a wonderful flavor and aroma. Coriander seeds are also used in some Mexican recipes, but the two should not be confused, nor should one be substituted for the other, as they have very different flavors.

Right: Vanilla

in Mexico in the 16th century as a flavoring for hot chocolate. Vanilla beans grow on vines, and until the 1800s, the spice was grown exclusively in Mexico. Good quality beans are very dark brown, waxy and malleable. The spice has a rich aroma and a sweet taste. It is perfect for adding to desserts and is also used to flavor drinks.

Epazote

This herb is widely used in Mexican cooking, but is, unfortunately, not available outside Mexico unless you grow it yourself. There is no real substitute for the distinctive, sharply pungent flavor of this fresh herb. *Epazote* is also useful because when it is cooked with beans such as black beans, it can help to relieve flatulence.

Oregano

There are several varieties of oregano grown in Mexico. The most popular type is from the verbena family; its flavor is stronger and more aromatic than that of the European varieties. Sold fresh or dried at markets across Mexico, oregano adds a delightful sweet note to *Escabeche*, stews and meat dishes.

Right: Tamarind

Vanilla Sugar

Place a vanilla bean in a large jar full of sugar. It gives the sugar a wonderful flavor, which is great in cakes and other desserts, and one pod will flavor several jars full of sugar before it is exhausted.

ALCOHOLIC DRINKS

Mexico has a large number of fermented beverages, mainly derived from fruit or a plant called the agave. Many of these are an acquired taste and not particularly popular outside the country.

BEER

Mexicans were introduced to the brewing process by the German settlers who came to their country, and many of the brewing companies in existence today have German roots. Mexican beer production centers largely around the north of the country, although there are breweries everywhere. The city of Monterrey in Nuevo León is renowned as the beer capital of Mexico. Many people are employed in brewing and subsidiary industries such as glass making, carton manufacturing and label printing,

Above: Beers

and the beer industry is an important part of the economy. Mexican beer brands such as Dos Equis, Sol and Corona are exported, although these are often brewed outside Mexico on licence. Other brands, such as Tecate, which are less readily available, are worth trying.

WINE

Wine production on a large scale was actively discouraged during the years of Spanish rule, as the conquerors wanted to promote wines and spirits from Spain. A wine industry finally did grow up, however, in Baja California, and even today, the major vineyards are in the northwest of the country, although there is some wine production further south. New World wines have become an important part of the wine market in recent years, and there is increased interest in wines from Mexico, which are very reasonably priced. The popular grapes for the production of white wine are Chardonnay, Sauvignon Blanc,

Left: Red wine

Right: White wine

Riesling and Chenin Blanc, while established red grape varieties include Cabernet Sauvignon, Pinot Noir and Grenache, as well as Merlot.

PULQUE

Records from the time of Cortés make reference to *pulque* being drunk by the Aztecs. It is a beer-like drink made from the sap of the agave plant, which is commonly called *maguey* in Mexico. While chocolate drinks were the preserve of the ruling classes in 16th century Mexico, *pulque* was drunk by the common people. The drink is still popular today, and *pulquerìas*, small bars selling *pulque* are widespread. These bars were once reputed to be wild, dangerous places, and women, children and people in uniform were not allowed to frequent them.

The traditional method for making *pulque* has changed little since the days of the Aztecs. The sap is extracted from the plant, allowed to ferment for a few weeks, then drunk. If left, it would continue to ferment and would quite soon become undrinkable. The short life span of the product means that it is seldom sold outside Mexico.

Pulque, which is between 6 and 8 percent proof, has a unique, slightly earthy flavor, and is very definitely an acquired taste. In Mexico, efforts to make it more universally acceptable include blending it with a fruit juice such as pineapple and selling it in cans.

Right: Pulque

KAHLÚA

This is a coffee liqueur made in Mexico city and popular throughout the world. It is added to fresh coffee to make after-dinner coffee and often features in cocktails. Kahlúa is delicious when drunk from a straight liqueur glass with a thin layer of cream floated on the top, and is also irresistible when blended with vanilla ice cream.

MESCAL

This is the generic name for agave spirit. Tequila, which will be discussed in more detail later, is just one type of *mescal*. Unfortunately, in western Europe, the name *mescal* is synonymous with one particular brand of the spirit, which has a *maguey* worm in the bottle. This has led to some monumental drinking sessions, as individuals competed to see who would land the worm, and the reputation of *mescal* suffered in the process. For the record, the worm was originally placed in the bottle to demonstrate the alcoholic proof of the *mescal*, the argument being that the preservation of the worm (actually a moth larva) proved the potency of the alcohol. Oaxaca is largely credited by aficionados as being one of the best areas for *mescal* production. The traditional way of producing the spirit involves taking the heart or *piña* from a number of plants and cooking them in a large pit. An average *piña* will weigh about 110 pounds. The procedure begins with the digging of the pit. A large fire is built in the bottom, and a layer of rocks is piled on top. When the fire has been burning under the rocks for about a day, the *piñas* are added. They are left to cook for 2–3 days. The cooking plays a large part in determining the flavor, aroma and smoothness of the *mescal*, and is a

Left: Kahlúa

skilled job. After cooking, the *piñas* are removed from the pit and crushed to release the juice. This, together with the fibrous part of the plant, is mixed with water and left to ferment. More modern methods, involving special ovens, are now used by commercial producers to cook the *piñas* and control the all-important fermentation process.

TEQUILA

Tequila is, without doubt, the Mexican spirit which is best known outside the country. A specific type of *mescal*, it is becoming steadily more popular, especially among younger drinkers.

The Spanish taught Mexicans the art of distilling. *Pulque*, the national drink made from the agave plant, was the perfect subject, and they began by distilling it to make *mescal*. This was then distilled a second time to produce tequila. If *mescal* is brandy, then tequila is Cognac, and is subject to similar

Left: Mescal

Right: Tequila

controls to those that are imposed by the French government on their famous spirit. There are also parallels with the production of Champagne, in that tequila production is tightly regulated and may only take place in specially designated areas.

Tequila takes its name from the eponymous town in Jalisco where it was first made. The name means "volcano" in the local Indian dialect. Jalisco is also the home of *mariachi* music, which possibly explains how tequila gained its image as a fun, party drink.

Production

Tequila is made from the sap of the blue agave plant, which is not a cactus, as is commonly believed, but is related to the amaryllis. The leaves of each plant are cut off to leave the *piña*,

which is then steam cooked. The juice is fermented, then distilled twice, the second time in a copper still, after which it is bottled or matured in casks. All aspects of the process are rigidly controlled and documented.

Flavor Variations

There are several different types of tequila, and innumerable brands of all of these. Each brand has a different flavor, determined by the soil and the climate where the agave was grown, the amount of sugar the agave contained and the finer details of the processing, including the cooking of the *piña* and the fermentation of the juice. Some tequilas are aged in casks, and the type of wood used, together with the duration of the aging process, will also influence the flavor of the finished product.

Not all tequilas are 100 percent agave spirit; some are blended with cane spirit, but by law tequila must contain at least 51 percent agave spirit. Blended tequilas are becoming less popular in foreign markets as consumers become more discriminating. At one time

Left: Tequila blanco

Below: Tequila and lime

*Right: A bottle of
Tequila anejo*

Types of Tequila

Joven or blanco tequila has been bottled immediately after distillation. It is usually clear, but can sometimes be golden in color. This classification also includes tequilas that have been aged for less than 60 days.

Reposada tequila is golden in color and has been aged in oak for 2–6 months. It has a more rounded flavor than joven tequila.

Anejo tequila has been aged in oak for a year or more and has a rich golden color.

Curados is the name given to blanco or joven tequila that has been naturally flavored. Cinnamon sticks, chillies, almonds and vanilla beans are among the whole flavorings used, but extracts and syrups can also be used.

Developing a Taste for Tequila

The best way to become a discriminating tequila drinker is to try as many different brands and types as possible. Compare and contrast them in terms of their appearance, bouquet, viscosity and flavor. Few tequilas taste of only one thing; most are a complex blend of flavors. They may taste sweet, earthy, woody, smooth or even smoky. It is a good idea to taste a new tequila against a familiar brand to give a standard for comparison.

Tequila Drinking

Drinking a shot of tequila in the classic manner, with a lick of salt beforehand and a wedge of lime after, is one of the best ways to sample this drink. The method was originally adopted because the spirit was so crude that salt and lime were deemed necessary to make it palatable.

A natural progression from the tequila shot was the margarita. The rim of the glass is dipped in salt, the lime juice and tequila are combined and

triple sec—orange liqueur—is added. A margarita may be served neat, as it comes out of the bottle, or over ice cubes, or "frozen" with crushed ice.

In Mexico, tequila is often sipped alternately with a glass of *sangrita*, a tomato juice flavored with chiles and other seasonings. When the tequila and tomato juice are combined, the drink becomes a Bloody Maria.

Below: Two types of Curados; bottles of blanco tequila that have had flavoring added. Here a few red chiles have been added to the bottle on the left, and three vanilla pods to the one on the right. The tequila will take on the flavor of the chile or vanilla in just a few days.

you could walk into a bar in Britain or Europe and find only one type of tequila—and that was primarily used for making margaritas. However, the increasing popularity of Mexican food has led to a gradual rise in the popularity of tequila and a greater appreciation of the various types, and in some places today there are even specialty tequila bars, which stock a vast range of different types and brands of this exciting spirit.

Left: Margarita

THE RECIPES

Mexican cooking is so much more than enchiladas and empanadas, although these are both worthy of mention. Until relatively recently, many Mexican restaurants outside the country tended to serve Tex-Mex food, which owed its origins to Mexico but had been modified by the country's northern neighbors. Today, discerning diners seek out places that serve true Mexican food—colorful, imaginative and not always fiery—and are eager to recreate their favorite dishes at home.

Supermarkets, gourmet stores and mail-order suppliers have responded to the changing market by stocking specialty ingredients—even such unusual items as tomatillos and the less common varieties of chile—and this has made it much easier for enthusiastic cooks. The recipes that follow are a cross-section of all the different regional dishes available in this exciting country and illustrate the diversity of flavors, textures and cooking methods that make Mexican cooking so fascinating and delicious.

SALSAS

Salsa simply means sauce, and Mexico is home to some of the finest. Hot and spicy, cool and refreshing, cooked or fresh, all are as versatile as they are varied. Some are poured onto food, others are served as relishes. There are a number of classic salsas that are widely used. Chief among the cooked sauces is Pumpkin Seed Sauce, or Pepián, in which the seeds are roasted to give a rich, nutty flavor. Green Tomatillo Sauce, known as Salsa Verde, is very tasty when served over enchiladas or with pork.

Of the many uncooked sauces, Classic Tomato Salsa, known as Salsa Ranchera, or Salsa Mexicana, is probably the most popular. This combination of tomatoes, onion, cilantro and lime makes a superb accompaniment that appears on almost every table. Unlike commercial sauces, many Mexican salsas contain neither oil nor added sugar, but rely for their flavor on fresh raw fruits and vegetables, making them an excellent choice for the health-conscious.

The bright colors, incomparable flavors and adaptability of salsas make them indispensable to any good cook, and their usefulness extends far beyond the boundaries of Mexican cuisine.

CLASSIC TOMATO SALSA

THIS IS THE TRADITIONAL TOMATO-BASED SALSA THAT MOST PEOPLE ASSOCIATE WITH MEXICAN FOOD. THERE ARE INNUMERABLE RECIPES FOR IT, BUT THE BASICS OF ONION, TOMATO, CHILE AND CILANTRO ARE COMMON TO EVERY ONE OF THEM. SERVE THIS SALSA AS A CONDIMENT WITH A WIDE VARIETY OF DISHES.

SERVES SIX AS AN ACCOMPANIMENT

INGREDIENTS
3–6 fresh serrano chiles
1 large white onion
grated zest and juice of 2 limes, plus
   strips of lime zest, to garnish
8 ripe, firm tomatoes
large bunch of cilantro
¼ teaspoon sugar
salt

1 Use three chiles for a salsa of medium heat, up to six if you like it hot. To peel the chiles, spear them on a long-handled metal skewer and roast them over the flame of a gas burner until the skins blister and darken. Do not let the flesh burn. Alternatively, dry-fry them in a griddle until the skins are scorched.

2 Place the roasted chiles in a strong plastic bag and tie the top of the bag to keep the steam in. Set aside for about 20 minutes.

3 Meanwhile, chop the onion finely and put it in a bowl with the lime rind and juice. The lime juice will soften the onion.

4 Remove the chiles from the bag and peel off the skins. Cut off the stalks, then slit the chiles and scrape out the seeds with a sharp knife. Chop the flesh roughly and set aside.

5 Cut a small cross in the bottom of each tomato. Place the tomatoes in a heatproof bowl and pour in boiling water to cover.

6 Leave the tomatoes in the water for 3 minutes, then lift them out using a slotted spoon and plunge them into a bowl of cold water. Drain. The skins will have begun to peel back from the crosses. Remove the skins completely.

7 Dice the peeled tomatoes and put them in a bowl. Add the chopped onion which should have softened, together with the lime mixture. Chop the cilantro finely.

8 Add the cilantro to the salsa, with the chiles and the sugar. Mix gently until the sugar has dissolved and all the ingredients are coated in lime juice. Cover and chill for 2–3 hours to let the flavors blend. The salsa will keep for 3–4 days in the refrigerator. Garnish with the strips of lime zest just before serving.

VARIATIONS
Use scallions or mild red onions instead of white onion. For a smoky flavor, use chipotle chiles instead of fresh serrano chiles.

GREEN TOMATILLO SAUCE

This sauce, with its distinctive green color and sharp taste, is a popular choice for pouring onto enchiladas. When the cream is added, it is perfect for poached fish or with chicken breasts. Fresh tomatillos are difficult to obtain outside Mexico, but the sauce can be made with canned tomatillos. Instructions for both versions are given here.

SERVES FOUR AS A SAUCE
FOR A MAIN COURSE

INGREDIENTS
11 ounces fresh tomatillos,
  plus ½ cup stock or water **or**
11 ounces drained canned
  tomatillos, plus ¼ cup stock
  or water
2 fresh serrano chiles
4 garlic cloves, crushed
1 tablespoon vegetable oil
small bunch of cilantro
½ cup heavy cream
  (optional)
salt

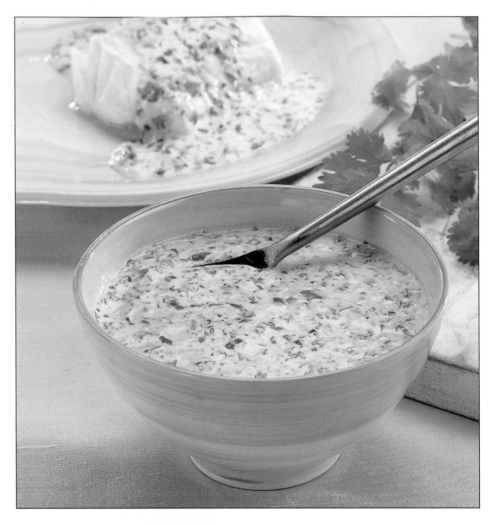

1 If using fresh tomatillos, remove the husks and cut the tomatillos into quarters. Place them in a saucepan and add the stock or water. Cook over medium heat for 8–10 minutes, until the flesh is soft and transparent.

2 Remove the stems from the chiles, slit them and scrape out the seeds with a small knife. Chop the flesh roughly and place it in a food processor or blender with the garlic.

3 Add the tomatillos to the processor or blender with their cooking liquid and process for a few minutes until almost smooth. If using drained canned tomatillos, simply quarter and put in the blender or food processor with the smaller amount of stock or water and the chopped chiles and garlic. Process until almost smooth.

4 Heat the oil in a heavy frying pan and add the processed tomatillo purée. Reduce the heat and cook gently, stirring, for about 5 minutes, until the sauce thickens. Be sure to keep stirring the sauce all the time, since it can easily stick and burn.

5 Chop the cilantro and add it to the sauce, with salt to taste. Cook for a few minutes, stirring occasionally.

6 Stir in the cream, if using, and warm the sauce through. Do not let it boil after adding the cream. Serve immediately.

GUACAMOLE

ONE OF THE BEST LOVED MEXICAN SALSAS, THIS BLEND OF CREAMY AVOCADO, TOMATOES, CHILES, CILANTRO AND LIME NOW APPEARS ON TABLES ALL OVER THE WORLD. PURCHASED GUACAMOLE USUALLY CONTAINS MAYONNAISE, WHICH HELPS TO PRESERVE THE AVOCADO, BUT THIS IS NOT AN INGREDIENT IN TRADITIONAL RECIPES.

SERVES SIX TO EIGHT

INGREDIENTS
    4 medium tomatoes
    4 ripe avocados
    juice of 1 lime
    ½ small onion
    2 garlic cloves
    small bunch of cilantro,
        chopped
    3 fresh red fresno chiles
    salt
    tortilla chips, to serve

1 Cut a cross in the bottom of each tomato. Place the tomatoes in a heatproof bowl and pour in boiling water to cover.

2 Leave the tomatoes in the water for 3 minutes, then lift them out using a slotted spoon and plunge them into a bowl of cold water. Drain. The skins will have begun to peel back from the crosses. Remove the skins completely. Cut the tomatoes in half, remove the seeds with a teaspoon, then chop the flesh roughly and set it aside.

COOK'S TIP
Smooth-skinned fuerte avocados are native to Mexico, so would be ideal for this dip. If they are not available, use any avocados, but make sure they are ripe. To test, gently press the top of the avocado; it should give a little.

3 Cut the avocados in half, then remove the pits. Scoop the flesh out of the shells and place it in a food processor or blender. Process until almost smooth, then scrape into a bowl and stir in the lime juice.

4 Chop the onion finely, then crush the garlic. Add both to the avocado and mix well. Stir in the cilantro.

5 Remove the stems from the chiles, slit them and scrape out the seeds with a small sharp knife. Chop the chiles finely and add them to the avocado mixture, with the chopped tomatoes. Mix well.

6 Check the seasoning and add salt to taste. Cover closely with plastic wrap or a tight-fitting lid and chill for 1 hour before serving as a dip with tortilla chips. If it is well covered, guacamole will keep in the refrigerator for 2–3 days.

BLACK BEAN SALSA

This salsa has a very striking appearance. It is rare to find a black sauce, and it provides a wonderful contrast to the more common reds and greens on the plate. The pasado chiles add a subtle citrus flavor. Use the salsa a day or two after making to let the flavors develop fully.

SERVES FOUR AS AN ACCOMPANIMENT

INGREDIENTS

generous ½ cup black beans,
   soaked overnight in water
   to cover
1 pasado chile
2 fresh red fresno chiles
1 red onion
grated zest and juice of 1 lime
2 tablespoons Mexican beer
   (optional)
1 tablespoon olive oil
small bunch of cilantro, chopped
salt

1 Drain the beans and put them in a large saucepan. Pour in water to cover and place the lid on the pan. Bring to a boil, lower the heat slightly and simmer the beans for about 40 minutes or until tender. They should still have a little bite and should not have begun to disintegrate. Drain, rinse under cold water, then drain again and leave the beans until cold.

2 Soak the pasado chile in hot water for about 10 minutes, until softened. Drain, remove the stalk, then slit the chile and scrape out the seeds with a small sharp knife. Chop the flesh finely.

COOK'S TIP
Mexican beer is a lager-type beer. Few brands are to be found in this country, but the most popular, *Dos Equis* (Double X), is readily available.

3 Spear the fresno chiles on a long-handled metal skewer and roast them over the flame of a gas burner until the skins blister and darken. Do not let the flesh burn. Alternatively, dry-fry them on a griddle until the skins are scorched. Then place the roasted chiles in a strong plastic bag and tie the top to keep the steam in. Set aside for 20 minutes.

4 Meanwhile, chop the red onion finely. Remove the chiles from the bag and peel off the skins. Slit them, remove the seeds and chop them finely.

5 Transfer the beans to a bowl and add the onion and both types of chile. Stir in the lime zest and juice, beer, oil and cilantro. Season with salt and mix well. Chill before serving.

PINTO BEAN SALSA

THESE BEANS HAVE A PRETTY, SPECKLED APPEARANCE. THE SMOKY FLAVOR OF THE CHIPOTLE CHILES AND THE HERBAL TASTE OF THE PASILLA CHILE CONTRAST WELL WITH THE TART TOMATILLOS.

2 Soak the chipotle and pasilla chiles in hot water for about 10 minutes, until softened. Drain, reserving the soaking water. Remove the stems, then slit each chile and scrape out the seeds with a small sharp knife. Chop the flesh finely and mix into a smooth paste with a little of the soaking water.

3 Roast the garlic in a dry frying pan over medium heat for a few minutes, until the cloves start to turn golden. Crush them and add them to the beans.

4 Chop the onion and tomatillos and stir them into the beans. Add the chile paste and mix well. Add salt to taste, cover and chill before serving.

SERVES FOUR AS AN ACCOMPANIMENT

INGREDIENTS
    generous ½ cup pinto beans,
      soaked overnight in water
      to cover
    2 chipotle chiles
    1 pasilla chile
    2 garlic cloves, peeled
    ½ onion
    7 ounces fresh tomatillos
    salt

1 Drain the beans and put them in a large saucepan. Pour in water to cover and place the lid on the pan. Bring to a boil, lower the heat slightly and simmer the beans for 45–50 minutes or until tender. They should still have a little bite and should not have begun to disintegrate. Drain, rinse under cold water, then drain again and transfer into a bowl. Leave the beans until cold.

COOK'S TIP
Canned tomatillos can be substituted, but to keep a clean, fresh flavor, add a little lime juice.

CHIPOTLE SAUCE

THE SMOKY FLAVOR OF THIS SAUCE MAKES IT IDEAL FOR GRILLED FOOD, EITHER AS A MARINADE OR AS AN ACCOMPANIMENT. IT IS ALSO WONDERFUL STIRRED INTO CREAM CHEESE AS A SANDWICH FILLING WITH CHICKEN. CHIPOTLE CHILES ARE SMOKED DRIED JALAPEÑO CHILES.

SERVES SIX AS AN ACCOMPANIMENT

INGREDIENTS
1¼ pounds tomatoes
5 chipotle chiles
3 garlic cloves, roughly chopped
⅔ cup red wine
1 teaspoon dried oregano
4 tablespoons honey
1 teaspoon American mustard
½ teaspoon ground black pepper
salt

1 Preheat the oven to 400°F. Cut the tomatoes into quarters and place them in a roasting pan. Roast for 45 minutes–1 hour, until they are charred and softened.

2 Meanwhile, soak the chiles in a bowl of cold water to cover for about 20 minutes or until soft. Remove the stalks, slit the chiles and scrape out the seeds with a small sharp knife. Chop the flesh roughly.

3 Remove the tomatoes from the oven, let them cool slightly, then remove the skins. If you prefer a smooth sauce, remove the seeds. Chop the tomatoes and put them in a blender or food processor. Add the chopped chiles and garlic with the red wine. Process until smooth, then add the oregano, honey, mustard and black pepper. Process briefly to mix, then taste and season with salt.

4 Scrape the mixture into a small saucepan. Place over medium heat and stir until the mixture boils. Lower the heat and simmer the sauce for about 10 minutes, stirring occasionally, until it has reduced and thickened. Spoon into a bowl and serve hot or cold.

GUAJILLO CHILI SAUCE

THIS SAUCE CAN BE SERVED OVER ENCHILADAS OR STEAMED VEGETABLES. IT IS ALSO GOOD WITH MEATS, SUCH AS PORK, AND A LITTLE MAKES A FINE SEASONING FOR SOUPS OR STEWS. MADE FROM DRIED CHILES, IT HAS A WELL ROUNDED, FRUITY FLAVOR AND IS NOT TOO HOT.

SERVES FOUR AS AN ACCOMPANIMENT

INGREDIENTS
2 tomatoes, total weight about 7 ounces
2 red bell peppers, cored, seeded and quartered
3 garlic cloves, in their skins
2 ancho chiles
2 guajillo chiles
2 tablespoons tomato paste
1 teaspoon dried oregano
1 teaspoon dark brown sugar
1¼ cups chicken stock

1 Preheat the oven to 400°F. Cut the tomatoes into quarters and place them in a roasting pan with the peppers and whole garlic cloves. Roast for 45 minutes–1 hour, until the tomatoes and peppers are slightly charred and the garlic has softened.

2 Put the peppers in a strong plastic bag and tie the top to keep the steam in. Set aside for 20 minutes. Remove the skin from the tomatoes. Meanwhile, soak the chiles in boiling water for 15 minutes, until soft.

3 Remove the peppers from the bag and rub off the skins. Cut them in half, remove the cores and seeds, then chop the flesh roughly and put it in a food processor or blender. Drain the chiles, remove the stems, then slit them and scrape out the seeds with a sharp knife. Chop the chiles roughly and add them to the peppers.

4 Add the roasted tomatoes to the food processor or blender. Squeeze the roasted garlic out of the skins and add to the tomato mixture, with the tomato paste, oregano, brown sugar and stock. Process until smooth.

5 Pour the mixture into a saucepan, place over medium heat and bring to a boil. Lower the heat and simmer for 10–15 minutes, until the sauce has reduced to about half. Transfer to a bowl and serve immediately or, if serving cold, cover, let cool, then chill until needed. The sauce will keep in the refrigerator for up to a week.

ROASTED TOMATO SALSA

Slow roasting these tomatoes to a semi-dried state results in a very rich, full-flavored sweet sauce. The costeno amarillo chile is mild and has a fresh light flavor, making it the perfect partner for the rich tomato taste. This salsa is great with tuna or sea bass and makes a great sandwich filling when teamed with creamy cheese.

SERVES SIX AS AN ACCOMPANIMENT

INGREDIENTS
1¼ pounds tomatoes
8 small shallots
5 garlic cloves
sea salt
1 fresh rosemary sprig
2 costeno amarillo chiles
grated zest and juice of ½ small
   lemon
2 tablespoons extra virgin olive oil
¼ teaspoon dark brown sugar

1 Preheat the oven to 325ºF. Cut the tomatoes into quarters and place them on a baking tray.

2 Peel the shallots and garlic and add them to the roasting pan. Sprinkle with sea salt. Roast for 1¼ hours or until the tomatoes are beginning to dry. Do not let them burn or blacken or they will have a bitter taste.

3 Let the tomatoes cool, then peel off the skins and chop the flesh finely. Place in a bowl. Remove the outer layer of skin from any shallots that have toughened.

4 Using a large, sharp knife, chop the shallots and garlic roughly, place them with the tomatoes in a bowl and mix.

5 Strip the rosemary leaves from the woody stem and chop them finely. Add half to the tomato and shallot mixture and mix lightly.

6 Soak the chiles in hot water for about 10 minutes, until soft. Drain, remove the stems, slit them and scrape out the seeds with a sharp knife. Chop the flesh finely and add it to the tomato mixture.

7 Stir in the lemon zest and juice, the olive oil and the sugar. Mix well, taste and add more salt if needed. Cover and chill for at least an hour before serving, sprinkled with the remaining rosemary. It will keep for up to a week in the refrigerator.

COOK'S TIP
Use plum tomatoes or vine tomatoes, which have more flavor than tomatoes that have been grown for their keeping properties rather than their flavor. Cherry tomatoes make delicious roast tomato salsa, and there is no need to peel them after roasting.

JICAMA SALSA

The jicama is a round, brown root vegetable with a texture somewhere between that of a water chestnut and a crisp apple. It can be eaten raw or cooked, and is always peeled. Look for jicamas at ethnic food stores.

SERVES FOUR AS AN ACCOMPANIMENT

INGREDIENTS
  1 small red onion
  juice of 2 limes
  3 small oranges
  1 *jicama*, about 1 pound
  ½ cucumber
  1 fresh red fresno chile

1 Cut the onion in half, then slice each half finely. Place in a bowl, add the lime juice and let soak while you prepare the remaining ingredients.

2 Slice the top and bottom off each orange. Stand an orange on a board, then carefully slice off all the peel and pith. Hold the orange over a bowl and cut carefully between the membranes so that the segments fall into the bowl. Having cut out all the segments, squeeze the pulp over the bowl to extract the remaining juice.

3 Peel the *jicama* and rinse it in cold water. Cut it into quarters, then slice finely. Add to the bowl of orange juice.

COOK'S TIP
The juices of citrus fruits are very useful in preserving color and freshness, and add more than flavoring to a recipe. For instance, lemon juice added to sliced apples keeps them white. Guacamole retains its color for two to three days if lime juice is added. In this recipe the lime juice will slightly soften the finely sliced onion.

4 Cut the cucumber in half lengthwise, then use a teaspoon to scoop out the seeds. Slice the cucumber and add to the bowl. Remove the stem from the chile, slit it and scrape out the seeds with a small sharp knife. Chop the flesh finely and add to the bowl.

5 Add the sliced onion to the bowl, with any remaining lime juice, and mix well. Cover and let stand at room temperature for at least 1 hour before serving. If not serving immediately, put the salsa in the refrigerator; it will keep for 2–3 days.

SWEET POTATO SALSA

*VERY COLORFUL AND DELIGHTFULLY SWEET, THIS SALSA MAKES THE PERFECT ACCOMPANIMENT
TO HOT, SPICY MEXICAN DISHES.*

SERVES FOUR AS AN ACCOMPANIMENT

INGREDIENTS
  1½ pounds sweet potatoes
  juice of 1 small orange
  1 teaspoon crushed dried
    jalapeño chiles
  4 small scallions
  juice of 1 small lime (optional)
  salt

COOK'S TIP
This fresh and tasty salsa is also very
good served with a simple grilled salmon
fillet or other fish dishes, and is a
delicious accompaniment to veal cutlets
or grilled chicken breasts.

1 Peel the sweet potatoes and dice the
flesh finely. Bring a saucepan of water
to a boil. Add the sweet potato and cook
for 8–10 minutes, until just soft. Drain
off the water, cover the pan and put it
back on the stove, having first turned
off the heat. Let the sweet potato dry
out for about 5 minutes, then transfer
to a bowl and set aside.

2 Mix the orange juice and crushed
dried chiles in a bowl. Chop the
scallions finely and add them to
the juice and chiles.

3 When the sweet potatoes are cool,
add the orange juice mixture and toss
carefully until all the pieces are coated.
Cover the bowl and chill for at least
1 hour, then taste and season with
salt. Stir in the lime juice, if you
prefer a fresher taste. The salsa will
keep for 2–3 days in a covered bowl in
the refrigerator.

NOPALES SALSA

NOPALES ARE THE TENDER, FLESHY LEAVES OR "PADDLES" OF AN EDIBLE CACTUS KNOWN VARIOUSLY AS THE CACTUS PEAR AND THE PRICKLY PEAR CACTUS. THIS GROWS WILD IN MEXICO, BUT IS ALSO CULTIVATED. THE MOST FAMILIAR TYPE SOLD IN MEXICAN MARKETS HAS DARK GREEN OVALS WITH TINY THORNS. FRESH NOPALES ARE DIFFICULT TO TRACK DOWN OUTSIDE MEXICO, BUT IF YOU DO LOCATE A SUPPLY, LOOK FOR PADDLES THAT ARE FIRM AND SMOOTH SKINNED.

SERVES FOUR AS AN ACCOMPANIMENT

INGREDIENTS
    2 fresh red fresno chiles
    9 ounces *nopales* (cactus paddles)
    3 scallions
    3 garlic cloves, peeled
    ½ red onion
    3½ ounces fresh tomatillos
    ½ teaspoon salt
    ⅔ cup cider vinegar

1 Spear the chiles on a long-handled metal skewer and roast them over the flame of a gas burner until the skins blister and darken. Do not let the flesh burn. Alternatively, dry-fry them in a griddle until the skins are scorched. Place the roasted chiles in a strong plastic bag and tie the top to keep the steam in. Set aside for 20 minutes.

2 Remove the chiles from the bag and peel off the skins. Cut off the stems, then slit the chiles and scrape out the seeds. Chop the chiles roughly and set them aside.

COOK'S TIP
Fresh *nopales* are sometimes available at specialty fruit and vegetable stores. Like okra, they yield a sticky gum and are best boiled before being used. Fresh cactus will lose about half its weight during cooking. Look for canned *nopales* (sometimes sold as *nopalitos*) packed in water or vinegar.

3 Carefully remove the thorns from the nopales. Wearing gloves or holding each cactus paddle in turn with kitchen tongs, cut off the bumps that contain the thorns with a sharp knife.

4 Cut off and discard the thick base from each cactus paddle. Rinse the paddles well and cut them into strips, then cut the strips into small pieces.

5 Bring a large saucepan of lightly salted water to a boil. Add the cactus paddle strips, scallions and garlic. Boil for 10–15 minutes, until the paddle strips are just tender.

6 Drain the mixture in a colander, rinse under cold running water to remove any remaining stickiness, then drain again. Discard the scallions and garlic.

7 Chop the red onion and the tomatillos finely. Place in a bowl and add the cactus and chiles.

8 Spoon the mixture into a large preserving jar, add the salt, pour in the vinegar and seal. Put the jar in the refrigerator for at least 1 day, turning the jar occasionally to ensure that the *nopales* are marinated. The salsa will keep in the refrigerator for up to 10 days.

MANGO SALSA

THIS HAS A FRESH, FRUITY TASTE AND IS PERFECT WITH FISH OR AS A CONTRAST TO RICH, CREAMY DISHES. THE BRIGHT COLORS MAKE IT AN ATTRACTIVE ADDITION TO ANY TABLE.

SERVES FOUR AS AN ACCOMPANIMENT

INGREDIENTS
    2 fresh red fresno chiles
    2 ripe mangoes
    ½ white onion
    small bunch of cilantro
    grated zest and juice of 1 lime

1 To peel the chiles, spear them on a long-handled metal skewer and roast them over the flame of a gas burner until the skins blister and darken. Do not let the flesh burn. Alternatively, dry-fry them in a griddle until the skins are scorched.

2 Place the roasted chiles in a strong plastic bag and tie the top to keep the steam in. Set aside for 20 minutes.

COOK'S TIP
Mangoes, in season, are readily available nowadays, but are usually sold unripe. Keep in a warm room for 24 hours or until they are just soft to the touch. Do not let ripen beyond this point.

3 Meanwhile, put one of the mangoes on a board and cut off a thick slice close to the flat side of the pit. Turn the mango around and repeat on the other side. Score the flesh on each thick slice with criss-cross lines at ½ inch intervals, taking care not to cut through the skin. Repeat with the second mango.

4 Fold the mango halves inside out so that the mango flesh stands proud of the skin, in neat dice. Carefully slice these off the skin and into a bowl. Cut off the flesh adhering to each pit, dice it and add it to the bowl.

5 Remove the roasted chiles from the bag and carefully peel off the skins. Cut off the stems, then slit the chiles and scrape out the seeds.

6 Chop the white onion and the cilantro finely and add them to the diced mango. Chop the chile flesh finely and add it to the mixture in the bowl, together with the lime zest and juice. Stir well to mix, cover and chill for at least 1 hour before serving. The salsa will keep for 2–3 days in the refrigerator.

ROASTED TOMATO AND CILANTRO SALSA

ROASTING THE TOMATOES GIVES A GREATER DEPTH TO THE FLAVOR OF THIS SALSA, WHICH ALSO BENEFITS FROM THE WARM, ROUNDED FLAVOR OF ROASTED CHILES.

SERVES SIX AS AN ACCOMPANIMENT

INGREDIENTS
    1¼ pounds tomatoes
    2 fresh serrano chiles
    1 onion
    juice of 1 lime
    large bunch of cilantro
    salt

1 Preheat the oven to 400°F. Cut the tomatoes into quarters and place them in a roasting pan. Add the chiles. Roast for 45 minutes–1 hour, until the tomatoes and chiles are charred and softened.

2 Place the roasted chiles in a strong plastic bag. Tie the top to keep the steam in and set aside for 20 minutes. Let the tomatoes cool slightly, then remove the skins and dice the flesh.

3 Chop the onion finely, then place in a bowl and add the lime juice and the chopped tomatoes.

4 Remove the chiles from the bag and peel off the skins. Cut off the stalks, then slit the chiles and scrape out the seeds with a sharp knife. Chop the chiles roughly and add them to the onion mixture. Mix well.

5 Chop the cilantro and add most to the salsa. Add salt, cover and chill for at least 1 hour before serving, sprinkled with the remaining cilantro. This salsa will keep in the refrigerator for 1 week.

CHAYOTE SALSA

CHAYOTE—OR *VEGETABLE PEAR, AS IT IS SOMETIMES CALLED—IS A GOURD-LIKE FRUIT, SHAPED LIKE A LARGE PEAR. SEVERAL VARIETIES GROW IN MEXICO, THE MOST COMMON BEING WHITE-FLESHED AND SMOOTH-SKINNED, WITH A TASTE REMINISCENT OF CUCUMBER. CHAYOTES SHOULD BE PEELED BEFORE BEING EATEN RAW OR COOKED. THE SEED, WHICH LOOKS LIKE A LARGE, FLAT ALMOND, IS EDIBLE. THE CONTRAST BETWEEN THE CRISP CHAYOTE, COOL MELON AND HOT HABAÑERO SAUCE MAKES THIS A SPECTACULAR SALSA.*

SERVES SIX AS AN ACCOMPANIMENT

INGREDIENTS
    1 *chayote*, about 7 ounces
    ½ small Galia melon
    2 teaspoons habañero sauce or
      similar hot chili sauce
    juice of 1 lime
    ½ teaspoon salt
    ½ teaspoon sugar

COOK'S TIP
In some countries, *chayotes* are called *christophenes* or *choko*. They are also used in Chinese cooking, so will be found at Chinese food stores.

1 Peel the *chayote*, then cut slices of flesh away from the pit. Cut the slices into thin strips. Cut the melon in half, scoop the seeds out, and cut each half into two pieces. Remove the skin and cut the flesh into small cubes. Place in a bowl with the *chayote* strips.

2 Mix the chili sauce, lime juice, salt and sugar in a bowl or pitcher. Stir until all the sugar has dissolved. Pour onto the melon and *chayote* mixture and mix thoroughly. Chill for at least 1 hour before serving. The salsa will keep for up to 3 days in the refrigerator.

PUMPKIN SEED SAUCE

THE ANCESTORS OF MODERN-DAY MEXICANS DIDN'T BELIEVE IN WASTING FOOD, AS THIS TRADITIONAL RECIPE PROVES. IT IS BASED ON PUMPKIN SEEDS, THE FLESH HAVING BEEN USED FOR ANOTHER DISH, AND HAS A DELICIOUS NUTTY FLAVOR. IT IS GREAT SERVED OVER STEAMED OR BOILED NOPALES (CACTUS PADDLES) AND IS ALSO DELICIOUS WITH COOKED CHICKEN OR RACK OF LAMB.

SERVES FOUR AS AN ACCOMPANIMENT

INGREDIENTS

4½ ounces raw pumpkin seeds
1¼ pounds tomatoes
2 garlic cloves, crushed
1¼ cups chicken stock, preferably
  freshly made
1 tablespoon vegetable oil
3 tablespoons red chili sauce
salt (optional)

1 Preheat the oven to 400°F. Heat a heavy frying pan until very hot. Add the pumpkin seeds and dry-fry them, stirring constantly over the heat. The seeds will start to swell and pop, but they must not be allowed to scorch (see Cook's Tip). When all the seeds have popped, remove the pan from heat.

2 Cut the tomatoes into quarters and place them on a baking sheet. Roast for 45 minutes–1 hour, until charred and softened. Let cool slightly, then remove the skins using a small sharp knife.

3 Put the pumpkin seeds in a food processor and process until smooth. Add the tomatoes and process for a few minutes, then add the garlic and stock and process for 1 more minute.

COOK'S TIP
When dry-frying the pumpkin seeds, don't stop stirring for a moment or they may scorch, which would make the sauce bitter. It is a good idea to stand back a little, as some of the hot seeds may fly out of the pan.

4 Heat the oil in a large frying pan. Add the red chili sauce and cook, stirring constantly, for 2–3 minutes. Add the pumpkin seed mixture and bring to a boil, stirring constantly.

5 Simmer the sauce for 20 minutes, stirring frequently, until the sauce has thickened and reduced by about half. Taste and add salt, if needed. Serve over meat or vegetables or cool and chill. The salsa will keep for up to a week in a covered bowl in the refrigerator.

ONION RELISH

THIS POPULAR RELISH, KNOWN AS CEBOLLAS EN ESCABECHE, IS TYPICAL OF THE YUCATAN REGION AND IS OFTEN SERVED WITH CHICKEN, FISH OR TURKEY DISHES. TRY IT WITH CRACKERS AND CHEESE— IT ADDS A SPICY, TANGY TASTE AND WON'T CONTRIBUTE ANY ADDITIONAL FAT OR SUGAR.

MAKES ONE SMALL JAR

INGREDIENTS
  2 fresh red fresno chiles
  1 teaspoon allspice berries
  ½ teaspoon black peppercorns
  1 teaspoon dried oregano
  2 white onions
  2 garlic cloves, peeled
  ⅓ cup white wine vinegar
  scant 1 cup cider vinegar
  salt

1 Spear the fresno chiles on a long-handled metal skewer and roast them over the flame of a gas burner until the skins blister. Do not let the flesh burn. Alternatively, dry-fry them in a griddle until the skins are scorched. Place the roasted chiles in a strong plastic bag and tie the top to keep the steam in. Set aside for 20 minutes.

2 Meanwhile, place the allspice, black peppercorns and oregano in a mortar or food processor. Grind slowly by hand with a pestle, or process until coarsely ground.

3 Cut the onions in half and slice them thinly. Put them in a bowl. Dry-roast the garlic in a heavy frying pan until golden, then crush and add to the onions in the bowl.

4 Remove the chiles from the bag and peel off the skins. Slit the chiles, scrape out the seeds with a small sharp knife, then chop them.

COOK'S TIP
White onions have a pungent flavor and are good in this salsa; Spanish onions can also be used. Shallots also make an exellent pickle.

5 Add the ground spices to the onion mixture, followed by the chiles. Stir in both vinegars. Add salt to taste and mix thoroughly. Cover the bowl and chill for at least 1 day before use.

CHILE STRIPS <u>WITH</u> LIME

THIS FRESH RELISH IS IDEAL FOR SERVING WITH STEWS, RICE DISHES OR BEAN DISHES. THE OREGANO ADDS A SWEET NOTE, AND THE ABSENCE OF SUGAR OR OIL MAKES THIS A VERY HEALTHY CHOICE.

2 Meanwhile, slice the onion very thinly and put it in a large bowl. Squeeze the limes and add the juice to the bowl, with any pulp that gathers in the strainer. The lime juice will soften the onion. Stir in the oregano.

3 Remove the chiles from the bag and peel off the skins. Slit them, scrape out the seeds with a small sharp knife, then cut the chiles into long strips, which are called "rajas."

4 Add the chile strips to the onion mixture and season with salt. Cover the bowl and chill for at least 1 day before serving, to let the flavors blend. The salsa will keep for up to 2 weeks in a covered bowl in the refrigerator.

MAKES ABOUT 4 TABLESPOONS

INGREDIENTS
    10 fresh green chiles
    ½ white onion
    4 limes
    ½ teaspoon dried oregano
    salt

COOK'S TIP
This method of roasting chiles is ideal if you need more than one or two, or if you do not have a gas burner. To roast over a burner, spear the chiles, four or five at a time, on a long-handled metal skewer and hold them over the flame until the skins blister.

1 Roast the chiles in a griddle over medium heat until the skins are charred and blistered. The flesh should not be allowed to blacken, as this might make the salsa bitter. Place the roasted chiles in a strong plastic bag and tie the top to keep the steam in. Set aside for 20 minutes.

HABAÑERO SALSA

THIS IS A VERY FIERY SALSA WITH AN INTENSE HEAT LEVEL. A DAB ON THE PLATE ALONGSIDE A MEAT OR FISH DISH ADDS A FRESH, CLEAN TASTE, BUT THIS IS NOT FOR THE FAINT-HEARTED. HABAÑERO CHILES, ALSO CALLED SCOTCH BONNETS, ARE VERY HOT. LANTERN-SHAPED, THEY RANGE IN COLOR FROM YELLOW TO A DEEP ORANGE-RED. COSTENO AMARILLO CHILES ARE YELLOW WHEN FRESH AND HAVE A SHARP CITRUS FLAVOR.

3 Put the chiles in a food processor and add a little of the soaking liquid. Purée into a fine paste. Do not lean over the processor—the fumes may burn your face. Remove the lid and scrape the mixture into a bowl.

4 Put the chopped scallions in another bowl and add the fruit juice, with the lime zest and juice. Roughly chop the cilantro.

USE SPARINGLY

INGREDIENTS
  5 dried roasted habañero chiles
  4 dried costeno amarillo chiles
  3 spring onions, finely chopped
  juice of ½ large grapefruit or
   1 Seville orange
  grated zest and juice of 1 lime
  small bunch of cilantro
  salt

1 Soak the habañero and costeno amarillo chiles in hot water for about 10 minutes, until softened. Drain, reserving the soaking water.

2 Wear rubber gloves to handle the habañeros. Remove the stems from all chiles, then slit them and scrape out the seeds with a small sharp knife. Chop the chiles roughly.

5 Carefully add to the cilantro to the chili mixture and mix very thoroughly. Add salt to taste. Cover and chill for at least 1 day before using. Serve the salsa very sparingly.

ADOBO SEASONING

ADOBO MEANS VINEGAR SAUCE, AND THIS ADOBO IS A CHILI VINEGAR PASTE USED FOR MARINATING PORK CHOPS OR STEAKS. ADOBOS ARE WIDELY USED IN THE COOKING OF THE YUCATAN.

MAKES ENOUGH TO MARINATE
SIX CHOPS OR STEAKS

INGREDIENTS
  1 small head of garlic
  5 ancho chiles
  2 pasilla chiles
  1 tablespoon dried oregano
  1 teaspoon cumin seeds
  6 cloves
  1 teaspoon coriander seeds
  4-inch piece cinnamon stick
  2 teaspoons salt
  ½ cup white wine vinegar

1 Preheat the oven to 350°F. Cut a thin slice off the top of the head of garlic, so that the inside of each clove is exposed. Wrap the head of garlic in aluminium foil. Roast for 45–60 minutes or until the garlic is soft.

2 Meanwhile, slit the chiles and scrape out the seeds. Put the chiles in a blender or a mortar. Add the oregano, cumin seeds, cloves, coriander seeds, cinnamon stick and salt. Process or grind with a pestle into a fine powder.

3 Remove the garlic from the oven. When it is cool enough to handle, squeeze the garlic pulp out of each clove and grind into the spice mix.

4 Add the wine vinegar to the spice and garlic mixture and process or grind until a smooth paste forms. Spoon into a bowl and let stand for 1 hour to allow the flavors to blend. Spread on pork chops or steaks as a marinade, before broiling or grilling.

RED RUB

THIS "RUB" OR DRY PASTE IS FREQUENTLY USED IN THE YUCATAN FOR SEASONING MEAT. THE MIXTURE IS RUBBED ON THE SURFACE OF THE MEAT, WHICH IS THEN WRAPPED IN BANANA LEAVES AND COOKED SLOWLY IN A PIB, A HEATED STONE-LINED HOLE IN THE GROUND. MEAT COOKED THIS WAY IS REFERRED TO AS PIBIL-STYLE. TRY USING THE RUB ON PORK CHOPS OR CHICKEN PIECES BEFORE BAKING OR GRILLING.

MAKES ENOUGH FOR ONE ROAST
OR FOUR CHICKEN BREASTS

INGREDIENTS
2 teaspoons achiote (annatto) seeds
1 teaspoon black peppercorns
1 teaspoon allspice berries
1 teaspoon dried oregano
½ teaspoon ground cumin
1 teaspoon freshly squeezed lime juice
1 small Seville orange or ½ grapefruit

1 Put the achiote (annatto) seeds in a mortar and grind them with a pestle into a fine powder. Alternatively, use a food processor. Add the peppercorns, grind again, then repeat the process with the allspice berries. Mix in the oregano and ground cumin.

2 Add the lime juice to the spice mixture. Squeeze the orange or grapefruit and add the juice to the spice mixture a teaspoonful at a time until a thick paste is produced. Don't be tempted to substitute a sweet orange if Seville oranges are out of season; the spice mixture must be tart.

3 Let the paste stand for at least 30 minutes so the spices absorb the juice. The correct consistency for the paste is slightly dry and crumbly. When ready to use, rub the paste on the surface of the meat, then let marinate for at least 1 hour before cooking, preferably overnight. The rub will keep for up to 1 week in a covered bowl in the refrigerator, after which time some of the flavor will be lost.

COOK'S TIP
Achiote is the rusty red seed of the annatto, a tropical American tree. It is used in Mexico for flavoring and coloring cheeses, butter and smoked fish. It is also used in Indian cooking and can be purchased at ethnic food stores.

RED SALSA

USE THIS AS A CONDIMENT WITH FISH OR MEAT DISHES, OR AS A DIPPING SAUCE FOR BAKED POTATO WEDGES. IT IS OFTEN ADDED TO RICE DISHES.

MAKES ABOUT 1 CUP

INGREDIENTS
3 large tomatoes
1 tablespoon olive oil
3 ancho chiles
2 pasilla chiles
2 garlic cloves, peeled and left whole
2 scallions
2 teaspoons dark brown sugar
2.5ml/½ teaspoon paprika
juice of 1 lime
½ teaspoon dried oregano
salt

1 Preheat the oven to 400°F. Quarter the tomatoes and place in a roasting pan. Drizzle on the oil. Roast for about 40 minutes, until slightly charred, then remove the skin.

2 Soak the chiles in hot water for about 10 minutes. Drain, remove the stalks, slit and then scrape out the seeds. Chop finely. Dry-roast the garlic in a heavy pan, until golden.

3 Finely chop most of the scallions, retaining the top part of one for garnishing. Place the chopped onion in a bowl with the sugar, paprika, lime juice and oregano. Slice the remaining scallion diagonally, take out slices and set aside for the garnish.

4 Put the skinned tomatoes and chopped chiles in a food processor or blender and add the garlic cloves. Process until smooth.

5 Add the sugar, paprika, lime juice, scallions and oregano to the blender. Process for a few seconds, then taste and add salt as required. spoon into a saucepan and warm through before serving, or place in a bowl, cover and chill until needed. Garnish with the sliced scallions. The salsa will keep, covered, for up to 1 week in the refrigerator.

SOUPS AND SNACKS

If you found the word "sopas" on a Mexican menu, you might, quite rightly, translate it to mean "soups." However, your order might not be quite what you were expecting. There are two classifications of soup in Mexico: those that conform to the accepted definition and consist of vegetables, meat or fish cooked in a liquid, and those that come under the heading of sopa seca, or "dry soup." This may sound like a contradiction in terms, but there is actually a perfectly logical explanation. A sopa seca starts out with plenty of liquid, but ingredients such as rice, vermicelli or corn tortilla strips soon absorb the surplus. What remains is a moist, thick, satisfying dish, which serves as a separate course in the comida—*the main meal— but may also be served solo.*

Bocaditos means "little bites," an apt description for a range of colorful little dishes that Mexicans snack on throughout the day. Several of these may be served together, like the Spanish tapas, to make an informal meal, or they may appear as appetizers, or on a brunch or buffet table. Most bocaditos can be prepared quickly and easily, so they make perfect packed lunches or picnic fare.

TLALPEÑO-STYLE SOUP

THIS SIMPLE CHICKEN SOUP ORIGINATES FROM TLALPAN, A SUBURB OF MEXICO CITY. THE SOUP IS MADE MORE SUBSTANTIAL BY THE ADDITION OF CHEESE AND CHICKPEAS.

SERVES SIX

INGREDIENTS
   6¼ cups chicken stock
   ½ chipotle chile, seeded
   2 skinless, boneless chicken breasts
   1 medium avocado
   4 scallions, finely sliced
   14-ounce can chickpeas, drained
   salt and ground black pepper
   ¾ cup grated Cheddar cheese,
      to serve

1 Pour the stock into a large saucepan and add the dried chile. Bring to a boil, add the whole chicken breasts, then lower the heat and simmer for about 10 minutes or until the chicken is cooked. Remove the chicken from the pan and let it cool a little.

2 Using two forks, shred the chicken into small pieces. Set it aside. Pour the stock and chile into a blender or food processor and process until smooth. Return the stock to the pan.

COOK'S TIP
When buying the avocado for this soup choose one that is slightly under-ripe, which makes it easier to handle when peeling and slicing.

3 Cut the avocado in half, remove the skin and pit, then slice the flesh into ¾-inch pieces. Add it to the stock, with the scallions and chickpeas. Return the shredded chicken to the pan, with salt and pepper to taste, and heat gently.

4 Spoon the soup into heated bowls. Sprinkle grated cheese on top of each portion and serve immediately.

CORN SOUP

QUICK AND EASY TO PREPARE, THIS COLORFUL SOUP HAS A SWEET FLAVOR. CHILDREN LOVE IT.

SERVES SIX

INGREDIENTS
   2 red peppers
   2 tablespoons vegetable oil
   1 medium onion, finely chopped
   3–4 cups corn niblets, thawed
      if frozen
   3 cups chicken stock
   ⅔ cup light cream
   salt and ground black pepper

1 Dry-fry the peppers in a griddle over medium heat, turning them frequently until the skins are blistered all over. Place them in a strong plastic bag and tie the top to keep the steam in. Set aside for 20 minutes, then remove the peppers from the bag and peel off the skin.

2 Cut the peppers in half and scoop out the seeds and cores. Set one aside. Cut the other into ½-inch dice.

3 Heat the oil in a large saucepan. Add the onion and sauté over low heat for about 10 minutes, until it is translucent and soft. Stir in the diced pepper and corn and cook for 5 minutes over medium heat.

4 Spoon the contents of the pan into a food processor, pour in the chicken stock and process until almost smooth. This processing can be done in batches if necessary.

5 Return the soup to the pan and reheat it. Stir in the cream, with salt and pepper to taste. Core, seed and cut the reserved pepper into thin strips and add half of these to the pan. Serve the soup in heated bowls, garnished with the remaining pepper strips.

COOK'S TIP
Look for roasted red peppers in jars. These come ready-skinned and are useful in all sorts of recipes. Used here, they make a quick soup even speedier.

TORTILLA SOUP

THERE ARE SEVERAL TORTILLA SOUPS. THIS ONE IS AN AGUADA—OR LIQUID—VERSION, AND IS INTENDED FOR SERVING AS AN APPETIZER OR LIGHT MEAL. IT IS VERY EASY AND QUICK TO PREPARE. YOU CAN ALSO MAKE IT IN ADVANCE AND FRY THE TORTILLA STRIPS AS IT REHEATS. THE CRISP TORTILLA PIECES ADD AN UNUSUAL TEXTURE.

SERVES FOUR

INGREDIENTS

    4 corn tortillas, freshly made or a few
      days old
    1 tablespoon vegetable oil, plus
      extra, for frying
    1 small onion, finely chopped
    2 garlic cloves, crushed
    14-ounce can plum tomatoes, drained
    4 cups chicken stock
    small bunch of cilantro
    salt and ground black pepper

3 Add a few tortilla strips to the hot oil and fry for a few minutes, until crisp and golden brown all over, turning them occasionally. Remove with a slotted spoon and drain on a double layer of paper towels. Cook the remaining tortilla strips in the same way.

5 Chop the tomatoes using a large sharp knife and add them to the onion mixture in the pan. Pour in the chicken stock and stir well. Bring to a boil, then lower the heat and let simmer for about 10 minutes, until the liquid has reduced slightly.

1 Using a sharp knife, cut each tortilla into four or five strips, each measuring about ¾ inch wide.

2 Pour vegetable oil to a depth of ¾ inch into a heavy frying pan. Heat until a small piece of tortilla, added to the oil, floats on the top and bubbles at the edges.

4 Heat the 1 tablespoon vegetable oil in a large heavy saucepan. Add the chopped onion and garlic and cook over medium heat for 2–3 minutes, stirring constantly with a wooden spatula, until the onion is soft and translucent. Do not let the garlic turn brown or it will give the soup a bitter taste.

6 Chop the cilantro. Add to the soup, reserving a little to use as a garnish. Season to taste.

COOK'S TIP
An easy way to chop the cilantro is to put the cilantro leaves in a mug and snip with a pair of scissors. Hold the scissors vertically in both hands and work the blades back and forth until the cilantro is finely chopped.

7 Place a few of the crisp tortilla pieces in the bottom of four warmed soup bowls. Ladle the soup on top. Sprinkle each portion with the reserved chopped cilantro and serve.

CHILLED COCONUT SOUP

REFRESHING, COOLING AND NOT TOO FILLING, THIS SOUP IS THE PERFECT ANTIDOTE TO HOT WEATHER. FOR A FORMAL MEAL, IT WOULD BE AN EXCELLENT CHOICE FOR SERVING AFTER AN APPETIZER, TO REFRESH THE PALATE BEFORE THE MAIN COURSE.

SERVES SIX

INGREDIENTS

   5 cups milk
   2⅔ cups unsweetened dry
     shredded coconut
   1⅔ cups coconut milk
   1⅔ cups chicken stock
   scant 1 cup heavy cream
   ½ teaspoon salt
   ½ teaspoon ground white pepper
   5ml/1 teaspoon sugar
   small bunch of cilantro

COOK'S TIP
Avoid using sweetened coconut, which would spoil the flavor of this soup.

1 Pour the milk into a large saucepan. Bring it to a boil, stir in the coconut, lower the heat and let simmer for 30 minutes. Spoon the mixture into a food processor and process until smooth. This may take a while—up to 5 minutes—so pause frequently and scrape down the sides of the bowl.

2 Rinse the pan to remove any coconut that remains, pour in the processed mixture and add the coconut milk. Stir in the chicken stock (homemade, if possible, which gives a better flavor), cream, salt, pepper and sugar. Bring the mixture to a boil, stirring occasionally, then lower the heat and cook for 10 minutes.

3 Reserve a few cilantro leaves to garnish, then chop the rest finely and stir into the soup. Pour the soup into a large bowl, let it cool, then cover and put into the refrigerator until chilled. Just before serving, taste the soup and adjust the seasoning, as chileng will alter the taste. Serve in chilled bowls, garnished with the cilantro leaves.

AVOCADO SOUP

THIS DELICIOUS AND VERY PRETTY SOUP IS PERFECT FOR DINNER PARTIES AND HAS A FRESH, DELICATE FLAVOR. YOU MIGHT WANT TO ADD A DASH MORE LIME JUICE JUST BEFORE SERVING FOR ADDED ZEST.

SERVES FOUR

INGREDIENTS
2 large ripe avocados
1¼ cups crème fraîche
4 cups well-flavored chicken stock
1 teaspoon salt
juice of ½ lime
small bunch of cilantro
½ teaspoon freshly ground
   black pepper

COOK'S TIP
Because this soup contains avocados, it may discolor if left to stand, so make it just before serving.

1 Cut the avocados in half, remove the peel and lift out the pits. Chop the flesh coarsely and place it in a food processor with 3–4 tablespoons of the crème fraîche. Process until smooth.

2 Heat the chicken stock in a saucepan. When it is hot, but still below simmering point, stir in the rest of the crème fraîche, with the salt.

3 Add the lime juice to the avocado mixture, process briefly to mix, then gradually stir the mixture into the hot stock. Heat gently but do not let the mixture approach the boiling point.

4 Chop the cilantro. Pour the soup into individual heated bowls and sprinkle each portion with cilantro and black pepper. Serve immediately.

CHILES RELLENOS

STUFFED CHILES ARE POPULAR ALL OVER MEXICO. THE TYPE OF CHILE USED DIFFERS FROM REGION TO REGION, BUT LARGER CHILES ARE OBVIOUSLY EASIER TO STUFF THAN SMALLER ONES. POBLANOS AND ANAHEIMS ARE QUITE MILD, BUT YOU CAN USE HOTTER CHILES IF YOU PREFER.

MAKES SIX

INGREDIENTS

6 fresh poblano or Anaheim chiles
2 potatoes, total weight about
  14 ounces
scant 1 cup cream cheese
1¾ cups grated aged
  Cheddar cheese
1 teaspoon salt
½ teaspoon ground black pepper
2 eggs, separated
1 cup all-purpose flour
½ teaspoon white pepper
oil, for frying
chile flakes to garnish, optional

1 Make a neat slit down one side of each chile. Place them in a dry frying pan over medium heat, turning them frequently until the skins blister.

2 Place the chiles in a strong plastic bag and tie the top to keep the steam in. Set aside for 20 minutes, then carefully peel off the skins and remove the seeds through the slits, keeping the chiles whole. Dry the chiles with paper towels and set them aside.

COOK'S TIP
Take care when making the filling; mix gently, trying not to break up the potato pieces.

VARIATION
Whole ancho (dried poblano) chiles can be used instead of fresh chiles, but will need to be reconstituted in water before they can be seeded and stuffed.

3 Scrub or peel the potatoes and cut them into ½ inch dice. Bring a large saucepan of water to the boil, add the potatoes and let the water return to the boiling point. Lower the heat and simmer for 5 minutes or until the potatoes are just tender. Do not overcook. Drain them thoroughly.

4 Put the cream cheese in a bowl and stir in the grated cheese, with ½ teaspoon of the salt and the black pepper. Add the potato and mix gently.

5 Spoon some of the potato filling into each chile. Put them on a plate, cover with plastic wrap and chill for 1 hour so that the filling becomes firm.

6 Put the egg whites in a clean, greasefree bowl and whisk them to firm peaks. In a separate bowl, beat the yolks until pale, then fold in the whites. Scrape the mixture onto a large, shallow dish. Spread out the flour in another shallow dish and season it with the remaining salt and the white pepper.

7 Heat the oil for deep frying to 375°F. Coat a few chiles first in flour and then in egg before adding carefully to the hot oil.

8 Fry the chiles in batches until golden and crisp. Drain on paper towels and serve hot, garnished with a sprinkle of chile flakes for extra heat, if desired.

TORTAS

THE MULTI-LAYERED FILLING OF TORTAS OFFERS LOTS OF DIFFERENT TASTES AND TEXTURES.
TRADITIONALLY THEY ARE MADE USING ROLLS CALLED TELERAS.

SERVES TWO

INGREDIENTS
   2 fresh jalapeño chiles
   juice of ½ lime
   2 French bread rolls or 2 pieces
     of French bread
   ⅔ cup Refried Beans
   5 ounces roast pork
   2 small tomatoes, sliced
   4 ounces Cheddar cheese, sliced
   small bunch of cilantro
   2 tablespoons crème fraîche

VARIATIONS
The essential ingredients of a *torta* are refried beans and chiles. Everything else is subject to change. Ham, chicken or turkey could all be used instead of pork, and lettuce is often added.

1 Cut the chiles in half, scrape out the seeds, then cut the flesh into thin strips. Put it in a bowl, pour in the lime juice and let stand.

2 If using rolls, slice them in half and remove some of the insides so that they are slightly hollowed. If using French bread, slice each piece in half lengthwise. Set the top of each piece of bread or roll aside and spread the bottom halves with the refried beans.

3 Cut the pork into thin shreds and put these on top of the refried beans. Top with the tomato slices. Drain the jalapeño strips and put them on top of the tomato slices. Add the cheese and sprinkle with cilantro leaves.

4 Turn the top halves of the bread or rolls over, so that the cut sides are facing up and spread these with crème fraîche. Sandwich back together again and serve.

TAQUITOS WITH BEEF

MINIATURE SOFT CORN TORTILLAS MOLDED AROUND A TASTY FILLING AND SERVED WARM. UNLESS YOU HAVE ACCESS TO MINIATURE FRESH CORN TORTILLAS, YOU WILL NEED A TORTILLA PRESS.

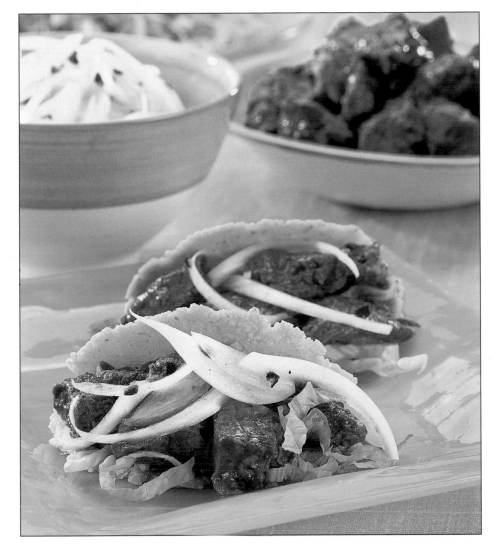

2 Mix the *masa harina* and salt in a large bowl. Add the warm water, a little at a time, to make a dough that can be worked into a ball. Knead this on a lightly floured surface for 3–4 minutes, until smooth, then wrap the dough in plastic wrap and let rest for 1 hour.

3 Divide the dough into 12 small balls. Open a tortilla press and line both sides with plastic (this can be cut from a new plastic sandwich bag). Put a ball on the press and bring the top down to flatten it into a 2–2½-inch round. Flatten the remaining dough balls in the same way to make more tortillas.

4 Heat a griddle or frying pan until hot. Cook each tortilla for 15–20 seconds on each side, and then for another 15 minutes on the first side. Keep the tortillas warm and soft by folding them inside a slightly damp dish towel.

5 Add the oregano, cumin, tomato paste and sugar to the pan containing the reserved beef cubes, with a couple of tablespoons of the reserved beef stock, or just enough to keep the mixture moist. Cook gently for a few minutes to combine the flavor.

SERVES TWELVE

INGREDIENTS
1¼ pounds rump steak, diced into
 ½-inch pieces
2 garlic cloves, peeled and left whole
3 cups beef stock
1 cup *masa harina*
pinch of salt
½ cup warm water
1½ teaspoons dried oregano
½ teaspoon ground cumin
2 tablespoons tomato paste
½ teaspoon sugar
salt and ground black pepper
shredded lettuce and Onion Relish,
 to serve

1 Put the beef and whole garlic cloves in a large saucepan and cover with the beef stock. Bring to a boil, lower the heat and simmer for 10–15 minutes, until the meat is tender. Using a slotted spoon, transfer the meat to a clean pan and set it aside. Reserve the stock.

6 Place a little of the lettuce on a warm tortilla. Top with a little of the filling and a little onion relish, fold in half and serve while still warm. Fill more tortillas in the same way.

EMPANADAS <u>WITH</u> ROPAS VIEJAS

THE FILLING FOR THESE EMPANADAS IS TRADITIONALLY MADE WITH MEAT THAT IS COOKED UNTIL IT IS SO TENDER THAT IT CAN BE TORN APART WITH FORKS. IT RESEMBLES TATTERED CLOTH, WHICH IS HOW IT CAME TO BE KNOWN AS ROPA VIEJA, WHICH MEANS "OLD CLOTHES."

<u>SERVES SIX (TWELVE EMPANADAS)</u>

INGREDIENTS

    1 cup *masa harina*
    2 tablespoons all-purpose flour
    ½ teaspoon salt
    ½–⅔ cup warm water
    1 tablespoon oil, plus extra,
      for frying
    9 ounces lean ground pork
    1 garlic clove, crushed
    3 tomatoes
    2 ancho chiles
    ½ small onion
    ½ teaspoon ground cumin
    ½ teaspoon salt

1 Mix the *masa harina*, flour and salt in a bowl. Gradually add enough of the warm water to make a smooth, but not sticky, dough. Knead briefly, then shape into a ball, wrap in plastic wrap and set aside.

2 Heat 1 tablespoon oil in a saucepan. Add the pork and cook, stirring frequently, until it has browned evenly. Stir in the garlic and cook for 2 more minutes. Remove from heat and set the pan aside.

3 Cut a cross in the bottom of each tomato, place them in a bowl and pour over boiling water. After 3 minutes plunge the tomatoes into a bowl of cold water. Drain. The skins will peel back easily from the crosses. Remove the skins completely. Chop the tomato flesh and put in a bowl.

4 Slit the ancho chiles and scrape out the seeds. Chop the chiles finely and add them to the tomatoes. Chop the onion finely and add it to the tomato mixture, with the ground cumin.

5 Stir the tomato mixture into the pan containing the pork and cook over medium heat for 10 minutes, stirring occasionally. Season with salt to taste.

6 To make the tortillas, divide the empanada dough into 12 pieces and roll each piece into a ball. Open a tortilla press and line both sides with plastic (this can be cut from a new plastic sandwich bag). Put a ball of dough on the press and bring the top down to flatten it into a 3-inch round. Use the remaining dough balls to make more tortillas in the same way.

COOK'S TIP

If the empanada dough proves difficult to handle, a little oil or melted lard can be kneaded into the dough to help make it more pliable.

7 Spoon a little of the meat mixture on one half of each tortilla, working quickly to keep the dough from drying out. Dampen the edges of the dough with a little water and fold, turnover-style, to make the empanadas.

8 Seal the edges on the empanadas by pinching them between the index finger and thumb of the left hand and the index finger of the right hand.

9 Heat a little oil in a large frying pan. When it is hot, fry the empanadas in batches until crisp and golden on both sides, turning at least once. Serve hot or cold.

PANUCHOS

THESE STUFFED TORTILLAS ARE A BIT FIDDLY TO MAKE, BUT WELL WORTH THE EFFORT. THIS DISH IS PARTICULARLY POPULAR IN THE YUCATÁN.

SERVES SIX (TWELVE *PANUCHOS*)

INGREDIENTS

    1 cup *masa harina*
    pinch of salt
    ½ cup warm water
    2 skinless, boneless chicken breasts
    1 teaspoon dried oregano
    about 1 cup *Frijoles de Olla*, blended
      to a smooth purée
    2 hard-boiled eggs, sliced
    oil, for shallow-frying
    salt and ground black pepper
    Onion Relish, to serve

1 Mix the *masa harina* and salt in a large bowl. Add the warm water, a little at a time, to make a dough that can be worked into a ball. Knead this on a lightly floured surface for 3–4 minutes, until smooth, then wrap the dough in plastic wrap and let rest for 1 hour.

2 Put the chicken in a saucepan, add the dried oregano and pour in water to cover. Bring to a boil, then lower the heat and simmer for 10 minutes or until the chicken is cooked. Remove the chicken from the pan, discard the water and let the chicken cool a little. Using two forks, shred the chicken into small pieces. Set it aside.

3 Divide the dough into 12 small pieces and roll into balls. Open a tortilla press and line both sides with plastic (this can be cut from a new plastic sandwich bag). Put a dough ball on the press and flatten it into a 2½-inch round. Use the remaining dough balls to make more tortillas in the same way.

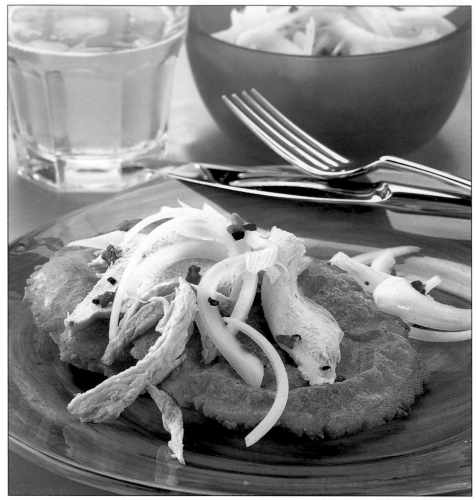

4 Cook each tortilla in a hot frying pan for 15–20 seconds on each side. After another 15 seconds on one side, remove and wrap in a clean dish towel.

5 Cut a slit in each tortilla, about ½ inch deep around the rim. Put a spoonful of the bean purée and a slice of hard-boiled egg in each slit.

6 Heat the oil for shallow frying in a large frying pan. Fry the tortilla pockets until they are crisp and golden brown on all sides, turning at least once during cooking. Drain them on paper towels and place on six individual serving plates. Top with a little of the shredded chicken and some onion relish. Season to taste and serve immediately.

SOPES WITH PICADILLO

THESE *ARE SMALL, THICK TORTILLAS MADE WITH* MASA HARINA *WITH CRIMPED EDGES, WHICH ARE FILLED LIKE TARTS. THEY ARE AN ACQUIRED TASTE AS THEY REMAIN "DOUGHY" WHEN COOKED, BUT THEY CAN BECOME QUITE ADDICTIVE. THE FILLING*—PICADILLO—*IS VERY POPULAR IN* MEXICO *AND IS USED IN MANY DIFFERENT RECIPES.*

SERVES SIX

INGREDIENTS
scant 2 cups *masa harina*
½ teaspoon salt
¼ cup chilled lard
1¼ cups warm water
1 tablespoon vegetable oil
9 ounces lean ground beef
2 garlic cloves, crushed
1 red pepper, seeded and chopped
¼ cup dry sherry
1 tablespoon tomato paste
½ teaspoon ground cumin
1 teaspoon ground cinnamon
¼ teaspoon ground cloves
½ teaspoon ground black pepper
3 tablespoon raisins
¼ cup slivered almonds
fresh parsley sprigs, to garnish

1 Put the *masa harina* and salt in a large bowl. Grate the chilled lard into the bowl and rub it into the dry ingredients until no visible pieces remain. Add the warm water, a little at a time, to make a dough that can be worked into a ball. Knead the dough on a lightly floured surface for 3–4 minutes, until smooth. Set aside.

2 Heat the oil in a large saucepan. Add the ground beef and cook over high heat, stirring until it has browned. Stir in the garlic and continue cooking for 2–3 minutes, stirring occasionally.

3 Stir in the red pepper, sherry, tomato purée and spices. Cook for 5 more minutes, then add the raisins and the slivered almonds. Lower the heat and simmer for 10 minutes. The meat should be cooked through and the mixture moist, but not wet. Keep hot.

4 Divide the dough into six balls. Open a tortilla press and line both sides with plastic (this can be cut from a new plastic sandwich bag). Put a ball on the press and bring the top down to flatten it into a 4-inch round, thicker than the conventional tortilla. Use the remaining dough balls to make five more rounds.

5 Heat a griddle or frying pan until hot. Add one of the rounds and fry until the underside is beginning to brown and blister. Turn the round over and cook the other side briefly, until the color is just beginning to change. Slide onto a plate and crimp the rim to form a raised edge. Fill with the spicy beef and keep hot while cooking and filling the remaining tartlets. Garnish with parsley.

COOK'S TIP
Take care that the dough for the *sopes* does not become dry. Wrap it in plastic wrap while it is set aside.

QUESADILLAS

THESE CHEESE-FILLED TORTILLAS ARE THE MEXICAN EQUIVALENT OF GRILLED CHEESE SANDWICHES. SERVE THEM AS SOON AS THEY ARE COOKED, OR THEY WILL BECOME CHEWY. IF YOU ARE MAKING THEM FOR A CROWD, FILL AND FOLD THE TORTILLAS AHEAD OF TIME, BUT ONLY COOK THEM TO ORDER.

SERVES FOUR

INGREDIENTS

7 ounces mozzarella, Monterey Jack
  or mild Cheddar cheese
1 fresh fresno chile (optional)
8 flour tortillas, about
  6-inches across
Onion Relish or Classic Tomato Salsa,
  to serve

VARIATIONS
Try spreading a thin layer of your favorite Mexican salsa on the tortilla before adding the cheese, or adding a few pieces of cooked chicken or shrimp before folding the tortilla in half.

1 If using mozzarella cheese, it must be drained thoroughly and then patted dry and sliced into thin strips. Monterey Jack and Cheddar cheese should both be coarsely grated, as finely grated cheese will melt and ooze out when cooking. Set the cheese aside in a bowl.

2 If using the chile, spear it on a long-handled metal skewer and roast it over the flame of a gas burner until the skin blisters and darkens. Do not let the flesh burn. Alternatively, dry-fry it in a griddle until the skin is scorched. Place the roasted chile in a strong plastic bag and tie the top to keep the steam in. Set aside for 20 minutes.

3 Remove the chile from the bag and peel off the skin. Cut off the stem, then slit the chile and scrape out the seeds. Cut the flesh into eight thin strips.

4 Warm a large frying pan or griddle. Place one tortilla on the pan or griddle at a time, sprinkle about an eighth of the cheese on one half and add a strip of chile, if using. Fold the tortilla over the cheese and press the edges together gently to seal. Cook the filled tortilla for 1 minute, then turn over and cook the other side for 1 minute.

5 Remove the filled tortilla from the pan or griddle, cut it into three triangles or four strips and serve immediately, with the onion relish or tomato salsa.

MEXICAN RICE

VERSIONS OF THIS DISH—A RELATIVE OF SPANISH RICE—ARE POPULAR ALL OVER SOUTH AMERICA.
CLASSIFIED AS A SOPA SECA OR DRY SOUP, IT IS A DELICIOUS MEDLEY OF RICE, TOMATOES AND
AROMATIC FLAVORINGS. THE STOCK IN WHICH THE RICE IS COOKED IS LARGELY ABSORBED BY THE
TIME THE DISH IS READY TO BE SERVED.

SERVES SIX

INGREDIENTS
 1 cup long-grain rice
 7-ounce can chopped tomatoes in
  tomato juice
 ½ onion, roughly chopped
 2 garlic cloves, roughly chopped
 2 tablespoons vegetable oil
 scant 2 cups chicken stock
 ½ teaspoon salt
 3 fresh fresno chiles or other fresh
  green chiles, trimmed
 1 cup frozen peas (optional)
 ground black pepper

1 Put the rice in a large heatproof bowl
and pour in boiling water to cover. Stir
once, then let stand for 10 minutes.
Transfer to a strainer over the sink,
rinse under cold water, then drain
again. Set aside to dry slightly.

2 Meanwhile, pour the tomatoes and
juice into a food processor or blender,
add the onion and garlic and process
until smooth.

3 Heat the oil in a large, heavy pan,
add the rice and cook over medium
heat until it becomes a delicate golden
brown. Stir occasionally to ensure that
the rice does not stick to the bottom
of the pan.

4 Add the tomato mixture and stir over
medium heat until all the liquid has
been absorbed. Stir in the stock, salt,
whole chiles and peas, if using.
Continue to cook the mixture, stirring
occasionally, until all the liquid has been
absorbed and the rice is just tender.

5 Remove the pan from the heat, cover
it with a tight-fitting lid and let it stand
in a warm place for 5–10 minutes.
Remove the chiles, fluff up the rice
lightly and serve, sprinkled with black
pepper. The chiles may be used as a
garnish, if desired.

COOK'S TIP
Do not stir the rice too often after adding
the stock or the grains will break down
and the mixture will become starchy.

CHICKEN FLAUTAS

CRISP FRIED TORTILLAS WITH A CHICKEN AND CHEESE FILLING MAKE A DELICIOUS LIGHT MEAL, ESPECIALLY WHEN SERVED WITH A SPICY TOMATO SALSA. THE SECRET OF SUCCESS IS TO MAKE SURE THAT THE OIL IS SUFFICIENTLY HOT TO PREVENT THE FLUTES FROM ABSORBING TOO MUCH OF IT.

MAKES TWELVE

INGREDIENTS
  2 skinless, boneless chicken breasts
  1 onion
  2 garlic cloves
  1 tablespoon vegetable oil
  3½ ounces feta cheese, crumbled
  12 corn tortillas, freshly made or a
    few days old
  oil, for frying
  salt and ground black pepper
For the salsa
  3 tomatoes, peeled, seeded
    and chopped
  juice of ½ lime
  small bunch of cilantro, chopped
  ½ small onion, finely chopped
  3 fresh fresno chiles or similar
    fresh green chiles, seeded
    and chopped

1 Start by making the salsa. Mix the tomatoes, lime juice, coriander, onion and chiles in a bowl. Season with salt to taste and set aside.

COOK'S TIP
You might find it easier to keep the cocktail sticks in place until after the flutes have been fried, in which case remove them before serving.

2 Put the chicken breasts in a large saucepan, add water to cover and bring to a boil. Lower the heat and simmer for 15–20 minutes or until the chicken is cooked. Remove the chicken from the pan and let it cool a little. Using two forks, shred the chicken into small pieces. Set it aside.

3 Chop the onion finely and crush the garlic. Heat the oil in a frying pan, add the onion and garlic and sauté over low heat for about 5 minutes or until the onion has softened but not colored. Add the shredded chicken, with salt and pepper to taste. Mix well, remove from heat and stir in the feta.

4 Before they can be rolled, soften the tortillas by steaming three or four at a time on a plate over boiling water for a few moments until they are pliable. Alternatively, wrap them in microwave-safe film and then heat them in a microwave oven on full power for about 30 seconds.

5 Place a spoonful of the chicken filling on one of the tortillas. Roll the tortilla tightly around the filling to make a neat cylinder. Secure with a toothpick. Immediately cover the roll with plastic wrap to prevent the tortilla from drying out and splitting. Fill and roll the remaining tortillas in the same way.

6 Pour oil into a frying pan to a depth of 1 inch. Heat it until a small cube of bread, added to the oil, rises to the surface and bubbles at the edges before turning golden. Remove the cocktail sticks, then add the flutes to the pan, a few at a time.

7 Fry the flutes for 2–3 minutes, until golden, turning frequently. Drain on paper towels and serve immediately, with the salsa.

EGGS WITH CHORIZO

IN MEXICO, THERE ARE TWO TYPES OF CHORIZO SAUSAGE. THE FIRST IS FRESHLY MADE AND SOLD LOOSE; THE SECOND IS PACKED IN SAUSAGE SKINS AND AIR-DRIED, LIKE SPANISH CHORIZO. THIS IS A RECIPE FOR THE FORMER. FRESHLY MADE CHORIZO CAN BE USED IN A NUMBER OF SAVORY DISHES, BUT IS PARTICULARLY GOOD WITH SCRAMBLED EGGS, AS HERE.

SERVES FOUR

INGREDIENTS
   2 tablespoons lard
   1¼ pounds ground pork
   3 garlic cloves, crushed
   2 teaspoons dried oregano
   1 teaspoon ground cinnamon
   ½ teaspoon ground cloves
   ½ teaspoon ground black pepper
   2 tablespoons dry sherry
   1 teaspoon caster sugar
   1 teaspoon salt
   6 eggs
   2 tomatoes, peeled, seeded and
      finely diced
   ½ small onion, finely chopped
   ¼ cup milk or light cream
   fresh oregano sprigs, to garnish
   warm corn or flour tortillas,
      to serve

1 Melt the lard in a large frying pan over medium heat. Add the pork mince and cook until browned, stirring frequently. Stir in the garlic, dried oregano, cinnamon, cloves and black pepper. Cook for 3–4 more minutes.

2 Add the sherry, sugar and salt to the pork, stir well and cook for 3–4 minutes, until the flavors are blended. Remove from heat.

3 Put the eggs in a bowl. Beat lightly to mix, then stir in the finely diced tomatoes and chopped onion.

4 Return the chorizo mixture to the heat. Heat it through and pour in the egg mixture. Cook, stirring constantly, until the egg is almost firm.

5 Stir in the milk or cream and check the seasoning. Garnish with fresh oregano and serve with warm corn or flour tortillas.

CHILES IN CHEESE SAUCE

THIS MAKES AN EXCELLENT APPETIZER, LIGHT LUNCH OR DIP TO SERVE WITH DRINKS. THE CHILES AND TEQUILA GIVE IT QUITE A KICK.

SERVES FOUR TO SIX

INGREDIENTS
   4 fresh fresno chiles or other fresh
      green chiles
   1 tablespoon vegetable oil
   ½ red onion, finely chopped
   5 cups grated Monterey Jack cheese
   2 tablespoons crème fraîche
   ⅔ cup heavy cream
   2 firm tomatoes, peeled
   1 tablespoon reposada tequila
   Tortilla Chips, to serve

COOK'S TIP
Cross-cut the bottom of a tomato and cover with boiling water. Plunge into cold water and the skin will peel off easily.

1 Place the chiles in a dry frying pan over medium heat, turning them frequently until the skin blisters and darkens. Place the chiles in a strong plastic bag and tie the top to keep the steam in. Set aside for 20 minutes, then carefully peel off the skins. Slit the chiles and scrape out the seeds, then cut the flesh into thin strips. Cut these in half lengthwise.

2 Heat the oil in a frying pan and sauté the onion over medium heat for 5 minutes, until it is beginning to soften. Add the cheese, crème fraîche and cream. Stir over low heat until the cheese melts and the mixture becomes a rich, creamy sauce. Stir in the thick chile strips.

3 Cut the tomatoes in half and scrape out the seeds. Cut the flesh into ½-inch pieces and stir these into the sauce.

4 Just before serving, stir in the tequila. Pour the sauce into a serving dish and serve warm, with the tortilla chips.

MOLETTES

THIS IS THE MEXICAN VERSION OF BEANS ON TOAST. SOLD BY STREET TRADERS AROUND MID-MORNING, THEY MAKE THE PERFECT SNACK FOR THOSE WHO HAVE MISSED BREAKFAST.

SERVES FOUR

INGREDIENTS
    4 crusty rolls
    ¼ cup butter, softened
    1⅓ cups Refried Beans
    1¼ cups grated Cheddar cheese
    green salad leaves, to garnish
    ½ cup Classic Tomato Salsa,
      to serve

1 Cut the rolls in half, then take a sliver off the bottom so that they lie flat. Remove a little of the insides. Spread them lightly with enough butter to crisp.

2 Arrange them on a baking sheet and broil for about 5 minutes or until they are crisp and golden. Meanwhile, heat the refried beans over low heat in a small saucepan.

3 Scoop the beans into the rolls, then sprinkle the grated cheese on top. Pop back under the broiler until the cheese melts. Serve with the tomato salsa and garnish with salad leaves.

EGGS MOTULENOS

A TASTY AND FILLING BREAKFAST OR MIDDAY SNACK, BLACK BEANS, WHICH ARE ALSO KNOWN AS TURTLE BEANS, ARE TOPPED WITH EGGS AND CHILI SAUCE AND SURROUNDED BY PEAS AND HAM.

SERVES FOUR

INGREDIENTS
    generous 1 cup black beans, soaked
      overnight in water
    1 small onion, finely chopped
    2 garlic cloves
    small bunch of cilantro, chopped
    1 cup frozen peas
    4 corn tortillas
    2 tablespoons oil
    4 eggs
    5 ounces cooked ham, diced
    4 tablespoons hot chili sauce
    3 ounces feta cheese, crumbled
    salt and ground black pepper
    Classic Tomato Salsa, to serve

1 Drain the beans, rinse them under cold water and drain again. Put them in a saucepan, add the onion and garlic and water to cover. Bring to a boil, then simmer for 40 minutes. Stir in the cilantro, with salt and pepper to taste, and keep the beans hot.

2 Cook the peas in a small saucepan of boiling water until they are just tender. Drain and set aside. Wrap the tortillas in aluminium foil and place them on a plate. Stand the plate over a pan of boiling water and steam them for about 5 minutes. Alternatively, wrap them in microwave plastic wrap and heat them in a micro-wave on full power for about 30 seconds.

3 Heat the oil in a frying pan and fry the eggs until the whites are set. Lift them onto a plate and keep them warm while you quickly heat the ham and peas in the oil remaining in the pan.

4 Place the tortillas on warmed plates and top each one with some beans. Place an egg on each tortilla, spoon on 1 tablespoon hot chili sauce, then surround each egg with some peas and ham. Sprinkle feta on the peas and serve immediately, with salsa on the side.

EGGS RANCHEROS

THERE ARE MANY VARIATIONS ON THIS POPULAR DISH, WHICH IS GREAT FOR BREAKFAST OR BRUNCH.
THE COMBINATION OF CREAMY EGGS WITH ONION, CHILE AND TOMATOES WORKS WONDERFULLY WELL.

SERVES FOUR FOR BREAKFAST

INGREDIENTS
    2 corn tortillas, several days old
    oil, for frying
    2 fresh green jalapeño chiles
    1 garlic clove
    4 scallions
    1 large tomato
    8 eggs, beaten
    ⅔ cup light cream
    small bunch of cilantro,
        finely chopped
    salt and ground black pepper

1 Cut the tortillas into long strips. Pour oil into a frying pan to a depth of ½ inch. Heat the oil until it is very hot, watching it closely.

2 Fry the tortilla strips in batches for a minute or two until they are crisp and golden, turning them occasionally, then drain on paper towels.

COOK'S TIP
When cooking the tortilla strips it is important that the oil is the correct temperature. To test if the oil is ready to use, carefully add a strip of tortilla. If the strip floats and the oil immediately bubbles around its edges, the oil is ready.

3 Spear the chiles on a long-handled metal skewer and roast them over the flame of a gas burner until the skins blister and darken. Do not let the flesh burn. Alternatively, dry-fry them in a griddle until the skins are scorched. Place them in a strong plastic bag and tie the top to keep the steam in. Set aside for 20 minutes.

4 Meanwhile, crush the garlic and chop the scallions finely. Cut a cross in the bottom of the tomato. Place it in a heatproof bowl and pour on boiling water to cover. After 3 minutes, lift the tomato out using a slotted spoon and plunge it into a bowl of cold water. Let sit for a few minutes to cool.

5 Drain the tomato, remove the skin and cut it into four pieces. Using a teaspoon scoop out the seeds and the core, then dice the flesh finely.

6 Remove the chiles from the bag and peel off the skins. Cut off the stems, then slit the chiles and scrape out the seeds. Chop the flesh finely. Put the eggs in a bowl, season with salt and pepper and beat lightly.

7 Heat 1 tablespoon oil in a large frying pan. Add the garlic and scallions and sauté gently for 2–3 minutes, until soft. Stir in the diced tomato and cook for 3–4 more minutes, then stir in the chiles and cook for 1 minute.

8 Pour the eggs into the pan and stir until they start to set. When only a small amount of uncooked egg remains visible, stir in the cream so that the cooking process is slowed down and the mixture cooks into a creamy mixture rather than a solid mass.

9 Stir the chopped cilantro into the scrambled eggs. Arrange the tortilla strips on four serving plates and spoon on the eggs. Serve immediately.

TORTILLA CHIPS

THESE ARE KNOWN AS TOTOPOS IN MEXICO, AND THE TERM REFERS TO BOTH THE FRIED TORTILLA STRIPS USED TO GARNISH SOUPS AND THE TRIANGLES OF CORN TORTILLA USED FOR SCOOPING SALSA OR DIPS. USE TORTILLAS THAT ARE A FEW DAYS OLD; FRESH ONES WILL NOT CRISP UP AS WELL.

SERVES FOUR

INGREDIENTS
4–8 corn tortillas
oil, for frying
salt

1 Cut each tortilla into six triangular wedges. Pour oil into a large frying pan to a depth of ½ inch, place the pan over medium heat and heat until very hot (see Cook's Tip).

2 Fry the tortilla wedges in the hot oil in small batches until they turn golden and are crisp. This will only take a few moments. Remove with a slotted spoon and drain on paper towels. Sprinkle with salt.

VARIATION
When fried, flour tortillas do not crisp up as well as corn tortillas, but they make a delicious sweet treat when sprinkled with ground cinnamon and sugar. Serve them hot with cream.

COOK'S TIP
The oil needs to be very hot for cooking the tortillas—test it by carefully adding one of the wedges. It should float and begin to bubble in the oil immediately.

3 *Totopos* should be served warm. They can be cooled completely and stored in an airtight container for a few days, but will need to be reheated in a microwave or a warm oven before being served.

PEPITAS

THESE LITTLE SNACKS ARE ABSOLUTELY IRRESISTIBLE, ESPECIALLY IF YOU INCLUDE CHIPOTLE CHILES. THEIR SMOKY FLAVOR IS THE PERFECT FOIL FOR THE NUTTY TASTE OF THE PUMPKIN SEEDS AND THE SWEETNESS CONTRIBUTED BY THE SUGAR. SERVE THEM WITH PRE-DINNER DRINKS.

SERVES FOUR

INGREDIENTS
1 cup pumpkin seeds
4 garlic cloves, crushed
¼ teaspoon salt
2 teaspoons crushed dried chiles
1 teaspoon sugar
a wedge of lime

COOK'S TIP
It is important to keep the pumpkin seeds moving as they cook. Watch them carefully and do not let them burn, or they will taste bitter.

1 Heat a small heavy frying pan, add the pumpkin seeds and dry-fry for a few minutes, stirring constantly as they swell.

2 When all the seeds have swollen, add the garlic and cook for a few more minutes, stirring constantly. Add the salt and the crushed chiles and stir to mix. Turn off the heat, but keep the pan on the stove. Sprinkle sugar on the seeds and shake the pan to ensure that they are all coated.

3 Transfer the *pepitas* to a bowl and serve with the wedge of lime for squeezing on the seeds. If the lime is omitted, the seeds can be cooled and stored in an airtight container for reheating later, but they are best served fresh.

SPICED PLANTAIN CHIPS

PLANTAINS ARE MORE STARCHY THAN THE BANANAS TO WHICH THEY ARE RELATED, AND MUST BE COOKED BEFORE BEING EATEN. IN LATIN AMERICA THE FRUIT IS USED MUCH AS A POTATO WOULD BE. THIS SNACK HAS A LOVELY SWEET TASTE, WHICH IS BALANCED BY THE HEAT FROM THE CHILI POWDER AND SAUCE. COOK THE CHIPS JUST BEFORE YOU PLAN TO SERVE THEM.

SERVES FOUR AS AN APPETIZER
OR SNACK

INGREDIENTS
   2 large plantains
   oil, for shallow-frying
   ½ teaspoon chili powder
   1 teaspoon ground cinnamon
   hot chili sauce, to serve

COOK'S TIP
Plantain skins are very dark, almost black, when the fruit is ready to eat. If they are green when you buy them, let them ripen at room temperature for a few days before use.

1 Peel the plaintains. Cut off and throw away the ends, then slice the fruit into rounds, cutting slightly on the diagonal to give larger, flatter slices.

2 Pour the oil for frying into a small frying pan, to a depth of about ½ inch. Heat the oil until it is very hot, watching it closely. Test by carefully adding a slice of plantain; it should float and the oil should immediately bubble up around it.

3 Fry the plantain slices in small batches or the temperature of the oil will drop. When they are golden brown, remove from the oil with a slotted spoon and drain on paper towels.

4 Mix the chili powder with the cinnamon. Put the plantain chips on a serving plate, sprinkle them with the chili and cinnamon mixture and serve immediately, with a small bowl of hot chili sauce for dipping.

POPCORN <u>WITH</u> LIME <u>AND</u> CHILI

IF THE ONLY POPCORN YOU'VE HAD CAME OUT OF A CARTON AT THE MOVIES, TRY THIS MEXICAN SPECIALTY. THE LIME JUICE AND CHILI POWDER ARE INSPIRED ADDITIONS, AND THE SNACK IS QUITE A HEALTHY CHOICE TO SERVE WITH DRINKS.

MAKES ONE LARGE BOWL

INGREDIENTS
  2 tablespoons vegetable oil
  1¼ cups corn kernels
    for popcorn
  2 teaspoons chili powder
  juice of 2 limes

1 Heat the oil in a large, heavy frying pan until it is very hot. Add the popcorn and immediately cover the pan with a lid and reduce the heat.

2 After a few minutes the corn should start to pop. Resist the temptation to lift the lid to check. Shake the pan occasionally so that all corn will be cooked and browned.

3 When the sound of popping corn has stopped, quickly remove the pan from the heat and let cool slightly. Take off the lid and with a spoon lift out and discard any corn kernels that have not popped. The uncooked corn will have fallen to the bottom of the pan and is completely inedible.

4 Add the chili powder. Shake the pan again and again to make sure that all of the corn is covered with a colorful dusting of chili.

5 Transfer the popcorn to a large bowl and keep warm. Add a squeeze of lime juice immediately before serving.

MEAT DISHES

Pork is undoubtedly the most popular meat in Mexico. Every part of the animal is processed for food, so it represents terrific value for money; traditionally a family keeps its own pig and feeds it on scraps from their table. Turkey was popular in pre-Columbian times and still features on the menu today, although chicken is widely used for everyday dishes. Beef is popular in the north, where cattle are raised, and lamb and goat are also eaten.

This chapter includes a wide range of favorite Mexican meat dishes, from Chicken Fajitas and Tacos with Shredded Beef to the aptly named Drunken Chicken. Classics such as Turkey Mole and Pork in Green Sauce with Cactus are included, along with Albondigas, delicious meatballs that can be served for a main course or—in miniature—as snacks.

BURRITOS WITH CHICKEN AND RICE

IN MEXICO, BURRITOS ARE A POPULAR STREET FOOD, EATEN ON THE RUN. THE SECRET OF A SUCCESSFUL BURRITO IS TO HAVE ALL THE FILLING NEATLY PACKAGED INSIDE THE TORTILLA FOR EASY EATING, SO THESE SNACKS ARE SELDOM SERVED WITH A POUR~ON SAUCE.

SERVES FOUR

INGREDIENTS
    ½ cup long grain rice
    1 tablespoon vegetable oil
    1 onion, chopped
    ½ teaspoon ground cloves
    1 teaspoon dried, or fresh oregano
    7-ounce can chopped tomatoes in
      tomato juice
    2 skinless, boneless chicken breasts
    1¼ cups grated Monterey Jack or
      mild Cheddar cheese
    4 tablespoons sour cream
      (optional)
    8 x 8–10-inch fresh flour tortillas
    salt
    fresh oregano, to garnish (optional)

1 Bring a saucepan of lightly salted water to a boil. Add the rice and cook for 8 minutes. Drain, rinse and then drain again.

2 Heat the oil in a large saucepan. Add the onion, with the ground cloves and oregano, and fry for 2–3 minutes. Stir in the rice and tomatoes and cook over low heat until all the tomato juice has been absorbed. Set the pan aside.

3 Put the chicken breasts in a large saucepan, pour in enough water to cover and bring to a boil. Lower the heat and simmer for about 10 minutes or until the chicken is cooked through. Lift the chicken out of the pan, put on a plate and cool slightly.

4 Preheat the oven to 325°F. Shred the chicken by pulling the flesh apart with two forks, then add the chicken to the rice mixture, with the grated cheese. Stir in the sour cream, if using.

COOK'S TIP
If you use very fresh tortillas, you may be able to dispense with the toothpicks. Secure the tortilla parcels by damping the final fold with a little water. When you lay the burritos in the dish, place them with the folded surfaces down.

5 Wrap the tortillas in aluminum foil and place them on a plate. Stand the plate over boiling water for about 5 minutes. Alternatively, wrap in microwave-safe plastic wrap and heat in a microwave on full power for 1 minute.

6 Spoon one-eighth of the filling into the center of a tortilla and fold in both sides. Fold the bottom up and the top down to form a parcel. Secure with a toothpick.

7 Put the filled burrito in a shallow dish or casserole, cover with foil and keep warm in the oven while you make seven more. Remove the toothpicks before serving, sprinkled with fresh oregano.

CHICKEN AND TOMATILLO CHIMICHANGAS

THESE FRIED BURRITOS ARE A COMMON SIGHT ON STREET STALLS AND IN CAFÉS ALONG THE MEXICAN BORDER WITH TEXAS, BUT ARE NOT SO WELL KNOWN FURTHER SOUTH.

SERVES FOUR

INGREDIENTS
2 skinless, boneless chicken breasts
1 chipotle chile, seeded
1 tablespoon vegetable oil
2 onions, finely chopped
4 garlic cloves, crushed
½ teaspoon ground cumin
½ teaspoon ground coriander
½ teaspoon ground cinnamon
½ teaspoon ground cloves
scant 2 cups drained canned
   tomatillos
2⅓ cups cooked pinto beans
8 x 8–10-inch fresh flour
   tortillas
oil, for frying
salt and ground black pepper

1 Put the chicken breasts in a large saucepan, pour in water to cover and add the chile. Bring to a boil, lower the heat and simmer for 10 minutes or until the chicken is cooked through and the chile has softened. Remove the chile and chop it finely. Lift the chicken breasts out of the pan and put them on a plate. Let cool slightly, then shred with two forks.

2 Heat the oil in a frying pan. Sauté the onions until translucent, then add the garlic and ground spices and cook for 3 more minutes. Add the tomatillos and pinto beans. Cook over medium heat for 5 minutes, stirring constantly to break up the tomatillos and some of the beans. Simmer gently for 5 more minutes. Add the chicken and seasoning.

3 Wrap the tortillas in aluminum foil and place them on a plate. Stand the plate over boiling water for about 5 minutes until they become pliable. Alternatively, wrap them in microwave-safe plastic wrap and heat them in a microwave on full power for 1 minute.

4 Spoon one-eighth of the bean filling into the center of a tortilla, fold in both sides, then fold the bottom of the tortilla up and the top down to form a neat parcel. Secure with a toothpick.

5 Heat the oil in a large frying pan and fry the chimichangas in batches until crisp, turning once. Remove them from the oil with a slotted spoon and drain on paper towels. Serve hot.

COOK'S TIP
The word "pinto" means speckled, which aptly describes these attractive dried beans. If you prepare them yourself, they will need to be soaked overnight in water, then cooked in unsalted boiling water for 1–1¼ hours, until tender.

DRUNKEN CHICKEN

TEQUILA IS THIS CHICKEN'S MAGIC INGREDIENT, AND THE DISH HAS A DELICIOUS SWEET-AND-SOUR FLAVOR. SERVE IT WITH GREEN OR YELLOW RICE AND FLOUR TORTILLAS TO MOP UP THE SAUCE.

2 Heat the remaining vegetable oil in a large, deep frying pan. Add the onion slices and crushed garlic and cook for 2–3 minutes. Meanwhile, peel, core and dice the apples.

3 Add the diced apple to the onion mixture with the almonds and plantain slices. Cook, stirring occasionally, for 3–4 minutes, then add the soaked raisins, with any remaining sherry. Add the chicken pieces to the pan.

4 Pour the stock and tequila over the chicken mixture. Cover the pan with a lid and cook for 15 minutes, then take off the lid and cook for 10 more minutes or until the sauce has reduced by about half.

SERVES FOUR

INGREDIENTS
  scant 1 cup raisins
  ½ cup sherry
  1 cup all-purpose flour
  ½ teaspoon salt
  ½ teaspoon ground black pepper
  3 tablespoons vegetable oil
  8 skinless chicken thighs, bone-in
  1 onion, halved and thinly sliced
  3 garlic cloves, crushed
  2 tart apples, such as
    Granny Smith
  1 cup slivered almonds
  1 ripe plantain, peeled and sliced
  1½ cups well-flavored chicken stock
  1 cup tequila
  fresh herbs, chopped, to garnish
    (optional)

1 Put the raisins in a bowl and pour in the sherry. Set aside to plump up. Season the flour with the salt and pepper and spread it out on a large, flat dish or soup plate. Heat 2 tablespoons of the oil in a large frying pan. Dip each chicken thigh in turn in the seasoned flour, then fry in the hot oil until browned, turning occasionally. Drain on paper towels.

5 Check that the chicken thighs are cooked by lifting one out of the pan and piercing it in the thickest part with a sharp knife or skewer. Any juices that come out should be clear. If necessary, cook the chicken for a little longer before serving, sprinkled with chopped fresh herbs, if desired.

CHICKEN FAJITAS

THE PERFECT DISH FOR CASUAL ENTERTAINING, FAJITAS ARE FLOUR TORTILLAS THAT ARE BROUGHT TO THE TABLE FRESHLY COOKED. GUESTS ADD THEIR OWN FILLINGS BEFORE FOLDING UP THE TORTILLAS.

SERVES SIX

INGREDIENTS
    3 skinless, boneless chicken breasts
    finely grated zest and juice of
      2 limes
    2 tablespoons sugar
    2 teaspoons dried oregano
    ½ teaspoon cayenne pepper
    1 teaspoon ground cinnamon
    2 onions
    3 bell peppers (1 red, 1 yellow or
      orange and 1 green)
    3 tablespoons vegetable oil
    guacamole, salsa and sour cream,
      to serve
For the tortillas
    2¼ cups all-purpose flour, sifted
    ¼ teaspoon baking powder
    pinch of salt
    ¼ cup lard
    ¼ cup warm water

1 Slice the chicken breasts into ¾-inch wide strips and place these in a large bowl. Add the lime zest and juice, sugar, oregano, cayenne and cinnamon. Mix thoroughly. Set aside to marinate for at least 30 minutes.

COOK'S TIP
Tortilla dough can be very difficult to roll out thinly. If the dough is breaking up, try placing each ball between two sheets of clean plastic wrap (this can be cut from a new sandwich bag). Roll out, turning over, still inside the plastic, until the tortilla is the right size.

2 Meanwhile, make the tortillas. Mix the flour, baking powder and salt in a large bowl. Rub in the lard, then add the warm water, a little at a time, to make a stiff dough. Knead this on a lightly floured surface for 10–15 minutes, until it is smooth and elastic.

3 Divide the dough into 12 small balls, then roll each ball into a 6-inch round. Cover the rounds with plastic wrap to keep them from drying out while you prepare the vegetables.

4 Cut the onions in half and slice them thinly. Cut the peppers in half, remove the cores and seeds, then slice the flesh into ½ inch wide strips.

5 Heat a large frying pan or griddle and cook each tortilla in turn for about 1 minute on each side or until the surface colors and begins to blister. Keep the cooked tortillas warm and pliable by wrapping them in a clean, dry dish towel.

6 Heat the oil in a large frying pan. Stir-fry the marinated chicken for 5–6 minutes, then add the peppers and onions and cook for 3–4 more minutes more, until the chicken strips are cooked through and the vegetables are soft and tender, but still juicy.

7 Spoon the chicken mixture into a serving bowl and take it to the table with the cooked tortillas, guacamole, salsa and sour cream. Keep the tortillas wrapped and warm.

8 To serve, each guest takes a warm tortilla, spreads it with a little salsa, adds a spoonful of guacamole and piles some of the chicken mixture in the center. The final touch is to add a small dollop of sour cream. The tortilla is then folded over the filling and eaten.

CHICKEN WITH CHIPOTLE SAUCE

IT IS IMPORTANT TO USE CHIPOTLE CHILES IN THIS RECIPE, AS THEY IMPART A WONDERFULLY RICH AND SMOKY FLAVOR TO THE CHICKEN BREASTS. THE PURÉE CAN BE MADE AHEAD OF TIME, MAKING THIS A VERY EASY RECIPE FOR ENTERTAINING.

SERVES SIX

INGREDIENTS
  6 chipotle chiles
  scant 1 cup water
  chicken stock (see method)
  3 onions
  6 boneless chicken breasts
  3 tablespoons vegetable oil
  salt and ground black pepper
  fresh oregano to garnish

1 Put the dried chiles in a bowl and pour in hot water to cover. Let stand for about 30 minutes, until very soft. Drain, reserving the soaking water in a measuring cup. Cut off the stem from each chile, then slit them lengthwise and scrape out the seeds with a small sharp knife.

2 Preheat the oven to 350°F. Chop the flesh of the chiles roughly and put it in a food processor or blender. Add enough chicken stock to the soaking water to make 1⅔ cups. Pour it into the processor or blender and process at maximum power until smooth.

3 Peel the onions. Using a sharp knife, cut them in half, then slice them thinly. Separate the slices.

4 Remove the skin from the chicken breasts and trim off any stray pieces of fat or membrane.

5 Heat the oil in a large frying pan, add the onions and cook over low to medium heat for about 5 minutes or until they have softened but not colored, stirring occasionally.

6 Using a slotted spoon, transfer the onion slices to a casserole that is large enough to hold all the chicken breasts in a single layer. Sprinkle the onion slices with a little salt and ground black pepper.

COOK'S TIP
If you are a lover of chipotle chiles, you may wish to use more than six.

7 Arrange the chicken breasts on top of the onion slices. Sprinkle with a little salt and several grindings of black pepper.

8 Pour the chipotle purée onto the chicken breasts, making sure that each piece is evenly coated.

9 Place the casserole in the preheated oven and bake for 45 minutes–1 hour or until the chicken is cooked through, but is still moist and tender. Garnish with fresh oregano and serve with boiled white rice, and *Frijoles de Olla*.

TURKEY MOLE

A MOLE IS A RICH STEW, TRADITIONALLY SERVED ON A FESTIVE OCCASION. THE WORD COMES FROM THE AZTEC "MOLLI," MEANING A CHILI-FLAVORED SAUCE. THERE ARE MANY DIFFERENT TYPES, INCLUDING THE FAMOUS MOLE POBLANO DE GUAJALOTE. TOASTED NUTS, FRUIT AND CHOCOLATE ARE AMONG THE CLASSIC INGREDIENTS; THIS VERSION INCLUDES COCOA POWDER.

SERVES FOUR

INGREDIENTS
    1 ancho chile, seeded
    1 guajillo chile, seeded
    ¾ cup sesame seeds
    ½ cup whole blanched almonds
    ½ cup shelled unsalted
      peanuts, skinned
    1 small onion
    2 garlic cloves
    ¼ cup lard or 4 tablespoons
      vegetable oil
    ⅓ cup canned tomatoes in
      tomato juice
    1 ripe plantain
    ⅓ cup raisins
    ½ cup ready-to-eat prunes, pitted
    1 teaspoon dried oregano
    ½ teaspoon ground cloves
    ½ teaspoon crushed
      allspice berries
    1 teaspoon ground cinnamon
    ¼ cup unsweetened cocoa powder
    4 turkey breasts
    fresh oregano, to garnish
      (optional)

1 Soak both types of dried chile in a bowl of hot water for 30 minutes, then lift them out and chop them roughly. Reserve 1 cup of the soaking liquid.

COOK'S TIP
It is important to use good quality cocoa powder, which is unsweetened.

2 Spread out the sesame seeds in a heavy frying pan. Toast them over medium heat, shaking the pan lightly so that they turn golden all over. Do not let them burn, or the sauce will taste bitter. Set aside 3 tablespoons of the toasted seeds for the garnish and put the rest in a bowl. Toast the almonds and peanuts in the same way and add them to the bowl.

3 Chop the onion and garlic finely. Heat half the lard or oil in a frying pan, cook the chopped onion and garlic for 2–3 minutes, then add the chiles and tomatoes. Cook gently for 10 minutes.

4 Peel the plantain and slice it into short diagonal slices. Add it to the onion mixture with the raisins, prunes, dried oregano, spices and cocoa. Stir in the 1 cup of the reserved water in which the chiles were soaked. Bring to a boil, stirring, then add the toasted sesame seeds, almonds and peanuts. Cook for 10 minutes, stirring frequently, then remove from heat and let cool slightly.

5 Blend the sauce in batches in a food processor or blender until smooth. The sauce should be fairly thick, but a little water may be added if necessary.

6 Heat the remaining lard or oil in a flameproof casserole. Add the turkey and brown over medium heat.

7 Pour the sauce onto the steaks and cover the casserole with aluminum foil and a tight-fitting lid. Cook over low heat for 20–25 minutes or until the turkey is cooked and the sauce has thickened. Sprinkle with sesame seeds and chopped oregano, and serve with a rice dish and warm tortillas.

ENCHILADAS WITH PORK AND GREEN SAUCE

THE GREEN TOMATILLO SAUCE PROVIDES A TART CONTRAST TO THE PORK FILLING IN THIS POPULAR DISH. CASCABELS ARE DRIED CHILES THAT RATTLE WHEN SHAKEN.

SERVES THREE TO FOUR

INGREDIENTS
- 1¼ pounds pork shoulder, diced
- 1 cascabel chilli
- 2 tablespoons oil
- 2 garlic cloves, crushed
- 1 onion, finely chopped
- scant 2 cups drained canned tomatillos
- 6 fresh corn tortillas
- ¾ cup grated Monterey Jack or mild Cheddar cheese

1 Put the diced pork in a saucepan and pour in water to cover. Bring to a boil, lower the heat and simmer for 40 minutes.

2 Meanwhile, soak the dried chile in hot water for 30 minutes until softened. Drain, remove the stem, then slit the chile and scrape out the seeds.

3 Drain the pork and let it cool slightly, then shred it, using two forks. Put the pork in a bowl and set it aside.

4 Heat the oil in a frying pan and sauté the garlic and onion for 3–4 minutes, until translucent. Chop and add the chile with the tomatillos. Cook, stirring constantly, until the tomatillos start to break up. Lower the heat and simmer the sauce for 10 more minutes. Cool slightly, then purée in a blender.

5 Preheat the oven to 350°F. Soften the tortillas by wrapping them in foil and steaming on a plate over boiling water for a few minutes, until they are pliable. Alternatively, wrap them in microwave-safe plastic wrap and heat in a microwave on full power for about 30 seconds.

6 Spoon one-sixth of the shredded pork onto the center of a tortilla and roll it up to make an enchilada. Place it in a shallow baking dish that is large enough to hold all the enchiladas in a single layer. Fill and roll the remaining tortillas and add them to the dish.

7 Pour the sauce onto the enchiladas to cover completely. Sprinkle evenly with cheese. Bake for 25–30 minutes or until the cheese bubbles. Serve immediately. Tomato salad makes a good accompaniment for this dish.

PORK <u>IN</u> GREEN SAUCE <u>WITH</u> CACTUS

CHILE VERDE IS A CLASSIC SAUCE. THE INCLUSION OF CACTUS PIECES—A POPULAR INGREDIENT IN MEXICAN COOKING—GIVES THIS DISH AN INTRIGUING FLAVOR THAT WILL DOUBTLESS PROVE A GOOD CONVERSATION STARTER AT THE DINNER TABLE.

SERVES FOUR

INGREDIENTS
    2 tablespoons vegetable oil
    1¼ pounds pork shoulder, cut in
      1-inch cubes
    1 onion, finely chopped
    2 garlic cloves, crushed
    1 teaspoon dried oregano
    3 fresh jalapeño chiles, seeded
      and chopped
    scant 2 cups drained
      canned tomatillos
    ⅔ cup vegetable stock
    11-ounce jar *nopalitos*, drained
    salt and ground black pepper
    warm fresh corn tortillas, to serve

COOK'S TIP
Nopalitos are cactus paddles that have been cut into strips and pickled in vinegar or packed in brine. Look for them at specialty food stores.

1 Heat the oil in a large saucepan. Add the pork cubes and cook over high heat, turning several times, until browned all over. Add the onion and garlic and sauté gently until soft, then stir in the oregano and chopped jalapeños. Cook for 2 more minutes.

2 Transfer the canned tomatillos to a blender, add the stock and process until smooth. Add to the pork mixture, cover and cook for 30 minutes.

3 Meanwhile, soak the *nopalitos* in cold water for 10 minutes. Drain, then add to the pork and continue cooking for about 10 minutes or until the pork is cooked through and tender.

4 Season the mixture with salt and plenty of ground black pepper. Serve with warm corn tortillas.

STUFFED LOIN OF PORK

PORK FEATURES TWICE IN THIS DELICIOUS AND LUXURIOUS DISH, WHICH CONSISTS OF A ROAST LOIN STUFFED WITH A RICH GROUND PORK MIXTURE. THE PERFECT CENTERPIECE FOR A SPECIAL OCCASION DINNER, IT IS SERVED IN MEXICO AT WEDDINGS AND SIMILAR CELEBRATIONS.

SERVES SIX

INGREDIENTS
  3–3½ pounds boneless pork loin,
    butterflied and ready for stuffing
For the stuffing
  ⅓ cup raisins
  ½ cup dry white wine
  1 tablespoon vegetable oil
  1 onion, diced
  2 garlic cloves, crushed
  ½ teaspoon ground cloves
  1 teaspoon ground cinnamon
  1¼ pounds ground pork
  ⅔ cup vegetable stock
  2 tomatoes
  ½ cup chopped almonds
  ½ teaspoon each salt and ground
    black pepper

3 While the pork is simmering, peel the tomatoes. Cut a cross in the bottom of each tomato, then put them both in a heatproof bowl. Pour in boiling water to cover. Leave the tomatoes in the water for 3 minutes, then lift them out on a slotted spoon and plunge them into a bowl of cold water. Drain. The skins will have begun to peel back from the crosses.

6 Preheat the oven to 350°F. Open out the pork loin and trim it neatly. Season the pork stuffing with salt and pepper to taste. Spread on the surface of the meat in a neat layer, taking it right to the edges and keeping it as even as possible.

1 Make the stuffing. Put the raisins and wine in a bowl. Set aside. Heat the oil in a large pan, add the onion and garlic and cook for 5 minutes over low heat.

4 Remove the skins completely, then chop the flesh.

7 Roll up the pork loin carefully and tie it at intervals with kitchen string. Weigh the pork and calculate the cooking time at 30 minutes per pound, plus another 30 minutes.

8 Put the stuffed pork joint in a roasting pan, season with salt and pepper and roast for the calculated time. When the joint is cooked, transfer it to a meat platter, place a tent of aluminum foil over it, and let it stand for 10 minutes before carving and serving with the roast vegetables of your choice.

2 Add the cloves and cinnamon, then the pork. Cook, stirring, until the pork has browned. Add the stock. Simmer, stirring frequently, for 20 minutes.

5 Stir the tomatoes and almonds into the pork mixture, add the raisins and wine. Cook until the mixture is reduced to a thick sauce. Let cool.

COOK'S TIP
Your butcher will prepare the pork loin for you, if you give plenty of notice.

CARNITAS

Succulent little pieces of meat (usually pork), carnitas, literally "little meats," can be eaten as part of a main dish or used to fill tacos or burritos. They are also served with salsa as snacks or antojitos (nibbles).

SERVES EIGHT AS AN APPETIZER,
SIX AS A MAIN COURSE

INGREDIENTS
  2 dried bay leaves
  2 teaspoons dried thyme
  1 teaspoon dried marjoram
  3–3½ pounds mixed boneless pork
   (loin and leg)
  3 garlic cloves
  ½ teaspoon salt
  scant 1 cup lard
  1 orange, cut into 8 wedges
  1 small onion, thickly sliced
  warm flour tortillas, to serve
For the salsa
  small bunch of cilantro
  1 white onion
  8–10 pickled jalapeño chile slices
  3 tablespoons freshly squeezed
   orange juice

2 Cut the pork into 2-inch cubes and place it in a nonmetallic bowl. Add the herbs and salt. Using your fingers, rub the spice mixture into the meat. Cover and marinate for at least 2 hours, preferably overnight.

5 Heat the lard in a flame-proof casserole. Add the pork mixture, with the oranges, garlic cloves and onion. Brown the pork cubes on all sides.

3 To make the salsa, remove the stems from the cilantro and chop the leaves roughly. Cut the onion in half, then slice each half thinly. Finely chop the jalapeño chile slices.

6 Using a slotted spoon, lift out the onion and garlic and discard. Cover the casserole and continue to cook over low heat for about 1½ hours.

1 Crumble the bay leaves into a mortar. Add the dried thyme and dried marjoram and grind the mixture with a pestle to a fine powder.

COOK'S TIP
If the *carnitas* are to be served in tacos or burritos, shred or chop them. Make the chunks about half the given size if serving them as *antojitos*. Reduce the cooking time accordingly.

4 Mix all the salsa ingredients in a bowl, pour in the freshly squeezed orange juice and toss gently to mix. Cover and chill until needed.

7 Remove the lid and lift out and discard the orange wedges. Continue to cook the mixture, uncovered, until all the meat juices have been absorbed and the pork cubes are crisp on the outside and tender and moist inside. Serve with warm tortillas and the salsa.

TORTILLA PIE WITH CHORIZO

THIS IS A POPULAR MEXICAN breakfast dish, known as Chilaquiles. The fried tortilla strips stay crisp in the tomatillo, cream and cheese sauce.

SERVES SIX

INGREDIENTS

    2 tablespoons lard or 2 tablespoons
      vegetable oil
    1¼ pounds ground pork
    3 garlic cloves, crushed
    2 teaspoons dried oregano
    1 teaspoon ground cinnamon
    ½ teaspoon ground cloves
    ½ teaspoon ground black pepper
    2 tablespoons dry sherry
    1 teaspoon caster sugar
    1 teaspoon salt
    12 corn tortillas, freshly made or a
      few days old
    oil, for frying
    3 cups grated Monterey Jack or mild
      Cheddar cheese
    1¼ cups crème fraîche
For the tomatillo sauce
    scant 2 cups drained canned
      tomatillos
    4 tablespoons stock or water
    2 fresh serrano chiles, seeded and
      roughly chopped
    2 garlic cloves
    small bunch of cilantro
    ½ cup sour cream

1 Preheat the oven to 350°F. Heat the lard or oil in a large saucepan. Add the pork and crushed garlic. Stir over medium heat until the meat has browned, then stir in the oregano, cinnamon, cloves and pepper. Cook for 3–4 more minutes, stirring constantly, then add the sherry, sugar and salt. Stir for 3–4 minutes, until all the flavors are blended, then remove the pan from heat.

2 Cut the tortillas into ¾-inch strips. Pour oil into a frying pan to a depth of ¾ inch and heat to 375°F. Fry the tortilla strips in batches until crisp and golden brown all over.

3 Spread half the pork mixture in a baking dish. Top with half the tortilla strips and grated cheese, then add dollops of crème fraîche. Repeat the layers. Bake for 20–25 minutes or until bubbling.

4 To make the sauce, put all the ingredients except the sour cream in a food processor or blender. Reserve a little cilantro for sprinkling. Process until smooth. Scrape into a saucepan, bring to a boil, then lower the heat and simmer for 5 minutes.

5 Stir the sour cream into the sauce, with salt and pepper to taste. Pour the mixture on top and serve immediately, sprinkled with cilantro.

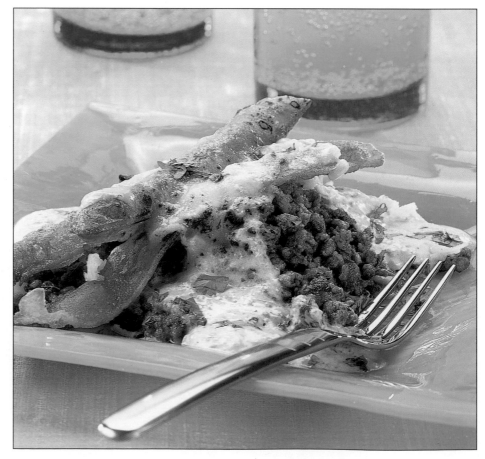

TOSTADAS <u>WITH</u> SHREDDED PORK <u>AND</u> SPICES

*CRISP FRIED TORTILLAS TOPPED WITH REFRIED BEANS AND SPICED SHREDDED PORK MAKE A
DELECTABLE TREAT AND ARE OFTEN SOLD AT STALLS IN MEXICAN CITY STREETS.*

SERVES SIX

INGREDIENTS
　6 corn tortillas, freshly made or a few
　　days old
　oil, for frying
For the topping
　1¼ pounds pork shoulder, cut into
　　1-inch cubes
　½ teaspoon salt
　1 tablespoon oil
　1 small onion, halved and sliced
　1 garlic clove, crushed
　1 pasilla chile, seeded and ground
　1 teaspoon ground cinnamon
　½ teaspoon ground cloves
　1 cup Refried Beans
　6 tablespoons sour cream
　2 tomatoes, seeded and diced
　4 ounces feta cheese, crumbled
　fresh oregano sprigs, to garnish

COOK'S TIP

In Mexico, the local fresh goat or cow's
milk cheese—*queso fresco*—would be
used, feta is the nearest equivalent.

1 Make the topping. Place the pork
cubes in a saucepan, pour in water to
cover and bring to a boil. Lower the
heat, cover and simmer for 40 minutes.
Drain, discarding the cooking liquid.
Shred the pork, using two forks. Put it
in a bowl and season with the salt.

2 Heat the oil in a large frying pan. Add
the onion, garlic, chile and spices. Stir
over the heat for 2–3 minutes, then add
the shredded meat and cook until the
meat is thoroughly heated and has
absorbed the flavorings. Heat the refried
beans in a separate, small pan.

3 Meanwhile, cook the tortillas. Pour oil
into a large frying pan to a depth of
¾ inch. Heat the oil and fry one tortilla
at a time, pressing down with a spatula
or a pair of tongs to keep it flat. As soon
as a tortilla is crisp, lift it out and drain
it on paper towels.

4 Place each tortilla on a plate. Top with
refried beans. Add a little of the meat
mixture, then spoon 1 tablespoon of the
sour cream on each. Divide the chopped
tomato among the tostadas and top with
the crumbled feta. Serve immediately,
garnished with fresh oregano.

TAMALES <u>FILLED WITH</u> SPICED PORK

THESE TAMALES ARE AMONG THE MOST ANCIENT OF MEXICAN FOODS. AT ONE TIME THE NEAT LITTLE CORN HUSK PARCELS FILLED WITH PLAIN, SAVORY OR SWEET MASA DOUGH WERE COOKED IN THE ASHES OF A WOOD FIRE. TODAY THEY ARE MORE LIKELY TO BE STEAMED, BUT THE THRILL OF UNWRAPPING THEM REMAINS THE SAME.

SERVES SIX

INGREDIENTS

    1¼ pounds lean pork, cut into
      2-inch cubes
    3 cups chicken stock
    4½ cups *masa harina*
    2 cups lard, softened
    2 tablespoons salt
    12 large or 24 small dried corn husks
    2 ancho chiles, seeded
    1 tablespoon vegetable oil
    ½ onion, finely chopped
    2–3 garlic cloves, crushed
    ½ teaspoon allspice berries
    2 dried bay leaves
    ½ teaspoon ground cumin
    lime wedges, to serve (optional)

1 Put the pork cubes in a large saucepan. Pour in water to cover. Bring to a boil, lower the heat and simmer for 40 minutes.

2 Meanwhile, heat the chicken stock in a separate pan. Put the *masa harina* in a large bowl and add the hot stock, a little at a time, to make a stiff dough.

3 Put the lard in another bowl and beat with an electric whisk until light and fluffy, as when beating butter for a cake. Test by dropping a small amount of the whipped lard into a cup of water. If it floats, it is ready for use.

4 Continue to beat the lard, gradually adding the *masa* dough. When all of it has been added and the mixture is light and spreadable, beat in the salt. Cover closely with plastic wrap to prevent the mixture from drying out.

5 Put the corn husks in a bowl and pour in boiling water to cover. Let soak for 30 minutes. Soak the seeded chiles in a separate bowl of hot water for the same time. Drain the pork, reserving 7 tablespoons of the cooking liquid, and chop the meat finely.

6 Heat the oil in a large saucepan and fry the onion and garlic over medium heat for 2–3 minutes. Drain the chiles, chop them finely and add them to the pan. Put the allspice berries and bay leaves in a mortar, grind them with a pestle, then work in the ground cumin. Add to the onion mixture and stir well. Cook for 2–3 more minutes. Add the chopped pork and reserved cooking liquid and continue cooking over medium heat until all the liquid is absorbed. Let cool slightly.

7 Drain the corn husks and pat them dry in a clean dish towel. Place one large corn husk (or overlap two smaller ones) on a board. Spoon about one-twelfth of the *masa* mixture onto the center of the husk wrapping and spread it almost to the sides.

8 Place a spoonful of the meat mixture on top of the *masa*. Fold the two long sides of the corn husk over the filling, then bring up each of the two shorter sides in turn, to make a neat parcel. Slide one of the two short sides inside the other, if possible, to prevent the parcel from unravelling, or tie with string or strips of the corn husk.

9 Place the *tamales* in a steamer basket over a pan of steadily simmering water and steam for 1 hour, adding water as needed. To test if the *tamales* are ready, unwrap one. The filling should separate from the husk cleanly. Pile the *tamales* on a plate, let stand for 10 minutes, then serve with lime wedges, if desired. Guests unwrap their own *tamales* at the table.

LAMB STEW WITH CHILI SAUCE

THE CHILES IN THIS STEW ADD DEPTH AND RICHNESS TO THE SAUCE, WHILE THE POTATO SLICES ENSURE THAT IT IS SUBSTANTIAL ENOUGH TO SERVE ON ITS OWN.

<u>SERVES SIX</u>

INGREDIENTS

6 guajillo chiles, seeded
2 pasilla chiles, seeded
1 cup hot water
3 garlic cloves, peeled
1 teaspoon ground cinnamon
½ teaspoon ground cloves
½ teaspoon ground black pepper
1 tablespoon vegetable oil
2¼ pounds lean boneless lamb
   shoulder, cut into ¾-inch cubes
14 ounces potatoes, scrubbed and
   cut into ½-inch thick slices
salt
strips of red bell pepper and fresh
   oregano to garnish

COOK'S TIP

When frying the lamb, don't be tempted to cook too many cubes at one time, as the meat will steam rather than fry.

1 Snap or tear the dried chiles into large pieces, put them in a bowl and pour in the hot water. Let soak for 30 minutes, then transfer the contents of the bowl to a food processor or blender. Add the garlic and spices. Process until smooth.

2 Heat the oil in a large saucepan. Add the lamb cubes, in batches, and stir-fry over high heat until the cubes are browned on all sides.

3 Return all the lamb cubes to the pan, spread them out, then cover them with a layer of potato slices. Add salt to taste. Put a lid on the pan and cook over medium heat for 10 minutes.

4 Pour over the chili mixture and mix well. Replace the lid and simmer over a low heat for about 1 hour or until the meat and the potato are tender. Serve with a rice dish, and garnish with strips of red bell pepper and fresh oregano.

ALBONDIGAS

DON'T BE DAUNTED BY THE LENGTH OF THE INGREDIENT LIST. THESE MEATBALLS ARE ABSOLUTELY DELICIOUS, AND THE CHIPOTLE CHILE GIVES THE SAUCE A DISTINCTIVE, SLIGHTLY SMOKY FLAVOR.

SERVES FOUR

INGREDIENTS
    8 ounces ground pork
    8 ounces lean ground beef
    1 onion, finely chopped
    1 cup fresh white breadcrumbs
    1 teaspoon dried oregano
    ½ teaspoon ground cumin
    ½ teaspoon salt
    ½ teaspoon ground black pepper
    1 egg, beaten
    oil, for frying
    fresh oregano sprigs,
      to garnish
For the sauce
    1 chipotle chilli, seeded
    1 tablespoon vegetable oil
    1 onion, finely chopped
    2 garlic cloves, crushed
    ¾ cup beef stock
    14-ounce can chopped tomatoes
      in tomato juice
    7 tablespoons passata

1 Mix the ground pork and beef in a bowl. Add the onion, bread crumbs, oregano, cumin, salt and pepper. Mix with clean hands until all the ingredients are well combined.

2 Stir in the egg, mix well, then roll into 1½-inch balls. Put these on a baking sheet and chill while you prepare the sauce.

3 Soak the dried chile in hot water to cover for 15 minutes. Heat the oil in a saucepan and sauté the onion and garlic for 3–4 minutes, until softened.

4 Drain the chile, reserving the soaking water, then chop it and add it to the onion mixture. Fry for 1 minute, then stir in the beef stock, tomatoes, passata and soaking water, with salt and pepper to taste. Bring to a boil, lower the heat and simmer, stirring occasionally, while you cook the meatballs.

5 Heat the oil for frying in a frying pan and fry the meatballs in batches for about 5 minutes, turning them occasionally, until browned.

6 Drain off the oil and transfer all the meatballs to a shallow casserole. Pour on the sauce and simmer for 10 minutes, stirring gently from time to time so that the meatballs are coated but do not disintegrate. Garnish with the oregano and serve. Plain white rice makes a good accompaniment.

COOK'S TIP
Dampen your hands before shaping the meatballs, and the mixture will be less likely to stick.

TACOS WITH SHREDDED BEEF

IN MEXICO TACOS ARE MOST OFTEN MADE WITH SOFT CORN TORTILLAS, WHICH ARE FILLED AND FOLDED IN HALF. IT IS UNUSUAL TO SEE THE CRISP SHELLS THAT ARE SO WIDELY USED IN TEX-MEX COOKING. TACOS ARE ALWAYS EATEN WITH THE HANDS.

3 Put the meat on a board, let it cool slightly, then shred it, using two forks. Put the meat in a bowl. Divide the tortilla dough into six equal balls.

4 Open a tortilla press and line both sides with plastic (this can be cut from a new plastic sandwich bag). Put each ball on the press and flatten it into a 6–8-inch round.

5 Heat a griddle or frying pan until hot. Cook each tortilla for 15–20 seconds on each side, and then for another 15 seconds on the first side. Keep the tortillas warm and soft by folding them inside a slightly damp dish towel.

6 Add the oregano and cumin to the shredded meat and mix well. Heat the oil in a frying pan and sauté the onion and garlic for 3–4 minutes, until softened. Add the spiced meat mixture and toss over the heat until heated through.

SERVES SIX

INGREDIENTS

    1 pound rump steak, diced
    1 cup *masa harina*
    ½ teaspoon salt
    ½ cup warm water
    2 teaspoons dried oregano
    1 teaspoon ground cumin
    2 tablespoons oil
    1 onion, thinly sliced
    2 garlic cloves, crushed
    cilantro, to garnish
    shredded lettuce, lime wedges and
        Classic Tomato Salsa, to serve

1 Put the steak in a deep frying pan and pour in water to cover. Bring to a boil, then lower the heat and simmer for 1–1½ hours.

2 Meanwhile, make the tortilla dough. Mix the *masa harina* and salt in a large mixing bowl. Add the warm water, a little at a time, to make a dough that can be worked into a ball. Knead the dough on a lightly floured surface for 3–4 minutes, until smooth, then wrap the dough in plastic wrap and let rest for 1 hour.

7 Place some shredded lettuce on a tortilla, top with shredded beef and salsa, fold in half and serve with lime wedges. Garnish with cilantro.

BEEF ENCHILADAS <u>WITH</u> RED SAUCE

ENCHILADAS ARE USUALLY MADE WITH CORN TORTILLAS, ALTHOUGH IN PARTS OF NORTHERN MEXICO FLOUR TORTILLAS ARE SOMETIMES USED.

SERVES THREE TO FOUR

INGREDIENTS

1¼ pounds rump steak, cut into
  2-inch cubes
2 ancho chiles, seeded
2 pasilla chiles, seeded
2 garlic cloves, crushed
2 teaspoons dried oregano
½ teaspoon ground cumin
2 tablespoons vegetable oil
7 fresh corn tortillas
shredded onion and flat-leaved
  parsley to garnish
Mango Salsa, to serve

1 Put the steak in a deep frying pan and cover with water. Bring to a boil, then lower the heat and simmer for 1–1½ hours or until very tender.

2 Meanwhile, put the dried chiles in a bowl and pour in the hot water. Let soak for 30 minutes, then put the contents of the bowl in a blender and whizz into a smooth paste.

3 Drain the steak and let it cool, reserving 1 cup of the cooking liquid. Meanwhile, fry the garlic, oregano and cumin in the oil for 2 minutes.

4 Stir in the chili paste and the reserved cooking liquid from the beef. Tear one of the tortillas into small pieces and add it to the mixture. Bring to a boil, then lower the heat. Simmer for 10 minutes, stirring occasionally, until the sauce has thickened. Shred the steak, using two forks, and stir it into the sauce, heat through for a few minutes.

5 Spoon some of the meat mixture onto each tortilla and roll it up to make an enchilada. Keep the enchiladas in a warmed dish until you have rolled them all. Garnish with shreds of onion and fresh flat-leaved parsley and then serve immediately with the Mango Salsa.

VARIATION

For a richer version, place the rolled enchiladas side by side in a gratin dish. Pour on 1¼ cups sour cream and ¾ cup grated Cheddar cheese. Place under a preheated broiler for 5 minutes or until the cheese melts and the sauce begins to bubble. Serve immediately, with the salsa.

STUFFED BEEF <u>WITH</u> CHEESE <u>AND</u> CHILI SAUCE

THIS RECIPE HAS ITS ORIGINS IN NORTHERN MEXICO, WHICH IS BEEF COUNTRY. IT IS A GOOD WAY TO COOK STEAKS, EITHER UNDER THE BROILER OR ON THE GRILL.

<u>SERVES FOUR</u>

INGREDIENTS
  4 fresh serrano chiles
  ½ cup full-fat soft cheese
  2 tablespoons reposada tequila
  2 tablespoons oil
  1 onion
  2 garlic cloves
  1 teaspoon dried oregano
  ½ teaspoon salt
  ½ teaspoon ground black pepper
  1½ cups grated Cheddar cheese
  4 fillet steaks, at least
    1 inch thick

3 Put the cream cheese in a small heavy saucepan and stir over low heat until it has melted. Add the chili strips and the tequila and stir to make a smooth sauce. Keep warm over very low heat.

6 Cut each steak almost but not quite in half across its width, so that it can be opened out, butterfly-style. Preheat the broiler to its highest setting.

1 Dry-roast the chiles in a griddle over medium heat, turning them frequently, until the skins are blistered but not burnt. Put them in a strong plastic bag and tie the top to keep the steam in. Set aside for 20 minutes.

4 Heat the oil in a frying pan and sauté the onion, garlic and oregano for about 5 minutes over medium heat, stirring frequently, until the onion has browned. Season with the salt and pepper.

7 Spoon a quarter of the cheese and onion filling on one side of each steak and close the other side over it. Place the steaks in a broiler pan and broil for 3–5 minutes on each side, depending on how you like your steak. Serve on heated plates with the vegetables of your choice, and with the cheese and chili sauce poured on top.

2 Remove the chilies from the bag, slit them and scrape out the seeds with a sharp knife. Cut the flesh into long narrow strips, then cut each strip into several shorter strips.

5 Remove the pan from heat and stir in the grated cheese so that it melts into the onion mixture.

COOK'S TIP
One of the easiest ways of testing whether a steak is cooked is by touch. A steak that is very rare or "blue" will feel soft to the touch; the meat will be relaxed. A rare steak will feel like a sponge, and will spring back when lightly pressed. A medium-rare steak offers more resistance, while a well-cooked steak will feel very firm.

FISH AND SHELLFISH

Mexico's delicious fish dishes are perhaps the country's best-kept secret. Asked to name the ten most popular Mexican dishes, few people would suggest seafood, yet the Pacific Ocean and the waters of the Gulf of Mexico are teeming with fish, and Mexican cooks put the bounty to excellent use. Tuna, swordfish, snapper and sea bass are just some of the varieties available at fish markets. Large succulent shrimp are a specialty, and crabs, crayfish and lobster are also available.

Between Ceviche, which requires no cooking at all, and Escabeche, which involves frying fish and then marinating it for 24 hours, there are a host of easy-to-cook dishes that take very little time to prepare. Some of these, such as Shrimp in Garlic Butter or Scallops with Garlic and Cilantro, make simple but delicious after-work meals, while others, such as Baked Salmon with Guava Sauce, are more elaborate and are perfect for entertaining.

ESCABECHE

A CLASSIC DISH THAT THE MEXICANS INHERITED FROM THE SPANISH, ESCABECHE IS OFTEN CONFUSED WITH CEVICHE, WHICH CONSISTS OF MARINATED RAW FISH. IN ESCABECHE, THE RAW FISH IS INITIALLY MARINATED IN LIME JUICE, BUT IS THEN COOKED BEFORE BEING PICKLED.

SERVES FOUR

INGREDIENTS

2 pounds whole fish fillets
juice of 2 limes
1¼ cups olive oil
6 peppercorns
3 garlic cloves, sliced
½ teaspoon ground cumin
½ teaspoon dried oregano
2 bay leaves
⅓ cup pickled jalapeño chile
    slices, chopped
1 onion, thinly sliced
1 cup white wine vinegar
1¼ cups green olives stuffed with
    pimiento, to garnish

1 Place the fish fillets in a single layer in a shallow nonmetallic dish. Pour on the lime juice, turn the fillets over once to ensure that they are completely coated, then cover the dish and let marinate for 15 minutes.

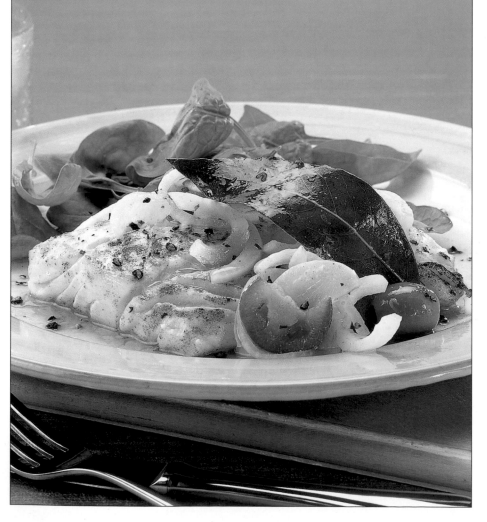

2 Drain the fish in a colander, then pat the fillets dry with paper towels. Heat 4 tablespoons of the oil in a large frying pan, add the fish fillets and sauté for 5–6 minutes, turning once, until they are golden brown. Use a spatula to transfer them to a shallow dish that will hold them in a single layer.

3 Heat 2 tablespoons of the remaining oil in a frying pan. Add the peppercorns, garlic, ground cumin, oregano, bay leaves and jalapeños, and cook over low heat for 2 minutes, then increase the heat, add the onion slices and vinegar and bring to a boil. Lower the heat and simmer for 4 minutes.

4 Remove the pan from heat and carefully add the remaining oil. Stir well, then pour the mixture onto the fish. Let cool, then cover the dish and marinate for 24 hours in the refrigerator.

5 When you are ready to serve, drain off the liquid and garnish the pickled fish with the stuffed olives. Salad leaves would make a good accompaniment.

COOK'S TIP
Use the largest frying pan you have when cooking the fish. If your pan is too small, it may be necessary to cook them in batches. Do not overcrowd the pan, as they will cook unevenly.

CEVICHE

THIS FAMOUS DISH IS PARTICULARLY POPULAR ALONG MEXICO'S WESTERN SEABOARD, IN PLACES SUCH AS ACAPULCO. IT CONSISTS OF VERY FRESH RAW FISH, "COOKED" BY THE ACTION OF LIME JUICE.

SERVES SIX

INGREDIENTS
7 ounces raw peeled shrimp
7 ounces shelled scallops
7 ounces squid, cleaned and cut
  into serving pieces
7 limes
3 tomatoes
1 small onion
1 ripe avocado
¼ cup chopped fresh oregano, or
  2 teaspoons dried
1 teaspoon salt
ground black pepper
fresh oregano sprigs, to garnish
crusty bread and lime wedges,
  to serve (optional)

1 Spread out the shrimp, scallops and squid in a non-metallic bowl. Squeeze six of the limes and pour the juice on the mixed seafood to cover it completely. Cover the dish with plastic wrap and set aside for 8 hours or overnight.

2 Drain the seafood in a colander to remove the excess lime juice, then pat it dry with paper towels. Place the shrimp, scallops and squid in a bowl.

3 Cut the tomatoes in half, squeeze out the seeds, then dice the flesh. Cut the onion in half, then slice it thinly. Cut the avocado in half lengthwise, remove the pit and peel, then cut the flesh into ½-inch dice.

4 Add the tomatoes, onion and avocado to the seafood with the oregano and seasoning. Squeeze the remaining lime and pour on the juice. Garnish with oregano and serve, with crusty bread and lime wedges, if desired.

SALT COD FOR CHRISTMAS EVE

THIS MEXICAN DISH IS MILDER THAN THE SIMILAR SPANISH DISH, BACALDO A LA VIZCAINA. IT IS EATEN ON CHRISTMAS EVE THROUGHOUT MEXICO.

SERVES SIX

INGREDIENTS
1 pound dried salt cod
7 tablespoons extra virgin olive oil
1 onion, halved and thinly sliced
4 garlic cloves, crushed
2 x 14-ounce cans chopped tomatoes
  in tomato juice
¾ cup slivered almonds
½ cup pickled jalapeño
  chile slices
1 cup green olives stuffed
  with pimiento
small bunch of fresh parsley,
  finely chopped
salt and ground black pepper
fresh flat-leaved parsley, to garnish
crusty bread, to serve

1 Put the cod in a large bowl and pour in enough cold water to cover. Soak for 24 hours, changing the water at least five times during this period.

2 Drain the cod and remove the skin using a large sharp knife. Shred the flesh finely using two forks, and put it into a bowl. Set it aside.

3 Heat half the oil in a large frying pan. Add the onion slices and sauté over medium heat until the onion has softened and is translucent.

4 Remove the onion from the pan and set aside. Make sure you transfer the oil with the onion, as it is an important flavoring in this dish and mustn't be discarded. In the same pan add the remaining olive oil. When the oil is hot but not smoking, add the crushed garlic and sauté gently for 2 minutes.

5 Add the canned tomatoes and their juice to the pan with the garlic. Cook over medium-high heat for about 20 minutes, stirring occasionally, until the mixture has reduced and thickened.

COOK'S TIPS
• Salt cod is available at specialty fishmongers, Spanish delicatessens and West Indian stores.
• Any leftovers can be used to fill burritos or empanadas.

6 Meanwhile, spread out the slivered almonds in a single layer in a large heavy frying pan. Toast them over medium heat for a few minutes, shaking the pan lightly throughout the process so that they turn golden brown all over. Do not let them burn.

7 Add the jalapeño chile slices and stuffed olives to the toasted almonds.

8 Stir in the shredded fish, mixing it in thoroughly, and cook for 20 more minutes, stirring occasionally, until the mixture is almost dry.

9 Season to taste, add the parsley and cook for another 2–3 minutes. Garnish with parsley leaves and serve in heated bowls, with crusty bread.

RED SNAPPER WITH CILANTRO AND ALMONDS

THIS SIMPLE TREATMENT IS PERFECT FOR RED SNAPPER, A FISH THAT IS VERY POPULAR IN MEXICO.

SERVES FOUR

INGREDIENTS
¾ cup all-purpose flour
4 red snapper fillets
salt and ground black pepper
6 tablespoons butter
1 tablespoon vegetable oil
¾ cup sliced almonds
grated zest and juice of 1 lime
small bunch of cilantro,
 finely chopped
warm flour tortillas, to serve

COOK'S TIP
Warm the tortillas by wrapping them in foil
and steaming them on a plate over boiling
water for a few minutes. Alternatively,
wrap them in microwave-safe plastic
wrap and heat them in a microwave on
full power for about 30 seconds.

1 Preheat the oven to 275°F. Spread
out the flour in a shallow dish and add
seasoning. Dry the fish fillets with
paper towels, then coat each fillet in
the seasoned flour.

2 Heat the butter and oil in a frying
pan. Add the snapper fillets, in batches
if necessary, and cook for 2 minutes.
Turn the fillets over carefully and cook
the other side until golden.

3 Using a spatula, carefully transfer the
fillets to a shallow dish and keep them
warm in the oven. Add the almonds to
the fat remaining and fry them for
3–4 minutes, until golden.

4 Add the lime zest, juice and cilantro
to the almonds in the frying pan and
stir well. Heat through for 1–2 minutes,
then pour the mixture onto the fish.
Serve with warm flour tortillas.

VERACRUZ-STYLE RED SNAPPER

THIS IS A CLASSIC MEXICAN DISH THAT BORROWS BAY LEAVES AND OLIVES FROM SPAIN TO GO WITH THE NATIVE CHILES.

SERVES FOUR

INGREDIENTS

4 whole red snapper, cleaned
juice of 2 limes
4 garlic cloves, crushed
1 teaspoon dried oregano
½ teaspoon salt
drained bottled capers, to garnish
lime wedges, to serve (optional)
For the sauce
½ cup olive oil
2 bay leaves
2 garlic cloves, sliced
4 fresh jalapeño chiles, seeded and
cut in strips
1 onion, thinly sliced
8 fresh tomatoes
½ cup pickled jalapeño
chilli slices
1 tablespoon soft dark brown sugar
½ teaspoon ground cloves
½ teaspoon ground cinnamon
1¼ cups green olives stuffed
with pimiento

1 Preheat the oven to 350°F. Rinse the fish inside and out, then pat dry with paper towels. Place in a large roasting pan in a single layer.

2 Mix the lime juice, garlic, oregano and salt in a small bowl. Pour the mixture onto the fish. Bake for about 30 minutes or until the flesh flakes easily when tested with the tip of a sharp knife.

3 Meanwhile, make the sauce. Heat the olive oil in a saucepan, add the bay leaves, garlic and chile strips; fry over low heat for 3–4 minutes.

4 Add the onion slices to the oil in the saucepan and cook for 3–4 more minutes, until all the onion is softened and translucent.

5 Cut a cross in the bottom of each tomato. Place them in a heatproof bowl and pour in boiling water to cover. After 3 minutes, lift the tomatoes out on a slotted spoon and plunge them into a bowl of cold water. Drain. The skins will have begun to peel back from the crosses.

6 Skin the tomatoes completely, then cut them in half and squeeze out the seeds. Chop the flesh finely and add it to the onion mixture. Cook for 3–4 minutes, until the tomato is starting to soften.

7 Add the pickled jalapeños, brown sugar, ground cloves and cinnamon to the sauce. Cook for 10 minutes, stirring frequently, then stir the olives into the sauce and pour a little onto each fish. Garnish with the capers and serve with lime wedges, if desired. A rice dish would make a good accompaniment.

RED SNAPPER BURRITOS

FISH MAKES A GREAT FILLING FOR A TORTILLA, ESPECIALLY WHEN IT IS SUCCULENT RED SNAPPER MIXED WITH RICE, CHILE AND TOMATOES.

SERVES SIX

INGREDIENTS
  3 red snapper fillets
  ½ cup long-grain white rice
  2 tablespoons vegetable oil
  1 small onion, finely chopped
  1 teaspoon ground achiote seed
    (annatto powder)
  1 pasilla or similar dried chile,
    seeded and ground
  ¾ cup slivered almonds
  7-ounce can chopped tomatoes in
    tomato juice
  1¼ cups grated Monterey Jack or
    mild Cheddar cheese
  8 x 8-inch flour tortillas
  fresh flat-leaved parsley to garnish
  lime wedges (optional)

1 Preheat the broiler. Broil the fish on an oiled rack for about 5 minutes, turning once. When cool, remove the skin and flake the fish into a bowl. Set it aside.

2 Meanwhile, put the rice in a saucepan, cover with cold water, cover and bring to a boil. Drain, rinse and drain again.

3 Heat the oil in a saucepan and sauté the onion until soft and translucent. Stir in the ground achiote (annatto powder) and the chile and cook for 5 minutes.

4 Add the rice, stir well, then stir in the fish and almonds. Add the tomatoes, with their juice. Cook over medium heat until the juice is absorbed and the rice is tender. Stir in the cheese and remove from the heat. Warm the tortillas.

6 Divide the filling among the tortillas and fold them as shown, to make neat parcels. Garnish with fresh parsley and serve with lime wedges, if desired. A green salad makes a good accompaniment.

SEA BASS WITH ORANGE CHILI SALSA

THE CITRUS SALSA HAS A FRESHNESS THAT PROVIDES THE PERFECT CONTRAST TO THE WONDERFUL FLAVOR OF FRESH SEA BASS.

SERVES FOUR

INGREDIENTS
4 sea bass fillets
salt and ground black pepper
cilantro, to garnish
For the salsa
2 fresh green chiles
2 oranges or pink grapefruit
1 small onion

1 Make the salsa. Roast the chiles in a dry griddle until the skins are blistered, being careful not to let the flesh burn. Put them in a strong plastic bag and tie the top to keep the steam in. Set aside for 20 minutes.

COOK'S TIP
If the fish has not been scaled, do this by running the back of a small filleting knife against the grain of the scales. They should come off cleanly. Rinse and pat dry with paper towels.

2 Slice the top and bottom off each orange or grapefruit and cut off all the peel and pith. Cut between the membranes and put each segment in a bowl.

3 Remove the chiles from the bag and peel off the skins. Cut off the stalks, then slit the chiles and scrape out the seeds. Chop the flesh finely. Cut the onion in half and slice it thinly. Add the onion and chiles to the orange pieces and mix lightly. Season and chill.

4 Season the sea bass fillets. Line a steamer with waxed paper, letting extra hang over the sides to enable the fish to be lifted out after cooking. Place the empty steamer over a pan of water and bring to a boil.

5 Place the fish in a single layer in the steamer. Cover with a lid and steam for about 8 minutes or until just cooked. Garnish with cilantro and serve with the salsa and a vegetable side dish of your choice.

FRIED SOLE WITH LIME

SIMPLE FISH DISHES LIKE THIS ONE CAPITALIZE ON THE DELICIOUS FLAVOR OF GOOD FRESH FISH.

SERVES FOUR

INGREDIENTS
  ¾ cup all-purpose flour
  2 teaspoons garlic salt
  1 teaspoon ground black pepper
  4 sole fillets
  oil, for frying
  juice of 2 limes
  small bunch of fresh parsley,
    chopped, plus extra sprigs,
    to garnish
  fresh salsa, to serve

COOK'S TIP
Make sure the oil is hot enough when you add the fish, or it will be absorbed by the fish and the dish will be too greasy.

1 Combine the flour, garlic salt and pepper. Spread out the seasoned flour mixture in a shallow dish. Pat the sole fillets dry with paper towels, then turn them in the seasoned flour until they are evenly coated.

2 Pour oil into a wide frying pan to a depth of ½ inch. Heat it until a cube of bread added to the oil rises to the surface and browns in 45–60 seconds.

3 Add the fish, in batches if necessary, and fry for 3–4 minutes. Lift each fillet out and drain it on paper towels. Transfer to a heated serving dish.

4 Squeeze the juice of half a lime onto each piece of fish and sprinkle with the chopped parsley. Serve immediately, with a fresh salsa to complement the fish. Garnish with parsley sprigs. New potatoes would also go well.

BAKED SALMON WITH GUAVA SAUCE

GUAVAS HAVE A CREAMY FLESH WITH A SLIGHT CITRUS TANG, WHICH MAKES THEM THE PERFECT FRUIT FOR A SAUCE TO SERVE WITH SALMON. THE SAUCE WORKS WELL WITH OTHER FISH AND IS ALSO GOOD WITH CHICKEN OR TURKEY.

SERVES FOUR

INGREDIENTS
  6 ripe guavas
  3 tablespoons vegetable oil
  1 small onion, finely chopped
  ½ cup well-flavored chicken stock
  2 teaspoons hot pepper sauce
  4 salmon steaks
  salt and ground black pepper
  strips of red bell pepper to garnish

COOK'S TIP
Ripe guavas have yellow skin and succulent flesh that ranges in color from white to deep pink or salmon red. They are exceptionally rich in vitamin C. Ripe fruit will keep in the refrigerator for a few days; green guavas will need to be placed in a warm spot until they ripen.

1 Cut each guava in half. Scoop the seeded soft flesh into a sieve placed over a bowl. Press it through the sieve, discard the seeds and skin and set the pulp aside.

2 Heat 2 tablespoons of the oil in a frying pan. Sauté the chopped onion for about 4 minutes over medium heat until softened and turned translucent.

3 Stir in the guava pulp, with the chicken stock and hot pepper sauce. Cook, stirring constantly, until the sauce thickens. Keep it warm until needed.

4 Brush the salmon steaks on one side with a little of the remaining oil. Season them with salt and pepper. Heat a griddle or ridged pan until very hot and add the salmon steaks, oiled side down. Cook for 2–3 minutes, until the underside is golden, then brush the surface with oil, turn each salmon steak over and cook the other side until the fish is cooked and flakes easily when tested with the tip of a sharp knife.

5 Transfer each steak to a warmed plate. Serve, garnished with strips of red pepper on a pool of sauce. A fresh green salad is a good accompaniment.

SALMON <u>WITH</u> TEQUILA CREAM SAUCE

USE REPOSADA TEQUILA, WHICH IS LIGHTLY AGED, FOR THIS SAUCE. IT HAS A SMOOTHER, MORE ROUNDED FLAVOR, WHICH GOES WELL WITH THE CREAM.

SERVES FOUR

INGREDIENTS

   3 fresh jalapeño chillies
   3 tablespoons olive oil
   1 small onion, finely chopped
   ⅔ cup fish stock
   grated rind and juice of 1 lime
   ½ cup light cream
   2 tablespoons reposada tequila
   1 firm avocado
   4 salmon fillets
   salt and ground white pepper
   strips of green bell pepper and fresh
     flat-leaved parsley to garnish

1 Roast the chiles in a frying pan until the skins are blistered, being careful not to let the flesh burn. Put them in a strong plastic bag and tie the top to keep the steam in. Set aside for 20 minutes.

2 Heat 1 tablespoon of the oil in a saucepan. Add the onion and sauté for 3–4 minutes, then add the stock, lime rind and juice. Cook for 10 minutes, until the stock starts to reduce. Remove the chiles from the bag and peel off the skins, slit and scrape out the seeds.

3 Stir the cream into the onion and stock mixture. Slice the chile flesh into strips and add to the pan. Cook over low heat, stirring constantly, for 2–3 minutes. Season to taste with salt and white pepper.

4 Stir the tequila into the onion and chilli mixture. Leave the pan over very low heat. Peel the avocado, remove the pit and slice the flesh. Brush the salmon fillets on one side with a little of the remaining oil.

5 Heat a frying pan or ridged pan until very hot and add the salmon, oiled side down. Cook for 2–3 minutes, until the underside is golden, then brush the top with oil, turn each fillet over and cook the other side until the fish is cooked and flakes easily when tested with the tip of a sharp knife.

6 Serve on a pool of sauce, with the avocado slices. Garnish with strips of green pepper and fresh parsley This is good with Fried Potatoes.

YUCATAN-STYLE SHARK STEAK

A FIRM-FLESHED FISH, SHARK IS WIDELY AVAILABLE, EITHER FRESH OR FROZEN. IT NEEDS CAREFUL WATCHING, AS OVERCOOKING WILL MAKE IT DRY AND TOUGH, BUT THE FLAVOR IS EXCELLENT.

SERVES FOUR

INGREDIENTS

grated zest and juice of 1 orange
juice of 1 small lime
3 tablespoons white wine
2 tablespoons olive oil
2 garlic cloves, crushed
2 teaspoons ground achiote seed
  (annatto powder)
½ teaspoon cayenne pepper
½ teaspoon dried marjoram
1 teaspoon salt
4 shark steaks
fresh oregano leaves, to garnish
4 flour tortillas and any suitable
  salsa, to serve

COOK'S TIP

Shark freezes successfully, with little or no loss of flavor on thawing, so use frozen steaks if you can't find fresh.

1 Put the orange zest and juice in a shallow nonmetallic dish which is large enough to hold all the shark steaks in a single layer. Add the lime juice, white wine, olive oil, garlic, ground achiote (annatto powder), cayenne, marjoram and salt. Mix well.

2 Add the shark steaks to the dish and spoon the marinade on them. Cover and set aside for 1 hour, turning once.

3 Heat a griddle until very hot and cook the marinated shark steaks for 2–3 minutes on each side. Alternatively, they are very good cooked on the grill, as long as they are cooked after the coals have lost their fierce initial heat. Do not overcook.

4 Garnish the shark steaks with oregano and serve with the tortillas and salsa. A green vegetable would also go well.

SWORDFISH TACOS

IT IS IMPORTANT NOT TO OVERCOOK SWORDFISH, OR IT CAN BE TOUGH AND DRY. COOKED CORRECTLY, HOWEVER, IT IS ABSOLUTELY DELICIOUS AND MAKES A GREAT CHANGE FROM BEEF OR CHICKEN AS A TACO FILLING.

SERVES SIX

INGREDIENTS
   3 swordfish steaks
   2 tablespoons vegetable oil
   2 garlic cloves, crushed
   1 small onion, chopped
   3 fresh green chiles, seeded
     and chopped
   3 tomatoes
   small bunch cilantro, chopped
   6 fresh corn tortillas
   ½ iceberg lettuce, shredded
   salt and ground black pepper
   lemon wedges, to serve (optional)

1 Preheat the broiler. Put the swordfish on an oiled rack over a broiler pan and broil for 2–3 minutes on each side. When cool enough to handle, remove the skin and flake the fish into a bowl.

2 Heat the oil in a saucepan. Add the garlic, onion and chiles and sauté for 5 minutes or until the onion is soft and translucent.

3 Cut a cross in the bottom of each tomato and pour in boiling water. After 3 minutes plunge into cold water. Remove the skins and seeds and chop the flesh into ½ inch dice.

4 Add the tomatoes and swordfish to the onion mixture. Cook for 5 minutes over low heat. Add the cilantro and cook for 1–2 minutes. Season to taste.

5 Wrap the tortillas in foil and steam on a plate over boiling water until pliable. Place some shredded lettuce and fish mixture on each tortilla. Fold in half and serve with lemon wedges, if desired.

GRILLED SWORDFISH WITH CHILI AND LIME SAUCE

SWORDFISH IS A PRIME CANDIDATE FOR THE GRILL, AS LONG AS IT IS NOT OVERCOOKED. IT TASTES WONDERFUL WITH A SPICY SAUCE WHOSE FIRE IS TEMPERED WITH CRÈME FRAÎCHE.

SERVES FOUR

INGREDIENTS
   2 fresh serrano chiles
   4 tomatoes
   3 tablespoons olive oil
   grated zest and juice of 1 lime
   4 swordfish steaks
   ½ teaspoon salt
   ½ teaspoon ground black pepper
   ¾ cup crème fraîche
   fresh flat-leaved parsley to garnish

1 Roast the chiles in a dry griddle until the skins are blistered. Put in a strong plastic bag and tie the top. Set aside for 20 minutes, then peel off the skins. Cut off the stalks, then slit the chiles, scrape out the seeds and slice the flesh.

2 Cut a cross in the bottom of each tomato. Place them in a heatproof bowl and pour in boiling water to cover. After 3 minutes, lift the tomatoes out on a slotted spoon and plunge them into a bowl of cold water. Drain. The skins will have begun to peel back from the crosses. Remove all the skin from the tomatoes, then cut them in half and squeeze out the seeds. Chop the flesh into ½-inch pieces.

3 Heat 1 tablespoon of the oil in a small saucepan and add the strips of chile, with the lime zest and juice. Cook for 2–3 minutes, then stir in the tomatoes. Cook for 10 minutes, stirring the mixture occasionally, until the tomato is pulpy.

4 Brush the swordfish steaks with olive oil and season. Grill for 3–4 minutes or until just cooked, turning once. Meanwhile, stir the crème fraîche into the sauce, heat it through gently and pour onto the swordfish steaks. Serve garnished with fresh parsley. Grill some vegetables as well.

SHRIMP WITH ALMOND SAUCE

GROUND ALMONDS ADD AN INTERESTING TEXTURE TO THE CREAMY, PIQUANT SAUCE THAT ACCOMPANIES THESE SHRIMP.

SERVES SIX

INGREDIENTS

    1 ancho or similar dried chile
    2 tablespoons vegetable oil
    1 onion, chopped
    3 garlic cloves, roughly chopped
    8 tomatoes
    1 teaspoon ground cumin
    ½ cup chicken stock
    generous 1 cup
      ground almonds
    ¾ cup crème fraîche
    ½ limeshrimp
    2 pounds cooked peeled prawns
    salt
    cilantro and scallion strips,
      to garnish
    cooked rice and warm tortillas,
      to serve

1 Place the dried chile in a heatproof bowl and pour in boiling water to cover. Let soak for 30 minutes until softened. Drain, remove the stem, then slit the chile and scrape out the seeds with a small sharp knife. Chop the flesh roughly and set it aside.

2 Heat the oil in a frying pan and sauté the onion and garlic until soft.

VARIATIONS
Try this sauce with other types of fish, too. Adding just a few shrimp and serving it over steamed sole would make a very luxurious dish. The sauce is also very good with chicken.

3 Cut a cross in the bottom of each tomato. Place them in a heatproof bowl and pour in boiling water to cover. After 3 minutes, lift the tomatoes out on a slotted spoon and plunge them into a bowl of cold water. Drain. The skins will have begun to peel off.

4 Skin the tomatoes completely, then cut them in half and scoop out the seeds. Chop the flesh into ½-inch cubes and add it to the onion mixture, with the chopped chile. Stir in the ground cumin and cook for 10 minutes, stirring occasionally.

5 Put the mixture in a food processor or blender. Add the stock and process on high speed until smooth.

6 Pour the mixture into a large saucepan, add the ground almonds and stir over low heat for 2–3 minutes. Stir in the crème fraîche until it has been incorporated completely.

7 Squeeze the juice from the lime and stir it into the sauce. Season with salt to taste, then increase the heat and bring the sauce to the simmering point.

8 Add the shrimp and heat for 2–3 minutes, depending on size, until warmed through. Serve on a bed of rice and pass warm tortillas separately.

SHRIMP IN GARLIC BUTTER

THIS QUICK AND EASY DISH IS PERFECT FOR SERVING TO FRIENDS WHO DON'T MIND GETTING THEIR HANDS DIRTY. PROVIDE A PLATE FOR THE SHRIMP SHELLS AND PASS WARM TORTILLAS FOR MOPPING UP THE DELECTABLE JUICES.

SERVES SIX

INGREDIENTS

   2 pounds large jumbo shrimp, in
     their shells, thawed if frozen
   ½ cup butter
   1 tablespoon vegetable oil
   6 garlic cloves, crushed
   grated zest and juice of 2 limes
   small bunch of cilantro, chopped
   warm tortillas, to serve
   lemon slices, for the finger bowls

1 Rinse the shrimp in a colander, remove their heads and let them drain. Heat the butter and oil in a large frying pan, add the garlic and sauté over low heat for 2–3 minutes.

2 Add the lime zest and juice. Cook, stirring constantly, for 1 more minute.

COOK'S TIP
Cook the shrimp in a large frying pan or cast iron flameproof dish that can be taken directly to the table, so that they retain their heat until they are served.

3 Add the shrimp and cook them for 2–3 minutes, until they turn pink. Remove from heat, sprinkle with cilantro and serve with the warm tortillas. Give each guest a finger bowl filled with water and a slice of lemon, for cleaning their fingers after shelling the shrimp, and provide paper napkins.

SHRIMP SALAD

IN MEXICO, THIS SALAD WOULD FORM THE FISH COURSE IN A FORMAL MEAL, BUT IT IS SO GOOD THAT YOU'LL WANT TO SERVE IT ON ALL SORTS OF OCCASIONS. IT IS PERFECT FOR A BUFFET LUNCH.

SERVES FOUR

INGREDIENTS
1 pound cooked peeled shrimp
juice of 1 lime
3 tomatoes
1 ripe but firm avocado
2 tablespoons hot chili sauce
1 teaspoon sugar
⅔ cup sour cream
2 Boston lettuces, separated
   into leaves
salt and ground black pepper
fresh basil leaves and strips of green
   bell pepper to garnish

1 Put the shrimp in a large bowl, add the lime juice and salt and pepper. Toss lightly, then leave to marinate.

2 Cut a cross in the bottom of each tomato. Place them in a heatproof bowl and pour in boiling water to cover.

3 After 3 minutes, lift the tomatoes out on a slotted spoon and plunge them into a bowl of cold water. Drain. The skins will have begun to peel back easily from the crosses.

4 Skin the tomatoes completely, then cut them in half and squeeze out the seeds. Chop the flesh into ½-inch cubes and add it to the shrimp.

5 Cut the avocado in half, remove the skin and pit, then slice the flesh into ½-inch chunks. Add it to the shrimp and tomato mixture.

6 Mix the hot chili sauce, sugar and sour cream in a bowl. Fold into the shrimp mixture. Line a bowl with the lettuce leaves, then top with the shrimp mixture. Cover and chill for at least 1 hour, then garnish with fresh basil and strips of green pepper. Crusty bread makes a perfect accompaniment.

CRAB <u>WITH</u> GREEN RICE

THIS IS A POPULAR DISH IN THE WESTERN COASTAL AREAS OF MEXICO. SHRIMP CAN BE USED INSTEAD OF CRABMEAT IF YOU PREFER, AND THE DISH ALSO WORKS WELL WITH WARM CORN TORTILLAS.

SERVES FOUR

INGREDIENTS

generous 1 cup long-grain
  white rice
3⅓ cups drained
  canned tomatillos
large bunch of cilantro
1 onion, roughly chopped
3 poblano or other fresh green
  chiles, seeded and chopped
3 garlic cloves
3 tablespoons olive oil
1¼ pounds crabmeat
1¼ cups fish stock
¼ cup dry white wine
salt
sliced scallions, to garnish

1 Put the rice in a heatproof bowl, pour in boiling water to cover and let stand for 20 minutes. Drain thoroughly.

2 Put the tomatillos in a food processor or blender and process until smooth. Chop half the cilantro and add to the tomatillo purée, with the onion, chiles and garlic. Process again until smooth.

3 Heat the oil in a large saucepan. Add the rice and fry over medium heat for 5 minutes, until all the oil has been absorbed. Stir occasionally to prevent the rice from sticking.

4 Stir in the tomatillo mixture, with the crabmeat, stock and wine. Cover and cook over low heat for about 20 minutes or until all the liquid has been absorbed. Stir occasionally and add a little more liquid if the rice starts to stick to the pan. Add salt as required, then spoon into a dish and garnish with the remaining cilantro and the sliced scallions. Green salad and lime wedges make good accompaniments.

SCALLOPS WITH GARLIC AND CILANTRO

SHELLFISH IS OFTEN COOKED VERY SIMPLY IN MEXICO, HOT CHILI SAUCE AND LIME BEING POPULAR INGREDIENTS IN MANY FISH RECIPES.

SERVES FOUR

INGREDIENTS
20 scallops
2 zucchini
6 tablespoons butter
1 tablespoon vegetable oil
4 garlic cloves, chopped
2 tablespoons hot chili sauce
juice of 1 lime
small bunch of cilantro,
  finely chopped

COOK'S TIP
Oil can withstand higher temperatures than butter, but butter gives fried food added flavor. Using a mixture, as here, is the perfect compromise.

1 If you have bought scallops in their shells, open them. Hold a scallop shell in the palm of your hand, with the flat side facing up. Insert the blade of a knife close to the hinge that joins the shells and prise them apart. Run the blade of the knife across the inside of the flat shell to cut off the scallop. Only the white adductor muscle and the orange coral are eaten, so pull off and discard all other parts. Rinse the scallops under cold running water.

2 Cut the zucchinis in half, then into four pieces. Melt the butter in the oil in a large frying pan. Add the zucchini and cook until soft. Remove from the pan. Add the garlic and fry until golden. Stir in the hot chili sauce.

3 Add the scallops to the sauce. Cook, stirring constantly, for 1–2 minutes only. Stir in the lime juice, chopped cilantro and the zucchini pieces. Serve immediately on heated plates.

PUEBLO BAKED FISH

THE LIME JUICE IS A PERFECT PARTNER FOR THE TROUT, WHICH IS AN OILY FISH. MARINATING MEANS THAT THE FISH IS BEAUTIFULLY TENDER WHEN COOKED.

SERVES FOUR

INGREDIENTS
    2 fresh pasilla chiles
    4 rainbow trout, cleaned
    4 garlic cloves
    2 teaspoons dried oregano
    juice of 2 limes
    /½ cup slivered almonds
    salt and ground black pepper

1 Roast the chiles in a dry frying pan or griddle until the skins are blistered, being careful not to let the flesh burn. Put them in a strong plastic bag and tie the top to keep the steam in. Set aside for 20 minutes.

2 Meanwhile, rub a little salt into the cavities in the trout, to ensure that they are completely clean, then rinse them under cold running water. Drain and pat dry with paper towels.

COOK'S TIP
Cooking fish in a paper parcel means that it stays very moist. Trout cooks perfectly by this method, but you could use other fish; try tuna steaks, small mackerel or salmon fillets.

3 Remove the chiles from the bag and peel off the skins. Cut off the stems, then slit the chiles and scrape out the seeds. Chop the flesh roughly and put it in a mortar. Crush with a pestle until the mixture forms a paste.

4 Place the chili paste in a shallow dish that will hold all the trout in a single layer. Slice the garlic lengthwise and add to the dish.

5 Add the oregano and 2 teaspoons salt, then stir in the lime juice and pepper to taste. Add the trout, turning to coat them in the mixture. Cover the dish and set aside for at least 30 minutes, turning the trout again halfway through.

6 Preheat the oven to 400°F. Have ready four pieces of aluminum foil, each large enough to wrap a trout. Top each sheet with a piece of waxed paper of the same size.

7 Place one of the trout on one of the pieces of paper, moisten with the marinade, then sprinkle about a quarter of the almonds on the top.

8 Bring up the sides of the paper and fold over to seal in the fish, then fold the foil over to make a neat parcel. Make three more parcels in the same way, then place them side by side in a large roasting pan.

9 Transfer the parcels to the oven and bake for 25 minutes. Put each parcel on an individual plate, or open them in the kitchen and serve unwrapped if you prefer. This dish goes well with new potatoes and cooked fresh vegetables.

FISHERMAN'S STEW

THIS IS JUST THE SORT OF ONE-POT MEAL YOU CAN IMAGINE FISHERMEN COOKING FOR THEMSELVES,
USING FRESHLY CAUGHT FISH AND A FEW VEGETABLES.

SERVES SIX

INGREDIENTS
1¼ pounds mussels
3 onions
2 garlic cloves, sliced
1¼ cups fish stock
12 scallops
1 pound cod fillet
2 tablespoons olive oil
1 large potato, about 7 ounces
few sprigs of fresh thyme, chopped
1 red and 1 green bell pepper
½ cup dry white wine
1 cup crème fraîche
10 ounces peeled shrimp
¾ cup grated aged
  Cheddar cheese
salt and ground black pepper
fresh thyme sprigs, to garnish

1 Clean the mussel shells, removing any beards. Discard any that stay open when tapped. Rinse in cold water.

2 Pour water to a depth of 1 inch into a large, deep frying pan. Chop one onion and add it to the pan, with the sliced garlic. Bring to a boil, then add the mussels and cover the pan tightly.

3 Cook the mussels for 5–6 minutes, shaking the pan occasionally. Remove them as they open, discarding any that remain shut. Remove the mussels from their shells and set them aside.

4 Strain the cooking liquid from the mussels through a muslin-lined sieve to remove any remaining sand. Make up the liquid with fish stock to 1¼ cups.

5 If you have bought scallops in their shells, open them: hold a scallop shell in the palm of your hand, with the flat side facing up. Insert the blade of a knife close to the hinge that joins the shells and prise apart. Run the blade of the knife across the inside of the flat shell to cut off the scallop. Only the white adductor muscle and the orange coral are eaten, so pull off and discard all other parts. Rinse the scallops under cold running water to remove any grit or sand, then put them in a bowl and set them aside.

6 Cut the cod into large cubes and put it in a bowl. Season with salt and pepper and set aside.

7 Cut the remaining onions into small wedges. Heat the olive oil in a large saucepan and fry the onion wedges for 2–3 minutes. Slice the potato about ½ inch thick and add to the pan, with the fresh chopped thyme. Cover and cook for about 15 minutes, until the potato has softened.

8 Core the peppers, remove the cores and seeds, then dice the flesh. Add to the onion and potato mixture and cook for a few minutes. Stir in the mixed mussel and fish stock, with the wine and crème fraîche.

9 Bring to just below the boiling point, then add the cod and scallops. Lower the heat and simmer for 5 minutes, then add the shrimp. Simmer for another 3–4 minutes, until all the seafood is cooked. Stir in the mussels and warm through for 1–2 minutes. Season the sauce if necessary. Spoon into bowls, garnish with the thyme sprigs and sprinkle on the cheese. Crusty bread would be an ideal accompaniment.

VEGETABLES

When the Spaniards arrived in Mexico they discovered that the indigenous people cultivated a wide range of vegetables including corn, which was a staple, several varieties of squash and pumpkin, avocados, bell peppers and green beans. Many of these vegetables have since been introduced into our diets—green beans were brought to England during the reign of Queen Elizabeth 1; others, such as jicama, the crisp textured vegetable that can be eaten raw or cooked, have been introduced to our diets through other cuisines such as Chinese. Many of these dishes could form the basis of a meal on their own, while side dishes such as green and yellow rice, fried potatoes, and Mexican-style green peas will add flavor and color to any meal. The wide range of recipes in this chapter is testimony to the great variety of vegetables that are still being eaten in Mexico today.

MEXICAN-STYLE GREEN PEAS

THIS IS A DELICIOUS WAY OF COOKING FRESH PEAS, AND MAKES AN EXCELLENT ACCOMPANIMENT TO ANY MEAL. THE FLAVOR COMES FROM THE VEGETABLES THEMSELVES, SO USE RIPE TOMATOES AND ORGANIC PEAS IF POSSIBLE.

SERVES FOUR

INGREDIENTS
 2 tomatoes
 ¼ cup butter
 2 garlic cloves, halved
 1 medium onion, halved and
  thinly sliced
 scant 3 cups shelled
  fresh peas
 2 tablespoons water
 salt and ground black pepper
 fresh chives, to garnish

1 Cut a cross in the bottom of each tomato. Place the tomatoes in a heatproof bowl and pour in boiling water to cover. Leave them in the water for 3 minutes, then lift the tomatoes out on a slotted spoon and plunge them into a bowl of cold water. Drain. The skins will have begun to peel back.

2 Remove the skins completely, then cut the tomatoes in half and squeeze out the seeds. Chop the flesh into ½-inch dice.

3 Melt the butter in a saucepan. Cook the garlic until golden. Do not overcook or it will add a bitter taste. Lift it out on a slotted spoon and discard it. Add the onion slices to the pan and sauté until transparent.

4 Add the tomato to the onion, mix well, then stir in the peas. Pour in the water, lower the heat and cover the pan tightly. Cook for 10 minutes, shaking the pan occasionally to stop the mixture from sticking to the bottom.

5 Check that the peas are cooked, then season with plenty of salt and pepper. Transfer the mixture to a heated dish and serve, garnished with fresh chives.

MUSHROOMS WITH CHIPOTLE CHILES

CHIPOTLE CHILES ARE JALAPEÑOS THAT HAVE BEEN SMOKE-DRIED. THEIR SMOKY FLAVOR IS THE PERFECT FOIL FOR THE MUSHROOMS IN THIS SIMPLE SALAD.

SERVES SIX

INGREDIENTS
 2 chipotle chiles
 6 cups button mushrooms
 ¼ cup vegetable oil
 1 onion, finely chopped
 2 garlic cloves, crushed or chopped
 salt
 small bunch of cilantro, to garnish

COOK'S TIP
Baby button mushrooms are perfect for this dish, if you can get them. You can, of course, use any white mushrooms, but larger ones may be better halved or quartered.

1 Soak the dried chiles in a bowl of hot water for about 10 minutes until they are softened. Drain, cut off the stems, then slit the chiles and scrape out the seeds. Chop the flesh finely.

2 Trim the mushrooms, then clean them with a damp cloth or paper towels. If they are large, cut them in half.

3 Heat the oil in a large frying pan. Add the onion, garlic, chiles and mushrooms and stir until evenly coated in the oil. Fry for 6–8 minutes, stirring occasionally, until the onion and mushrooms are tender. Season to taste and spoon into a serving dish. Chop some of the cilantro, leaving some whole leaves, and use to garnish. Serve hot.

STUFFED CHILES IN WALNUT SAUCE

THE POTATO AND MEAT FILLING IN THESE CHILES IS A GOOD PARTNER FOR THE RICH, CREAMY SAUCE THAT COVERS THEM.

SERVES FOUR

INGREDIENTS
    8 ancho chillies
    1 large potato, about 7 ounces
    3 tablespoons vegetable oil
    4 ounces lean ground pork
    1 onion, chopped
    1 teaspoon ground cinnamon
    1 cup walnuts, roughly chopped
    ½ cup chopped almonds
    ⅔ cup cream cheese
    ½ cup soft goat cheese
    ½ cup light cream
    ½ cup dry sherry
    ½ cup all-purpose flour
    ½ teaspoon ground white pepper
    2 eggs, separated
    oil, for deep-frying
    salt
    chopped fresh herbs,
      to garnish

1 Soak the dried chiles in a bowl of hot water for 30 minutes, until softened. · Drain, cut off the stems, then slit them down one side. Scrape out the seeds with a small sharp knife, taking care to keep the chiles intact for stuffing.

2 Peel the potato and cut it into ½-inch cubes. Heat 1 tablespoon of the oil in a large frying pan, add the pork and cook, stirring, until it has browned evenly.

COOK'S TIP
The potatoes must not break or become too floury. Do not overcook. For the best results buy waxy potatoes.

3 Add the potato cubes and mix well. Cover and cook over low heat for 25–30 minutes, stirring occasionally. Do not worry if the potato sticks to the bottom of the pan. Season with salt, remove from heat and set aside.

4 Heat the remaining oil in a separate frying pan and sauté the onion with the cinnamon for 3–4 minutes or until softened. Stir in the nuts and cook for 3–4 more minutes.

5 Add both types of cheese to the pan, with the cream and sherry. Mix well. Reduce the heat to the lowest setting and cook until the cheese melts and the sauce starts to thicken. Taste and season if necessary.

6 Spread out the flour on a plate or in a shallow dish. Season with the white pepper. Beat the egg yolks in a bowl until they are pale and thick.

7 In a separate, greasefree bowl, whisk the whites until they form soft peaks. Add a generous pinch of salt, then fold in the yolks, a little at a time.

8 Spoon some of the filling into each chilli. Pat the outside dry with paper towels. Heat the oil for deep-frying to a temperature of 350°F.

9 Coat a chile in flour, then dip it in the egg batter, covering it completely. Drain for a few seconds, then add to the hot oil. Add several more battered chiles, but do not overcrowd the pan. Fry the chiles until golden, then drain on paper towels and keep hot while cooking successive batches.

10 Reheat the sauce over low heat, if necessary. Arrange the chiles on individual plates, spoon a little sauce on each and serve immediately, sprinkled with chopped fresh herbs. A green salad goes well with this dish.

POTATOES <u>WITH</u> CHORIZO <u>AND</u> GREEN CHILLS

MEXICANS MAKE THEIR OWN CHORIZO SAUSAGE, SOMETIMES USING IT FRESH, BUT ALSO PUTTING IT INTO CASINGS TO DRY, WHEN IT RESEMBLES THE SPANISH VERSION THAT IS NOW POPULAR ALL OVER THE WORLD. THIS RECIPE MAKES A DELICIOUS BRUNCH DISH. TYPICAL OF PEASANT FOOD, IT IS BASED ON THE COMBINATION OF PLENTY OF POTATOES MIXED WITH STRONGLY FLAVORED MEAT TO HELP IT GO FURTHER.

SERVES FOUR TO SIX

INGREDIENTS

  2 pounds potatoes, peeled and diced
  2 tablespoons vegetable oil
  2 garlic cloves, crushed
  4 scallions, chopped
  2 fresh jalapeño chiles, seeded
    and diced
  11 ounces chorizo sausage, skinned
  1¼ cups grated Monterey Jack or
    Cheddar cheese
  salt (optional)

1 Bring a large saucepan of water to a boil and add the potatoes. When the water returns to a boil, lower the heat and simmer the potatoes for 5 minutes. Put the potatoes in a colander and drain thoroughly.

COOK'S TIP
Use firm-textured potatoes for this dish. Instead of Monterey Jack, you can also use Gouda or Cheddar.

2 Heat the oil in a large frying pan, add the garlic, scallions and chiles and cook for 3–4 minutes. Add the diced potato and cook until the cubes begin to brown a little.

3 Cut the chorizo into small cubes and add these to the pan. Cook the mixture for 5 minutes more, until the sausage has heated through.

4 Season with salt if necessary, then add the cheese. Mix quickly and carefully, trying not to break up the cubes of potato. Serve immediately, while the cheese is still melting.

RED CAULIFLOWER

VEGETABLES ARE SELDOM SERVED PLAIN IN MEXICO. THE CAULIFLOWER HERE IS FLAVORED WITH A SIMPLE TOMATO SALSA AND FRESH CHEESE. THE SALSA COULD BE ANY TABLE SALSA; TOMATILLO IS PARTICULARLY GOOD. THE CONTRAST WITH THE TEXTURE AND MILD FLAVOR OF THE CAULIFLOWER MAKES FOR A TASTY DISH.

SERVES SIX

INGREDIENTS
1 small onion
1 lime
1 medium cauliflower
14 ounces can chopped tomatoes
4 fresh serrano chiles, seeded and finely chopped
¼ teaspoon sugar
3 ounces feta cheese, crumbled
salt
chopped fresh flat-leaved parsley, to garnish

COOK'S TIP
Use a zester for the lime, if have you have one. This handy little tool enables you to pare off tiny strips of the zest, leaving the pith behind.

1 Chop the onion very finely and place in a bowl. With a zester peel off the zest of the lime in thin strips. Add to the chopped onion.

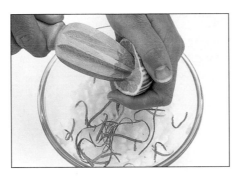

2 Cut the lime in half and add the juice from both halves to the onions and lime zest mixture. Set aside so that the lime juice can soften the onion. Cut the cauliflower into florets.

3 Put the tomatoes in a pan and add the chiles and sugar. Heat gently. Meanwhile, place the cauliflower in a pan of boiling water and cook gently for 5–8 minutes, until tender.

4 Add the onions to the tomato salsa, with salt to taste, stir in and heat through, then spoon about a third of the salsa into a serving dish.

5 Arrange the drained cauliflower florets on top of the salsa and spoon the remaining salsa on top.

6 Sprinkle with the feta, which should soften a little on contact. Serve immediately, sprinkled with chopped fresh flat-leaved parsley.

GREEN LIMA BEANS ᴵᴺ SAUCE

MAKE THE MOST OF LIMA BEANS OR FAVA BEANS BY TEAMING THEM WITH TOMATOES AND FRESH CHILES IN THIS SIMPLE ACCOMPANIMENT.

SERVES FOUR

INGREDIENTS
1 pound fresh lima beans or
  fava beans
2 tablespoons olive oil
1 onion, finely chopped
2 garlic cloves, crushed
14-ounce can plum tomatoes,
  drained and chopped
about 3 tablespoons drained pickled
  jalapeño chilli slices, chopped
salt
cilantro and lemon slices,
  to garnish

COOK'S TIP
Pickled chiles are often hotter than roasted chiles—taste one before adding to the recipe and adjust the quantity to suit your taste.

1 Bring a saucepan of lightly salted water to a boil. Add the lima beans or fava beans and cook for 15 minutes or until just tender.

2 Meanwhile, heat the olive oil in a frying pan, add the onion and garlic and sauté until the onion is translucent. Add the tomatoes and continue to cook, stirring, until the mixture thickens.

3 Add the chili slices and cook for 1–2 minutes. Season with salt to taste.

4 Drain the beans and return them to the pan. Pour in the tomato mixture and stir over the heat for a few minutes. If the sauce thickens too quickly, add a little water. Spoon into a serving dish, garnish with the cilantro and lemon slices and serve.

GREEN BEANS ᵂᴵᵀᴴ EGGS

THIS IS AN UNUSUAL WAY OF COOKING GREEN BEANS, BUT TASTES DELICIOUS. TRY THIS DISH FOR A LIGHT SUPPER OR AS AN ACCOMPANIMENT TO A SIMPLE ROAST.

SERVES SIX

INGREDIENTS
11 ounces string beans,
  trimmed and halved
2 tablespoons vegetable oil
1 onion, halved and
  thinly sliced
3 eggs
salt and ground black pepper
½ cup grated Monterey Jack or
  mild Cheddar cheese
strips of lemon zest, to garnish

VARIATION
Freshly grated Parmesan can be used instead of the Monterey Jack or Cheddar cheese for a sharper flavor.

1 Bring a saucepan of water to a boil, add the beans and cook for 5–6 minutes or until tender. Drain in a colander, rinse under cold water to preserve the bright color, then drain the beans once more.

2 Heat the oil in a frying pan and sauté the onion slices for 3–4 minutes, until soft and translucent. Break the eggs into a bowl and beat them with seasoning.

3 Add the egg mixture to the onion. Cook slowly over moderate heat, stirring constantly so that the egg is lightly scrambled. The egg should be moist throughout. Do not overcook.

4 Add the beans to the pan and cook for a few minutes until warmed through. Transfer the mixture to a heated serving dish, sprinkle on the grated cheese and lemon zest and serve.

ZUCCHINI WITH CHEESE AND GREEN CHILES

THIS IS A VERY TASTY WAY TO SERVE ZUCCHINI, OFTEN A RATHER BLAND VEGETABLE, AND THE DISH LOOKS GOOD TOO. SERVE IT AS A VEGETARIAN MAIN DISH OR AN UNUSUAL SIDE DISH.

SERVES SIX AS AN ACCOMPANIMENT

INGREDIENTS
    2 tablespoons vegetable oil
    ½ onion, thinly sliced
    2 garlic cloves, crushed
    1 teaspoon dried oregano
    2 tomatoes
    ⅓ cup drained pickled jalapeño
      chili slices, chopped
    1¼ pounds zucchini
    ½ cup cream cheese, cubed
    salt and ground black pepper
    fresh oregano sprigs,
      to garnish

1 Heat the oil in a frying pan. Add the onion, garlic and dried oregano. Sauté for 3–4 minutes, until the onion is soft and translucent.

2 Cut a cross in the bottom of each tomato. Place in a heatproof bowl and cover with boiling water. Leave in the water for 3 minutes, then lift out on a slotted spoon and plunge into a bowl of cold water. Drain. The skins will have begun to peel back from the crosses. Remove the skins and cut the tomatoes in half and squeeze out the seeds. Chop the flesh into strips.

3 Trim the zucchinis then cut them lengthwise into ½ inch wide strips. Slice the strips into matchsticks.

4 Stir the zucchini into the onion mixture and fry for 10 minutes, stirring occasionally, until just tender. Add the tomatoes and chopped jalapeños and cook for 2–3 more minutes.

5 Add the cream cheese. Reduce the heat to the lowest setting. As the cheese melts, stir gently to coat the zucchini. Season with salt, pile into a heated dish and serve, garnished with fresh oregano. If serving as a main dish, rustic bread makes a good accompaniment.

ZUCCHINI TORTE

THIS DISH LOOKS LIKE A SPANISH OMELET, WHICH IS TRADITIONALLY SERVED AT ROOM TEMPERATURE.
SERVE WARM OR PREPARE IT IN ADVANCE AND LET COOL, BUT DO NOT REFRIGERATE.

2 Slice the onion and add it to the oil remaining in the pan, with most of the jalapeño strips, reserving some for the garnish. Sauté until the onions have softened and are golden. Using a slotted spoon, add the onions and jalapeños to the zucchini.

3 Beat the eggs in a large bowl. Add the self-rising flour, cheese and cayenne. Mix well, then stir in the zucchini mixture, with salt to taste.

4 Grease a 9-inch round shallow ovenproof dish with the butter. Pour in the zucchini mixture and bake for 30 minutes, until risen, firm to the touch and golden. Let cool.

5 Serve the zucchini torte in thick wedges, garnished with the remaining jalapeño strips. A tomato salad, sprinkled with chives, makes a colorful accompaniment.

SERVES FOUR TO SIX

INGREDIENTS
  1¼ pounds zucchini
  ¼ cup vegetable oil
  1 small onion
  3 fresh jalapeño chiles, seeded
    and cut in strips
  3 large eggs
  ½ cup self-rising flour
  1 cup grated Monterey Jack or
    mild Cheddar cheese
  ½ teaspoon cayenne pepper
  1 tablespoon butter
  salt

1 Preheat the oven to 350°F. Trim the zucchini, then slice them thinly. Heat the oil in a large frying pan. Add the zucchini and cook for a few minutes, turning them over at least once, until they are soft and beginning to brown. Using a slotted spoon, transfer them to a bowl.

PUMPKIN <u>WITH</u> SPICES

ROASTED PUMPKIN HAS A WONDERFUL, RICH FLAVOR. EAT IT STRAIGHT FROM THE SKIN, EAT THE SKIN TOO, OR SCOOP OUT THE COOKED FLESH, ADD A SPOONFUL OF SALSA AND WRAP IT IN A WARM TORTILLA. IT ALSO MAKES FLAVORFUL SOUPS AND SAUCES.

SERVES SIX

INGREDIENTS

2¼ pounds pumpkin
¼ cup butter, melted
2 teaspoons hot chili sauce
½ teaspoon salt
½ teaspoon ground allspice
1 teaspoon ground cinnamon
chopped fresh herbs, to garnish
Classic Tomato Salsa and crème
  fraîche, to serve

COOK'S TIP
Green, gray or orange-skinned pumpkins all roast well. The orange-fleshed varieties are the most colorful when it comes to cooking.

1 Preheat the oven to 425°F. Cut the pumpkin into large pieces. Scoop out and discard the fiber and seeds, then put the pumpkin pieces in a roasting pan.

2 Mix the melted butter and chili sauce and drizzle the mixture evenly on the pumpkin pieces.

3 Put the salt in a small bowl and add the ground allspice and cinnamon. Sprinkle the mixture on the pumpkin.

4 Roast for 25 minutes or until the pumpkin flesh yields when pressed gently. Serve on a heated platter and pass the tomato salsa and crème fraîche separately.

POTATO CAKES

QUICK AND EASY TO MAKE, THESE POTATO CAKES ARE DELICIOUS. SERVE THEM WITH SALSA AS A LIGHT MEAL, OR AS AN ACCOMPANIMENT TO ROAST OR PAN-FRIED MEATS.

MAKES TEN

INGREDIENTS
   1 pound 6 ounces potatoes
   1 cup grated Cheddar cheese
   ½ teaspoon salt
   ⅓ cup drained pickled jalapeño
     chile slices, finely chopped
     (optional)
   1 egg, beaten
   small bunch of cilantro,
     finely chopped
   all-purpose flour, for shaping
   oil, for shallow frying
   fresh citrus salsa, to serve

1 Peel the potatoes and halve them if large. Add them to a saucepan of cold water. Bring to a boil and cook for about 30 minutes, until tender. Drain, return to the saucepan and mash. The mixture should not be smooth.

2 Scrape the potatoes into a bowl and stir in the grated cheese, with the salt and the chopped jalapeños, if using. Stir in the beaten egg and most of the chopped cilantro and mix into a dough.

3 When the dough is cool enough to handle, put it on a board. With floured hands, divide it into ten pieces of equal size. Shape each piece into a ball, then flatten to a cake.

4 Heat the oil in a large frying pan. Fry the potato cakes, in batches if necessary, for 2–3 minutes over medium heat. Turn them over and cook until both sides are golden. Pile on a platter, sprinkle with salt and the remaining chopped cilantro and serve with salsa.

FRIED PLANTAINS

THESE ARE THE PERFECT ACCOMPANIMENT TO HIGHLY SPICED AND SEASONED FOODS. THEIR SWEET FLAVOR PROVIDES AN INTERESTING CONTRAST.

SERVES FOUR

INGREDIENTS
   4 ripe plantains
   6 tablespoons butter
   2 teaspoons vegetable oil
   strips of scallion and red bell pepper,
      to garnish

COOK'S TIP
Ripe plantains have dark, almost black skins. Do not use under-ripe plantains, which are very hard and do not soften on cooking.

1 Peel the plantains, cut them in half lengthwises, then cut them in half again. Melt the butter with the oil in a large frying pan.

2 Add the plantains to the pan in a single layer and fry for 8–10 minutes, turning halfway through. Spoon into a heated dish and serve, garnished with strips of scallion and red pepper.

FRIED POTATOES

THESE MAKE THE PERFECT ACCOMPANIMENT FOR CHORIZO, AND ALSO GO VERY WELL WITH EGGS AND BACON.

SERVES FOUR

INGREDIENTS
   6 fresh jalapeño chiles
   4 tablespoons vegetable oil
   1 onion, finely chopped
   1 pound waxy potatoes, scrubbed
      and cut in ½-inch cubes
   few sprigs of fresh oregano, chopped
      plus extra sprigs, to garnish
   1 cup freshly grated Parmesan
      cheese (optional)

1 Dry-roast the jalapeños in a griddle pan, turning them frequently so that the skins blacken but do not burn. Place them in a strong plastic bag and tie the top to keep the steam in. Set aside for 20 minutes.

2 Remove the jalapeños from the bag, peel off the skins and remove any stems. Cut them in half, scrape out the seeds, then chop the flesh finely.

COOK'S TIP
If your frying pan does not have a lid, use aluminum foil instead.

3 Meanwhile, heat half the oil in a large heavy frying pan that has a lid. Add the onion and sauté, stirring occasionally, for 3–4 minutes, until translucent, then add the potato cubes.

4 Stir to coat the potato cubes in oil, then cover the pan and cook over medium heat for 20–25 minutes, until the potatoes are tender. Shake the pan occasionally to stop them from sticking to the bottom.

5 When the potatoes are tender, push them to the side of the frying pan, then add the remaining oil.

6 When the oil is hot, spread out the potatoes again and add the chopped jalapeños. Cook over high heat for 5–10 minutes, stirring carefully so that the potatoes turn golden brown all over but do not break up.

7 Add the chopped oregano, with the grated Parmesan, if using. Mix gently, spoon onto a heated serving dish and garnish with extra oregano sprigs. Serve as part of a cooked breakfast or brunch.

CORN <u>WITH</u> CREAM

IN MEXICO, THIS WOULD BE MADE WITH HEAVY CREAM, BUT THE SAUCE HAS A BETTER CONSISTENCY WHEN MADE WITH CREAM CHEESE.

SERVES SIX AS A SIDE DISH

INGREDIENTS

4 ears of corn
¼ cup butter
1 small onion, finely chopped
⅔ cup drained pickled jalapeño
   chile slices
⅔ cup cream cheese
⅓ cup freshly grated Parmesan
   cheese, plus shavings,
   to garnish
salt and ground black pepper

1 Strip off the husks from the corn and pull off the silks. Place the ears in a bowl of water and use a vegetable brush to remove any remaining silks. Stand each ear in turn on a board and slice off the kernels, cutting as close to the cob as possible.

2 Melt the butter in a saucepan, add the chopped onion and sauté for 4–5 minutes, stirring occasionally, until the onion has softened and is translucent.

3 Add the corn kernels and cook for 4–5 minutes, until they are just tender. Chop the jalapeños finely and stir them into the corn mixture.

4 Stir in the cream cheese and the grated Parmesan. Cook over low heat until both cheeses have melted and the corn kernels are coated in the mixture. Season to taste, transfer into a heated dish and serve, topped with shredded Parmesan.

VARIATION

A simplified version of this dish is sold at street stalls in Mexico. Whole cooked ears of corn are dipped in cream, then sprinkled with crumbled fresh cheese. Next time you grill, try this as an appetizer. Alternatively, put whole ears of corn in a shallow baking dish and bake them in an oven preheated to 400°F for 30 minutes, until tender and golden. Pour in ½ cup sour cream or crème fraîche, then sprinkle the corn with 2 tablespoons freshly grated Parmesan cheese and serve. The corn can also be brushed with butter and broiled, but it must have plenty of room below the heat, or it will burn.

FRIJOLES DE OLLA

Travelers often say that "beans in a pot," as it is translated, taste different in Mexico from those cooked anywhere else. The secret is, quite literally, in the pot. Traditionally, clay pots are used, which give the beans a wonderful, slightly earthy flavor. This dish would be served as just one of the courses in a formal Mexican meal.

3 While the beans are cooking, prepare the toppings. Spear the chiles on a long-handled metal skewer and roast them over the flame of a gas burner until the skins blister and darken. Do not let the flesh burn. Alternatively, dry-fry them in a griddle until the skins are scorched. Put the roasted chiles in a strong plastic bag and tie the top immediately to keep the steam in. Set aside for 20 minutes.

4 Remove the chiles from the bag and peel off the skins. Cut off the stems, then slit the chiles and scrape out the seeds. Cut the flesh into thin strips and put it in a bowl. Spoon all the other toppings into separate bowls.

5 Ladle about 1 cup of the beans and liquid into a food processor or blender. Process into a smooth purée. If you prefer, simply mash the beans with a potato masher.

6 Return the bean purée to the pan, and stir it in. Chop the cilantro, reserving some leaves to garnish, season with salt and mix well. Ladle the beans into warmed individual bowls and take them to the table with the toppings.

7 Serve the beans with the toppings and add cilantro to garnish. Traditionally, each guest spoons a little of the chiles, tomatoes and scallions over the beans, then adds a spoonful of sour cream. The finishing touch is a little feta cheese, crumbled on each portion.

SERVES FOUR

INGREDIENTS
  1¼ cups dried pinto beans, soaked
    overnight in water to cover
  7½ cups water
  2 onions
  10 garlic cloves, peeled and
    left whole
  small bunch of cilantro
  salt
For the toppings
  2 fresh red fresno chillies
  1 tomato, peeled and chopped
  2 scallions, finely chopped
  4 tablespoons sour cream
  2 ounces feta cheese

COOK'S TIP
In Mexico, the local fresh cheese—*queso fresco*—would be used as the topping, but feta makes an acceptable substitute.

1 Drain the beans, rinse them under cold water and drain again. Put the water in a large saucepan, bring to a boil and add the beans.

2 Cut the onions in half and add them to the pan, with the whole garlic cloves. Bring to a boil again, then lower the heat and simmer for 1½ hours, until the beans are tender and there is only a little liquid remaining.

REFRIED BEANS

THESE ARE NOT ACTUALLY FRIED TWICE, BUT THEY ARE COOKED TWICE, FIRST AS FRIJOLES DE OLLA AND THEN BY FRYING IN LARD. IF THE ONLY REFRIED BEANS YOU'VE TRIED HAVE BEEN THE CANNED ONES, YOU MAY HAVE FOUND THEM RATHER BLAND. THESE, HOWEVER, ARE SUPERB.

SERVES FOUR

INGREDIENTS
  2 tablespoons lard
  2 onions, finely chopped
  1 teaspoon ground cumin
  1 teaspoon ground coriander
  1 batch *Frijoles de Olla*, without
    the toppings
  3 garlic cloves, crushed
  small bunch of cilantro or
    4–5 dried avocado leaves
  2 ounces feta cheese
  salt

1 Melt the lard in a large frying pan. Add the onions, cumin and ground coriander. Cook gently over low heat for about 30 minutes or until the onions caramelize and become soft.

2 Add a ladleful of the soft, cooked beans. Fry them for only a few minutes simply to heat. Mash the beans into the onions as they cook, using a fork or a potato masher. Continue until all the beans have been added, a little at a time, then stir in the crushed garlic.

3 Lower the heat and cook the beans to form a thick paste. Season with salt and spoon into a warmed serving dish. Chop the cilantro or crumble the avocado leaves, and sprinkle most of them on the beans. Crumble the feta cheese on top, then garnish with the reserved sprigs or leaves.

FRIJOLES CHARROS

THESE "COWBOY BEANS" TASTE LIKE BOSTON BAKED BEANS, BUT WITH MORE PUNCH. THE FLAVOR IMPROVES OVER TIME, SO MAKE IT THE DAY BEFORE YOU INTEND TO SERVE IT.

SERVES SIX

INGREDIENTS
  2 x 14-ounce cans pinto beans
  ½ cup Mexican beer
  ⅔ cups drained pickled jalapeño
    chile slices
  2 tomatoes, peeled and chopped
  1 teaspoon ground cinnamon
  6 ounces bacon fat
  1 onion, chopped
  2 garlic cloves, crushed
  6 ounces lean bacon, diced
  3 tablespoons dark brown sugar
  wheat flour tortillas, to serve

2 Lower the heat slightly and stir in the chopped jalapeños chile, then add the tomatoes and cinnamon. Continue to cook, stirring occasionally, for about 10 minutes.

3 Meanwhile, heat the bacon in a frying pan until the fat runs. The quantity suggested should yield about 3 tablespoons bacon fat.

1 Put the drained pinto beans in a saucepan. Stir in the beer and cook over high heat for 5 minutes, until some of the beer has been absorbed.

4 Discard the bacon, then add the onion and garlic to the pan and fry for about 5 minutes, until browned. Using a slotted spoon, lift out the garlic and onions and stir them into the beans.

5 Add the diced bacon to the fat remaining in the frying pan and fry until crisp. Add the bacon and any remaining fat to the beans and mix well.

6 Stir in the sugar. Cook the bean and bacon mixture over low heat, stirring constantly, until the sugar is dissolved. Serve immediately or spoon into a bowl, let cool, cover, then chill for reheating the next day. Serve with warmed flour tortillas.

GREEN RICE

THIS RICE IS RARELY FEATURED ON MENUS IN MEXICAN RESTAURANTS, BUT IS OFTEN MADE IN THE HOME. EXTRA CHILES AND GREEN BELL PEPPER CAN BE DICED AND ADDED AT THE END, IF DESIRED.

SERVES FOUR

INGREDIENTS

   2 fresh green chiles, preferably
     poblanos
   1 small green bell pepper
   1 cup long-grain white rice
   1 garlic clove, roughly chopped
   large bunch of cilantro
   small bunch of fresh flat-leaf parsley
   2 cups chicken stock
   2 tablespoons vegetable oil
   1 small onion, finely chopped
   salt

1 Dry roast the chiles and green pepper in a griddle pan, turning them frequently so that the skins blacken but the flesh does not burn. Place them in a strong plastic bag, tie the top securely and set aside for 20 minutes.

2 Put the rice in a heatproof bowl, pour in boiling water to cover and let stand for 20 minutes.

3 Drain the rice, rinse well under cold water and drain again. Remove the chiles and peppers from the bag and peel off the skins. Remove any stems, then slit the vegetables and scrape out the seeds with a sharp knife.

4 Put the roasted vegetables in a food processor, with the garlic. Strip off the leaves from the cilantro and parsley stalks, reserve some for the garnish and add the rest to the processor. Pour in half the chicken stock and process until smooth. Add the rest of the stock and process the purée again.

5 Heat the oil in a saucepan, add the onion and rice and fry for 5 minutes over medium heat until the rice is golden and the onion translucent. Stir in the purée. Lower the heat, cover and cook for 25–30 minutes or until all the liquid is absorbed and the rice is just tender. Add salt and garnish with the reserved herbs. Served with lime wedges, this rice goes extremely well with fish.

YELLOW RICE

THIS RICE DISH OWES ITS STRIKING COLOR AND DISTINCTIVE FLAVOR TO GROUND ACHIOTE SEED, WHICH IS DERIVED FROM ANNATTO.

SERVES SIX

INGREDIENTS

   1 cup long-grain white rice
   2 tablespoons vegetable oil
   1 teaspoon ground achiote seed
     (annatto powder)
   1 small onion, finely chopped
   2 garlic cloves, crushed
   2 cups chicken stock
   ⅓ cup drained pickled jalapeño chile
     slices, chopped
   salt
   cilantro leaves, to garnish

COOK'S TIP

Achiote, the seed of the annatto tree, is used as a food coloring and flavoring throughout Latin America. You can buy it at specialty spice shops and ethnic food stores. It is sometimes called annatto powder.

1 Put the rice in a heatproof bowl, pour in boiling water to cover and let stand for 20 minutes. Drain, rinse under cold water and drain again.

2 Heat the oil in a saucepan, add the ground achiote seed (annatto powder) and cook for 2–3 minutes. Add the onion and garlic and cook for another 3–4 minutes or until the onion is translucent. Stir in the rice and cook for 5 minutes.

3 Pour in the stock, mix well and bring to a boil. Lower the heat, cover the pan with a tight-fitting lid and simmer for 25–30 minutes, until all the liquid has been absorbed.

4 Add the chopped jalapeños to the pan and stir to distribute them evenly. Add salt to taste, then spoon into a heated serving dish and garnish with the cilantro leaves. Serve immediately.

CHAYOTES WITH CORN AND CHILES

*SHAPED LIKE PEARS OR AVOCADOS, CHAYOTES ARE MEMBERS OF THE SQUASH FAMILY AND HAVE A
BLAND TASTE. HOWEVER, THEY GO EXTREMELY WELL WITH OTHER INGREDIENTS, SUCH AS THE CORN
AND ROASTED JALAPEÑOS IN THIS MEDLEY.*

SERVES SIX

INGREDIENTS
   4 fresh jalapeño chiles
   3 *chayotes*
   oil, for frying
   1 red onion, finely chopped
   3 garlic cloves, crushed
   1⅓ cups corn kernels, thawed
     if frozen
   ⅔ cup cream cheese
   1 teaspoon salt (optional)
   ⅓ cup freshly grated
     Parmesan cheese

1 Dry-roast the fresh jalapeño chiles in
a griddle, turning them frequently so
that the skins blacken but do not burn.
Place them in a plastic bag, tie the
top securely, and set them aside for
20 minutes.

2 Meanwhile, peel the *chayotes*, cut
them in half and remove the seed
from each of them. Cut the flesh into
½-inch cubes.

COOK'S TIP
Chayotes go by several names, including
christophene and *choko*. Store them in a
plastic bag in the refrigerator and they
will keep for up to 1 month.

3 Heat the oil in a frying pan. Add the
onion, garlic, *chayote* cubes and corn.
Fry over medium heat for 10 minutes,
stirring occasionally.

4 Remove the jalapeños from the bag,
peel off the skins and remove any
stems. Cut them in half, scrape out the
seeds, then cut the flesh into strips.

5 Add the chiles and cream cheese to
the pan, stirring gently, until the cheese
melts. Place in a serving dish.

6 Stir in salt, if needed, then spoon into
a warmed dish. Sprinkle with Parmesan
cheese and serve. This makes a good
accompaniment for cold roast meats.

SPINACH SALAD

YOUNG SPINACH LEAVES MAKE A WELCOME CHANGE FROM LETTUCE AND ARE EXCELLENT IN SALADS. THE ROASTED GARLIC IS AN INSPIRED ADDITION TO THE DRESSING.

SERVES SIX

INGREDIENTS
    1¼ pounds baby spinach leaves
    ⅓ cup sesame seeds
    ¼ cup butter
    2 tablespoons olive oil
    6 shallots, sliced
    8 fresh serrano chiles, seeded
        and cut into strips
    4 tomatoes, sliced
For the dressing
    6 roasted garlic cloves
    ½ cup white wine vinegar
    ½ teaspoon ground white pepper
    1 bay leaf
    ½ teaspoon ground allspice
    2 tablespoons chopped fresh thyme,
        plus extra sprigs, to garnish

COOK'S TIP
To roast individual garlic cloves simply
place in a roasting tray in a medium
oven for about 15 minutes until soft.

1 Make the dressing. Remove the skins
from the garlic when cool, then chop
and combine with the vinegar, pepper,
bay leaf, allspice and chopped thyme in
a jar with a screw-top lid. Close the lid
tightly, shake well, then put the dressing
in the refrigerator until needed.

2 Wash the spinach leaves and dry
them in a salad spinner or clean dish
towel. Put them in a plastic bag in
the refrigerator.

3 Toast the sesame seeds in a dry frying
pan, shaking frequently over medium
heat until golden. Set aside.

4 Heat the butter and oil in a frying
pan. Sauté the shallots for 4–5 minutes,
until softened, then stir in the chile
strips and fry for 2–3 more minutes.

5 In a large bowl, layer the spinach with
the shallot and chili mixture, and the
tomato slices. Pour on the dressing.
Sprinkle with sesame seeds and serve,
garnished with thyme sprigs.

NOPALITOS SALAD

NOPALITOS—*STRIPS OF PICKLED CACTUS PADDLES—ARE SOLD IN CANS OR JARS, AND ARE VERY USEFUL FOR MAKING QUICK AND EASY SALADS LIKE THIS ONE.*

SERVES FOUR

INGREDIENTS
 scant 2 cups drained
  canned *nopalitos*
 1 red pepper
 2 tablespoons olive oil
 2 garlic cloves, sliced
 ½ red onion, thinly sliced
 ½ cup cider vinegar
 small bunch of cilantro, chopped
 salt

1 Preheat the broiler. Put the *nopalitos* in a bowl. Pour in water to cover and set aside for 30 minutes. Drain, replace with fresh water and let soak for another 30 minutes.

2 Place the halves of the red pepper cut side down in a broiler. Broil the peppers until the skins blister and char, then put the pepper halves in a strong plastic bag, tie the top securely to keep the steam in, and set aside for 20 minutes.

3 Heat the oil in a small frying pan and fry the garlic over low heat until the slices start to turn golden. Using a slotted spoon, transfer them to a salad bowl. Pour the garlic-flavored oil into a pitcher and set it aside to cool.

4 Add the red onion slices to the salad bowl, then pour on the vinegar. Remove the red pepper from the bag, peel off the skins, then cut the flesh into thin strips. Add to the salad bowl.

5 Drain the *nopalitos* thoroughly and add them to the salad, with the cool garlic-flavored oil and a little salt, to taste. Toss lightly, then chill until needed. Sprinkle on the chopped cilantro just before serving. This is delicious served with crusty bread.

JICAMA, CHILE <u>AND</u> LIME SALAD

A VERY TASTY, CRISP VEGETABLE, THE JICAMA IS SOMETIMES CALLED THE MEXICAN POTATO. UNLIKE POTATO, HOWEVER, IT CAN BE EATEN RAW AS WELL AS COOKED. THIS MAKES A GOOD SALAD OR AN APPETIZER TO SERVE WITH DRINKS.

<u>SERVES FOUR</u>

INGREDIENTS
  1 *jicama*
  ½ teaspoon salt
  2 fresh serrano chiles
  2 limes

1 Peel the *jicama* with a potato peeler or knife, then cut it into ¾-inch cubes. Put these in a large bowl, add the salt and toss well.

2 Cut the chiles in half, scrape out the seeds with a sharp knife, then cut the flesh into fine strips. Grate one of the limes thinly, removing only the colored part of the skin, then cut the lime in half and squeeze the juice.

3 Add the chiles, lime zest and juice to the *jicama* and mix thoroughly to ensure that all the *jicama* cubes are coated. Cut the other lime into wedges.

4 Cover and chill for at least 1 hour before serving with lime wedges. If the salad is to be served as an appetizer with drinks, transfer the *jicama* cubes to little bowls and pass them with toothpicks for spearing.

COOK'S TIP
Look for *jicama* at Asian supermarkets, as it is widely used in Chinese cooking. It goes by several names, and you may find it labelled as either yam bean or Chinese turnip.

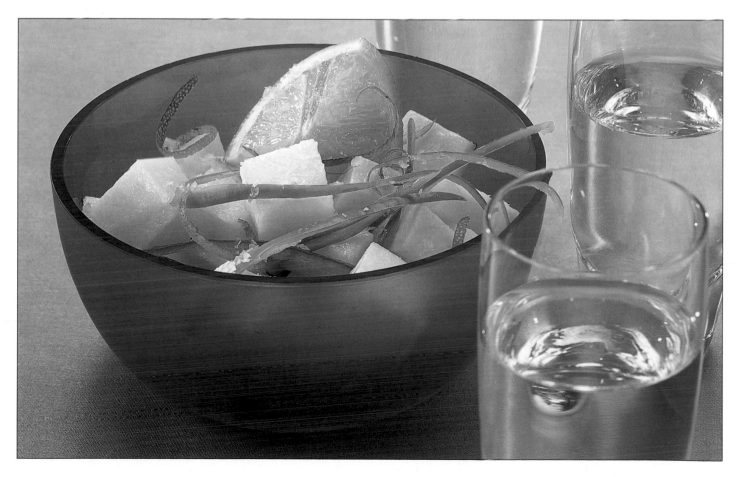

CHAYOTE SALAD

*COOL AND REFRESHING, THIS SALAD IS IDEAL ON ITS OWN OR WITH FISH OR CHICKEN DISHES.
THE SOFT FLESH OF THE CHAYOTES ABSORBS THE FLAVOR OF THE DRESSING BEAUTIFULLY.*

SERVES FOUR

INGREDIENTS
    2 *chayotes*
    2 firm tomatoes
    1 small onion, finely chopped
    finely sliced strips of fresh red and
        green chile, to garnish
For the dressing
    ½ teaspoon Dijon mustard
    ½ teaspoon ground anise
    6 tablespoons white wine vinegar
    ¼ cup olive oil
    salt and ground black pepper

1 Bring a pan of water to a boil. Peel
the *chayotes*, cut them in half and
remove the seeds. Add them to a
boiling water. Lower the heat and simmer
for 20 minutes or until the *chayotes* are
tender. Drain and set them aside to cool.

2 Meanwhile, peel the tomatoes. Cut a
cross in the bottom of each tomato.
Place them in a heatproof bowl and
pour in boiling water to cover. After
3 minutes, lift the tomatoes out on a
slotted spoon and plunge them into
a bowl of cold water. Drain. The skins
will have begun to peel back from the
crosses. Remove the skins completely
and cut the tomatoes into wedges.

3 Make the dressing by combining
all the ingredients in a screw top jar.
Close the lid tightly and shake the
jar vigorously.

4 Cut the *chayotes* into wedges and
place in a bowl with the tomato and
onion. Pour over the dressing and serve
garnished with strips of fresh red and
green chile.

CAESAR SALAD

*ALTHOUGH THIS IS WIDELY REGARDED AS AN AMERICAN CLASSIC, CAESAR SALAD ACTUALLY
ORIGINATED IN MEXICO, AND TAKES ITS NAME FROM THE CHEF, CAESAR CARDINI, WHO INVENTED IT
IN HIS RESTAURANT IN TIJUANA IN 1924. PREGNANT WOMEN AND YOUNG CHILDREN ARE ADVISED TO
AVOID EATING RAW EGGS.*

SERVES FOUR

INGREDIENTS

2 large garlic cloves, peeled and
  left whole
¼ cup extra virgin olive oil
4 slices of bread, crusts
  removed, cubed
1 Romaine lettuce, separated into
  leaves
6 drained canned anchovy fillets
shavings of Parmesan cheese,
  to garnish
For the dressing
1 egg
2 teaspoons Dijon mustard
generous dash of Worcestershire
  sauce
2 tablespoons lemon juice
2 tablespoons extra virgin olive oil
salt and ground black pepper

1 Cut one garlic clove in half and rub it
around the inside of a salad bowl. Put
the remaining garlic in a large frying
pan. Add the oil and heat gently for
5 minutes, then discard the garlic.
Add the bread cubes to the hot oil, in
batches if necessary, and fry them until
they are crisp on all sides. Drain on
paper towels.

2 Line the salad bowl with the Romaine
leaves. Carefully cut the anchovy
fillets in half lengthwise and distribute
them among the lettuce leaves.
Toss the leaves to spread the flavor of
the anchovies.

3 Crack the egg into a food processor
or blender, with the Dijon mustard,
Worcestershire sauce and lemon juice.
Season and process to blend briefly,
then add the oil with the motor running.

4 Pour the dressing onto the salad in
the bowl and toss lightly. Add the garlic
croûtons. Transfer to individual bowls
or carry to the table in the salad bowl.
Sprinkle on Parmesan shavings and serve.

DESSERTS

Mexicans love sweet things. Ever since Hernàn Cortèz introduced sugar cane
to the country, desserts have been very much on the menu and the array of
cakes and pastries in a Mexican pastelerìa would rival any display
at a European cake shop.

Special cakes and cookies are made for feast days and
festivals, like the Day of the Dead or Twelfth Night.
Kings' Day Bread is traditionally served to celebrate
Epiphany, on January 6th, while Mexican Wedding Cookies,
with their generous coating of confectioners' sugar, are a
familiar sight at marriage celebrations.

The most famous Mexican dessert is Flan, a caramel custard which is
also very popular in Spain. Rice puddings of various types are often served,
and rich puddings made from pumpkin or plantains are popular too,
especially with children.

However, with the wonderful produce at their disposal, Mexicans
often opt to end a meal with a simple platter of colorful fresh
fruit, served with salt, chili powder and fresh lime juice,
as they did in the days before Spanish and French cooks
introduced them to puddings and pastries.

CHURROS

THESE DELECTABLE TREATS ARE TRADITIONALLY MADE BY FORCING DOUGH THROUGH A CHURRERA, WHICH IS A UTENSIL FITTED WITH A WOODEN PLUNGER. AN ICING BAG FITTED WITH A LARGE STAR NOZZLE MAKES A GOOD SUBSTITUTE. CHURROS ARE USUALLY SERVED WITH CAFE DE OLLA OR MEXICAN HOT CHOCOLATE AND ARE PERFECT FOR DIPPING.

MAKES ABOUT TWENTY-FOUR

INGREDIENTS
   3 cups all-purpose flour
   1 teaspoon baking powder
   2½ cups water
   ½ teaspoon salt
   3 tablespoons dark brown sugar
   2 egg yolks
   oil, for deep-frying
   2 limes, cut in wedges
   sugar, for dusting

COOK'S TIP
These are best eaten on the day they are made, preferably while still warm.

1 Sift the flour and baking powder into a bowl and set aside. Bring the measured water to a boil in a saucepan, add the salt and brown sugar, stirring constantly, until both have dissolved. Remove from heat, add all the flour and baking powder and beat the mixture continuously until smooth.

2 Beat in the egg yolks, one at a time, until the mixture is smooth and glossy. Set the batter aside to cool. Have ready a piping bag fitted with a large star nozzle, which will give the *churros* their traditional shape.

3 Pour oil into a deep-fryer or suitable saucepan to a depth of about 2 inches. Heat to 375ºF, or until a cube of dried bread, added to the oil, floats and turns golden after 1 minute.

4 Spoon the batter into the piping bag. Pipe five or six 4-inch lengths of the mixture into the hot oil, using a knife to slice off each length as it emerges from the nozzle. Fry for 3–4 minutes or until they are golden brown. Drain the *churros* on paper towels while cooking successive batches, then arrange on a plate with the lime wedges, dust them with sugar and serve warm.

SOPAIPILLAS

THESE GOLDEN PILLOWS OF PUFF PASTRY CAN BE SERVED AS A DESSERT, WITH HONEY, OR PLAIN WITH SOUPS. THEY ARE ALSO IDEAL FOR BUFFETS.

MAKES ABOUT THIRTY

INGREDIENTS
   2 cups all-purpose flour
   1 teaspoon baking powder
   1 teaspoon salt
   2 tablespoons white cooking fat
     or margarine
   ¾ cup warm water
   oil, for deep-frying
   clear honey, for drizzling
   ground cinnamon for sprinkling
   crème fraîche or thick heavy cream,
     to serve

VARIATION
Instead of drizzling honey on the *sopaipillas*, use a mixture of ¼ cup sugar and 2 teaspoons ground cinnamon.

1 Sift the flour, baking powder and salt into a bowl. Rub in the cooking fat or margarine until the mixture resembles fine bread crumbs. Gradually add enough of the water to form a dough. Wrap the dough in plastic wrap and let sit 1 hour.

2 Working with half the dough at a time, roll it out into a square, keeping it as even and as thin as possible. Cut into 3-inch squares. When both pieces of the dough have been rolled and cut, set the squares aside.

3 Heat the oil for deep-frying to 375ºF, or until a cube of dried bread, added to the oil, floats and turns golden after 1 minute. Add a few pastry squares, using tongs to push them down into the oil. Cook in batches until golden on both sides, turning them once, and drain on paper towels.

4 When all the *sopaipillas* have been cooked, arrange on a large serving plate, drizzle with honey and sprinkle with ground cinnamon Serve warm, with crème fraîche or thick heavy cream.

CARAMEL CUSTARD

THIS EXTREMELY POPULAR DESSERT IS A COUSIN OF THE FRENCH CRÈME CARAMEL,
AND HAS ITS ORIGINS IN SPAIN, WHERE THE SAME NAME IS USED.

SERVES SIX

INGREDIENTS
    4 cups milk
    1 vanilla bean, split
    6 eggs
    ½ cup sugar
    1 teaspoon vanilla extract
For the caramel
    ¾ cup sugar

1 Put six ramekins or dariole molds in a pan full of hot water. Make the caramel. Spread out the sugar evenly on the bottom of a large saucepan. Heat it slowly, without stirring, tilting the pan backward and forward until the sugar melts.

2 Lift the heated ramekins or molds out of the water and dry them quickly. Watch the melted sugar closely, and when it turns a rich golden color, pour the mixture into the dishes and simply turn until they are coated, or brush the caramel on the insides of the dishes. Set them aside.

3 Preheat the oven to 350°F. Pour the milk into a saucepan, add the vanilla bean and bring the milk to just below boiling point. Pour it into a bowl and set it aside to cool.

4 Put the eggs in a bowl, beat them lightly, then gradually beat in the sugar. Remove the vanilla from the milk, then gradually mix the milk into the egg.

5 Strain the egg mixture into the caramel-lined ramekins or molds and stand them in a roasting pan. Pour boiling water into the roasting pan until it comes halfway up the sides of the dishes, then carefully put the pan in the oven.

6 Bake the caramel custards for about 40 minutes. The custards are done when a slender knife blade, inserted in one of them, comes out clean.

7 Lift the dishes out of the water, let them cool, then chill them for several hours in the refrigerator.

8 To serve, run a round-bladed knife around the edge of each custard, place a dessert plate upside down on top of the dish and turn the dish and plate over together. Lift off the dish. Some of the caramel will settle in a puddle around the custard, so it is important not to choose dessert dishes that are too shallow. Try serving these custards with fresh fruit.

VARIATIONS
Flavor the custard with cinnamon, cocoa or rum instead of vanilla. In the Tabasco region, where chestnuts grow, chestnut purée is sometimes added.

RICE PUDDING

RICE IS A POPULAR DESSERT INGREDIENT IN MEXICO. ONE WAY OF SERVING IT IS TO COOK IT IN MILK UNTIL SOFT AND THICK, THEN SHAPE IT INTO BALLS. THESE ARE COATED IN EGG AND BREAD CRUMBS, FRIED IN OIL, THEN ROLLED IN CINNAMON SUGAR TO MAKE SWEET TREATS. THIS IS A LIGHT, EASY-TO-MAKE RICE PUDDING, WHICH IS FULL OF FLAVOR.

SERVES FOUR

INGREDIENTS

½ cup raisins
5 tablespoons dry sherry
½ cup short- grain (pudding) rice
3 or 4 strips of pared lemon peel
1 cup water
2 cups milk
1 cup sugar
pinch of salt
1 cinnamon stick, about 3-inches in
   length, plus 3 more, to decorate
2 egg yolks
1 tablespoon butter, diced
toasted sliced almonds, to decorate
chilled orange segments, to serve

COOK'S TIP
Cut strips of lemon peel and add them
to the rice.

1 Put the raisins and sherry in a small saucepan. Heat gently until warm, then set the pan aside, which will let the raisins swell.

2 Mix the rice, lemon peel and water in a heavy saucepan and bring to a boil. Lower the heat, cover the pan and simmer for about 20 minutes. Remove the lemon peel.

3 Add the milk and the cinnamon stick to the pan, then stir until the rice has absorbed the milk. Stir in the sugar and salt. Add the egg yolks and butter. Stir constantly until the butter has melted.

4 Drain the raisins and stir into the rice mixture. Cook for 2–3 minutes, top with the toasted almonds and serve with the orange segments. Place a cinnamon stick in each bowl.

ALMOND PUDDING <u>WITH</u> CUSTARD

THIS DISH MAY WELL DATE FROM THE TIME OF THE FRENCH OCCUPATION OF MEXICO, FOR IT BEARS A CLOSE RESEMBLANCE TO ÎLE FLOTTANTE—FLOATING ISLANDS—ALTHOUGH IN THAT RECIPE THE MERINGUES ARE ACTUALLY POACHED IN THE CUSTARD. DELICIOUS AND VERY LIGHT, IT MAKES THE PERFECT DESSERT TO FOLLOW A SUBSTANTIAL MAIN COURSE.

SERVES SIX

INGREDIENTS

1 cup water
½ ounce envelope powdered gelatin
1¼ cups sugar
½ teaspoon almond essence
6 eggs, separated
pinch of salt
2 cups light cream
½ teaspoon vanilla extract
ground cinnamon, for dusting

1 Pour the water into a saucepan and sprinkle the gelatin on the surface. When it has softened, add 1 cup of the sugar and place the pan over low heat. Stir until both the gelatin and the sugar have dissolved, then stir in the almond extract. Pour the mixture into a bowl and chill in the refrigerator until it starts to thicken.

2 Whisk the egg whites until they are stiff. Whisk the gelatin mixture until is frothy, then fold in the egg whites carefully. Chill until firm.

3 Meanwhile, make the custard. Put the egg yolks, remaining sugar and salt in a heavy saucepan. Stir in the cream and vanilla. Cook over very low heat, stirring constantly, until the custard thickens to a soft dropping consistency, enough to coat the back of a wooden spoon.

4 Pour the custard into dessert bowls. Cover each with a piece of dampened waxed paper until ready to serve to prevent the formation of a skin.

5 Serve each custard topped with a few spoonfuls of the meringue mixture and a sprinkle of ground cinnamon.

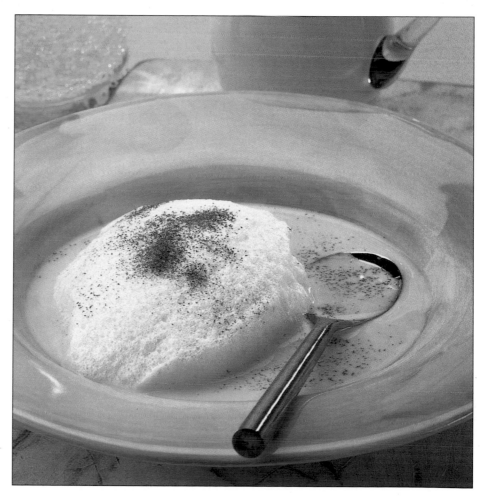

PUMPKIN IN BROWN SUGAR

RICH, STICKY AND SWEET, THIS DESSERT IS VERY ATTRACTIVE AND IS NOT AT ALL DIFFICULT TO PREPARE.

SERVES SIX

INGREDIENTS

    1 small pumpkin, about 1¾ pounds
    1½ cups dark brown sugar
    ½ cup water
    1 teaspoon ground cloves
    12 cinnamon sticks, each about
     4 inches in length
    fresh mint sprigs, to decorate
    thick yogurt or crème fraîche,
     to serve

1 Halve the pumpkin, remove the seeds and fibers and cut into wedges. Arrange in a single layer in a shallow, flameproof casserole or heavy pan. Fill the hollows with the sugar.

2 Pour the water carefully into the pan, taking care not to wash all the sugar to the bottom. Make sure that some of the water trickles down to the bottom to prevent the pumpkin from burning. Sprinkle on the ground cloves and add two of the cinnamon sticks.

3 Cover the pan tightly and cook over low heat for about 30 minutes or until the pumpkin is tender and the sugar and water have formed a syrup. Check the casserole or pan occasionally to make sure that the pumpkin does not dry out or stick to the bottom.

4 Transfer the pumpkin to a platter and pour on the hot syrup. Decorate each portion with mint and cinnamon sticks and serve with thick yogurt or crème fraîche.

COOK'S TIP
Pumpkin cooked in this way can be used to fill sweet empanadas, so cook all of it and use the rest as filling.

COCONUT CUSTARD

*LIGHT AND CREAMY, THIS IS THE PERFECT DESSERT FOR SERVING AFTER A SPICY MAIN COURSE.
CHILDREN LIKE IT, AND IT IS IDEAL FOR ENTERTAINING, AS IT CAN BE MADE AHEAD OF TIME AND
KEPT IN THE REFRIGERATOR OVERNIGHT.*

2 Add the coconut and cook over low heat, stirring occasionally, for 5 minutes. Stir in the milk until the mixture has thickened slightly. Remove the cinnamon stick. Remove from heat.

3 Whisk the eggs until light and fluffy. Gradually incorporate the coconut mixture, then scrape into a clean pan.

SERVES SIX

INGREDIENTS
    1 cup sugar
    1 cup water
    1 cinnamon stick, about 3 inches
      in length
    2 cups dry, shredded coconut
    3 cups milk
    4 eggs
    ¾ cup whipping cream
    ½ cup chopped almonds, toasted
    strips of orange zest, to decorate

VARIATION
Use about 1 cup fresh coconut, and grate it in a food processor before adding it to the cinnamon syrup.

1 To make the cinnamon syrup, place the sugar and water in a very large saucepan, add the cinnamon stick and bring to a boil. Lower the heat and simmer, uncovered, for 5 minutes.

4 Cook over low heat, stirring constantly, until the mixture becomes a thick custard. Cool, then chill. Just before serving, whip the cream. Transfer to individual bowls, top with the cream, chopped almonds and orange rind and serve. Toasted sliced almonds also go well with this.

BUÑUELOS

THESE LOVELY LITTLE PUFFS LOOK LIKE MINIATURE DOUGHNUTS AND TASTE SO GOOD IT IS HARD NOT TO OVER-INDULGE. MAKE THEM FOR BRUNCH, OR SIMPLY SERVE THEM WITH A CUP OF CAFE CON LECHE OR CAFE DE OLLA.

MAKES TWELVE

INGREDIENTS
2 cups all-purpose flour
pinch of salt
1 teaspoon baking powder
½ teaspoon ground anise
½ cup sugar
1 large egg
½ cup milk
¼ cup butter
oil, for deep-frying
2 teaspoons ground cinnamon
cinnamon sticks, to decorate

1 Sift the flour, salt, baking powder and ground anise into a mixing bowl. Add 2 tablespoons of the sugar.

2 Place the egg and milk in a small pitcher and whisk well with a fork. Melt the butter in a small pan.

COOK'S TIP
Buñuelos are sometimes served with syrup for dunking, although they are perfectly delicious without. To make the syrup, mix ¾ cup dark brown sugar and scant 2 cups water in a small saucepan. Add a cinnamon stick and heat, stirring until the sugar has dissolved. Bring to a boil, then lower the heat and simmer for 15 minutes without stirring. Cool slightly before serving with the *buñuelos*.

3 Pour the egg mixture and milk gradually into the flour, stirring constantly, until well blended, then add the melted butter. Mix first with a wooden spoon and then with your hands to make a soft dough.

4 Lightly flour a work surface, put the dough on it and knead for about 10 minutes, until smooth.

5 Divide the dough into 12 pieces and roll into balls. Slightly flatten each ball with your hand and then make a hole in the center with the floured handle of a wooden spoon.

6 Heat the oil for deep-frying to a temperature of 375°F, or until a cube of dried bread, added to the oil, floats and then turns a golden color in 30–60 seconds. Fry the *buñuelos* in small batches until they are puffy and golden brown, turning them once or twice during cooking. As soon as they are golden, lift them out of the oil using a slotted spoon and lie them on a double layer of paper towels to drain.

7 Mix the remaining sugar with the ground cinnamon in a small bowl. Add the *buñuelos*, one at a time, while they are still warm, toss them in the mixture until they are lightly coated and either serve immediately or let cool. Decorate with cinnamon sticks.

CAPIROTADA

MEXICAN COOKS BELIEVE IN MAKING GOOD USE OF EVERYTHING AVAILABLE TO THEM. THIS PUDDING WAS INVENTED AS A WAY OF USING UP FOOD BEFORE THE LENTEN FAST, BUT IS NOW EATEN AT OTHER TIMES TOO.

SERVES SIX

INGREDIENTS
1 small loaf French bread, a few
  days old
⅓–½ cup butter, softened, plus extra
  for greasing
scant 1 cup dark brown sugar
1 cinnamon stick, about
  6 inches long
1⅔ cups water
3 tablespoons dry sherry
¾ cup sliced almonds, plus extra,
  to decorate
½ cup raisins
1 cup grated Monterey Jack or
  mild Cheddar cheese
light cream, for pouring

1 Slice the bread into about 30 rounds, each ½ inch thick. Lightly butter on both sides. Cook in batches in a warm frying pan until browned, turning over once. Set the slices aside.

2 Place the sugar, cinnamon stick and water in a saucepan. Heat gently, stirring all the time, until the sugar has dissolved. Bring to a boil, then lower the heat and simmer for 15 minutes without stirring. Remove the cinnamon stick, then stir in the sherry.

COOK'S TIP
This recipe works well with older bread that is quite dry. If you only have fresh bread, slice it and dry it out for a few minutes in a low oven.

3 Preheat the oven to 350°F. Grease an 8-inch square baking dish with butter. Layer the bread rounds, almonds, raisins and cheese in the dish, pour on the syrup, letting it soak into the bread. Bake the pudding for about 30 minutes, until golden brown.

4 Remove from the oven, let stand for 5 minutes, then cut into squares. Serve cold, with cream poured on top and decorated with the extra sliced almonds.

DRUNKEN PLANTAINS

MEXICANS ENJOY THEIR NATIVE FRUITS AND UNTIL THEIR CUISINE WAS INFLUENCED BY THE SPANISH AND THE FRENCH, THEY HAD NO PASTRIES OR CAKES, PREFERRING TO END THEIR MEALS WITH FRUIT, WHICH WAS ABUNDANT. THIS DESSERT IS QUICK AND EASY TO PREPARE, AND TASTES DELICIOUS.

SERVES SIX

INGREDIENTS
3 ripe plantains
¼ cup butter, diced
3 tablespoons rum
grated zest and juice of
  1 small orange
1 teaspoon ground cinnamon
¼ cup dark brown sugar
½ cup whole almonds, in their skins
fresh mint sprigs, to decorate
Crème fraîche or thick heavy cream,
  to serve

1 Preheat the oven to 350°F. Peel the plantains and cut them in half lengthwise. Put the pieces in a shallow baking dish, dot them all over with butter, then spoon on the rum and orange juice.

2 Mix the orange zest, cinnamon and brown sugar in a bowl. Sprinkle the mixture on the plantains.

3 Bake for 25–30 minutes, until the plantains are soft and the sugar has melted into the rum and orange juice to form a sauce.

4 Meanwhile, slice the almonds and dry-fry them in a heavy frying pan until the cut sides are golden. Serve the plantains in individual bowls, with some of the sauce spooned on top. Sprinkle the almonds on top, decorate with the fresh mint sprigs and pass crème fraîche or heavy cream separately.

FRUIT PLATTER

MEXICANS LIKE TO EAT FRUIT WITH CHILE AND LIME AS AN APPETIZER OR HORS D'OEUVRE, BUT THE COMBINATION ALSO MAKES A REFRESHING END TO A MEAL. THE SELECTION OF FRUIT BELOW IS JUST A SUGGESTION; USE ANY FRUIT IN SEASON, BEARING IN MIND THAT THE AIM IS TO PRODUCE A COLORFUL PLATTER WITH PLENTY OF FLAVOR.

SERVES SIX

INGREDIENTS
  ½ small watermelon
  2 mangoes
  2 papayas
  1 small pineapple
  1 fresh coconut
  1 jicama
  juice of 2 limes, plus lime wedges,
    to serve
  sea salt
  mild red chili powder

1 Slice the watermelon thinly, then cut each slice into bite-size triangles, removing as many of the seeds as possible. Take a large slice off the pit on either side of each mango, then cross-hatch the mango flesh on each slice. Turn the slices inside out so that the cubes of mango flesh stand proud. Slice these off and put them in a bowl.

2 Cut the payayas in half, scoop out the seeds, then cut each half into wedges, leaving the skin on. Cut the leafy green top off the pineapple, then slice off the base. With a sharp knife, remove the skin, using a spiral action and cutting deeply enough to remove most of the "eyes." Use a small knife to take out any remaining "eyes." Cut the pineapple lengthwise in quarters and remove the core from the center of each piece. Slice each of the pieces into bite-size wedges.

3 Make a hole in two of the "eyes" at the top of the coconut, using a nail and hammer. Pour out the liquid. Tap the coconut with a hammer until it breaks into pieces. Remove the hard outer shell, then use a potato peeler to remove the thin brown layer. Cut the coconut into neat pieces.

4 Peel and slice the jicama. Arrange all the fruits on a platter, sprinkle them with lime juice and serve with lime wedges and small bowls of sea salt and chili powder for sprinkling.

COOK'S TIP
Cut all the fruit into bite-size pieces, so that it can be speared on toothpicks and eaten.

ICE CREAM WITH MEXICAN CHOCOLATE

THIS RICH, CREAMY ICE CREAM HAS A WONDERFULLY COMPLEX FLAVOR, THANKS TO THE CINNAMON AND ALMONDS IN THE MEXICAN CHOCOLATE.

SERVES FOUR

INGREDIENTS
  2 large eggs
  ½ cup sugar
  2 bars Mexican chocolate, total
    weight about 4 ounces
  1⅔ cups heavy cream
  scant 1 cup milk
  chocolate curls, to decorate

1 Put the eggs in a bowl and whisk them with an electric beater until they are thick, pale and fluffy. Gradually whisk in the sugar.

2 Melt the chocolate in a heavy saucepan over low heat, then add it to the egg mixture and mix thoroughly. Whisk in the cream, then stir in the milk, a little at a time. Cool the mixture, then chill. Pour the mixture into an ice cream maker and churn until thick.

3 Alternatively, freeze it in a shallow plastic box in the fast-freeze section of the freezer for several hours, until ice crystals have begun to form around the edges. Process to break up the ice crystals, then freeze again. To serve, decorate with chocolate curls.

GARBANZO CAKE

THIS IS A MOIST CAKE, WITH A TEXTURE LIKE THAT OF CHRISTMAS PUDDING. IT IS FLAVORED WITH ORANGE AND CINNAMON AND TASTES WONDERFUL IN THIN SLICES, WITH FRESH MANGO OR PINEAPPLE AND A SPOONFUL OF YOGURT. AS IT CONTAINS NO FLOUR, IT IS A GOOD CHOICE FOR ANYONE ON A WHEAT-FREE DIET.

SERVES SIX

INGREDIENTS

    2 x 10-ounce cans chickpeas,
       drained
    4 eggs, beaten
    1 cup sugar
    1 teaspoon baking powder
    2 teaspoons ground cinnamon
    grated zest and juice of 1 orange
    cinnamon sugar (see Cook's Tip),
       for sprinkling

COOK'S TIP

To make the cinnamon sugar, mix ¼ cup sugar with 1 teaspoon ground cinnamon.

1 Preheat the oven to 350°F. Tip the chickpeas in a colander, drain them thoroughly, then rub them between the palms of your hands to loosen and remove the skins. Put the skinned chickpeas in a food processor and process until smooth.

2 Spoon the purée into a bowl and stir in the eggs, sugar, baking powder, cinnamon, orange rind and juice. Grease and line a 1-pound loaf pan.

3 Pour the cake mixture into the loaf pan, level the surface and bake for about 1½ hours or until a skewer inserted into the center comes out clean.

4 Remove the cake from the oven and let stand, in the pan, for about 10 minutes. Remove from the pan, place on a wire rack and sprinkle with the cinnamon sugar. Let cool completely before serving. Try serving this with sliced fresh pineapple.

PECAN CAKE

THIS CAKE IS AN EXAMPLE OF THE FRENCH INFLUENCE ON MEXICAN COOKING. IT IS TRADITIONALLY SERVED WITH CAJETA—SWEETENED BOILED MILK—BUT WHIPPED CREAM OR CRÈME FRAÎCHE CAN BE USED INSTEAD. TRY SERVING THE CAKE WITH A FEW RED CURRANTS FOR A SPLASH OF COLOR.

SERVES EIGHT TO TEN

INGREDIENTS
    1 cup pecans
    ½ cup butter, softened
    ½ cup light brown sugar
    1 teaspoon vanilla extract
    4 large eggs, separated
    ¾ cup all-purpose flour
    pinch of salt
    12 whole pecans, to decorate
    cajeta, whipped cream or crème
      fraîche, to serve
For drizzling
    ¼ cup butter
    scant ½ cup honey

1 Preheat the oven to 350°F. Grease an 8-inch round spring-form cake pan. Toast the pecans in a dry frying pan for 5 minutes, shaking frequently. Grind finely into a blender or food processor. Place in a bowl.

2 Cream the butter with the sugar in a mixing bowl, then beat in the vanilla and egg yolks.

3 Add the flour to the ground nuts and mix well. Whisk the egg whites with the salt in a greasefree bowl until soft peaks form. Fold the whites into the butter mixture, then gently fold in the flour and nut mixture. Spoon the mixture into the prepared cake pan and bake for 30 minutes or until a skewer inserted in the center comes out clean.

4 Cool the cake in the pan for 5 minutes, then remove the sides of the pan. Stand the cake on a wire rack until cool.

5 Remove the cake from the bottom of the pan if necessary, then return it to the rack and arrange the pecans on top. Transfer to a plate. Melt the butter in a small pan, add the honey and bring to a boil, stirring. Lower the heat and simmer for 3 minutes. Pour onto the cake. Serve with *cajeta*, whipped cream or crème fraîche.

KINGS' DAY BREAD

ON TWELFTH NIGHT, JANUARY 6TH, MEXICAN CHILDREN RECEIVE GIFTS TO MARK THE DAY THE THREE KINGS BROUGHT GIFTS TO THE INFANT JESUS. THIS SWEETENED RICH BREAD, DECORATED WITH CANDIED FRUIT, IS AN IMPORTANT PART OF THE CELEBRATIONS. A DOLL AND A BEAN ARE HIDDEN INSIDE THE CAKE, AND THE PERSON WHO GETS THE DOLL HAS TO HOST A PARTY ON FEBRUARY 2ND, ANOTHER FEAST DAY. THE PERSON WHO FINDS THE BEAN BRINGS THE DRINKS.

SERVES EIGHT

INGREDIENTS
   ½ cup lukewarm water
   6 eggs
   2 teaspoons active dry yeast
   2½ cups all-purpose flour
   ½ teaspoon salt
   ¼ cup sugar
   ½ cup butter, plus 2 tablespoons
     melted butter, for glazing
   1½ cups crystallized fruit and
     candied peel
   1½ cups confectioners' sugar, plus
     extra, for dusting
   2 tablespoons light cream
   crystallized fruit and candied
     cherries, to decorate

1 Pour the water into a small bowl, stir in the dried yeast and set in a warm place until frothy.

2 Crack four of the eggs and divide the yolks and the whites. Place the four yolks in a small bowl and discard the egg whites.

3 Put 1¼ cups of the flour in a mixing bowl. Add the salt and sugar. Break the remaining two eggs into the bowl, then add the four egg yolks.

4 Add ½ cup of the butter to the bowl together with the yeast and water mixture. Combine all the ingredients well.

5 Put the crystallized fruit and peel into a separate bowl. Add ½ cup of the remaining flour and toss the fruit with the flour to coat it.

6 Add the floured fruit to the egg mixture, with the rest of the flour. Mix into a soft, non-sticky dough. Knead the dough on a lightly floured surface for about 10 minutes, until smooth.

7 Shape the dough into a ball. Using the floured handle of a wooden spoon, make a hole in the center, and enlarge.

8 Put the dough ring onto a greased baking sheet and cover lightly with oiled plastioc wrap. Set in a warm place for about 2 hours or until doubled in bulk.

9 Preheat the oven to 350°F. Brush the dough with the melted butter and bake for about 30 minutes or until it has risen well and is cooked through and springy.

10 Mix the confectioners' sugar and cream in a bowl. Drizzle the mixture on the bread when it is cool and decorate it with the crystallized fruit and candied cherries. Dust with confectioners' sugar.

PAN DULCE

THESE "SWEET BREADS" OF VARIOUS SHAPES ARE MADE THROUGHOUT MEXICO, AND ARE EATEN AS A SNACK OR WITH JAM OR MARMALADE FOR BREAKFAST.

MAKES TWELVE

INGREDIENTS
   ½ cup lukewarm milk
   2 teaspoons active dry yeast
   4 cups strong all-purpose flour
   6 tablespoons sugar
   2 tablespoons butter, softened
   4 large eggs, beaten
   oil, for greasing
For the topping
   6 tablespoons butter, softened
   ½ cup sugar
   1 egg yolk
   1 teaspoon ground cinnamon
   1 cup all-purpose flour

1 Pour the milk into a small bowl, stir in the dried yeast and set in a warm place until frothy.

2 Put the flour and sugar in a mixing bowl, add the butter and beaten eggs and mix into a soft, sticky dough.

3 Place the dough on a lightly floured surface and dredge it with more flour. Using floured hands, turn the dough over and over until it is completely covered in a light coating of flour. Cover it with lightly oiled plastic wrap and let rest for 20 minutes.

4 Meanwhile, make the topping. Cream the butter and sugar in a bowl, then mix in the egg yolk, cinnamon and flour. The mixture should have a slightly crumbly texture.

5 Divide the dough into 12 equal pieces and shape each of them into a round. Space well apart on greased baking sheets. Sprinkle the topping onto the breads, dividing it more or less equally among them, then press it lightly into the surface.

6 Set the rolls in a warm place to stand for about 30 minutes, until they are about one-and-a-half times their previous size. Preheat the oven to 400°F and bake the breads for about 15 minutes. Let cool slightly before serving.

ALMOND COOKIES

CONFECTIONERS' SUGAR AND BUTTER COMBINE TO GIVE THESE COOKIES A LIGHT, DELICATE TEXTURE. THEY CAN BE MADE DAYS IN ADVANCE, AND ARE DELICIOUS WITH DESSERTS OR COFFEE.

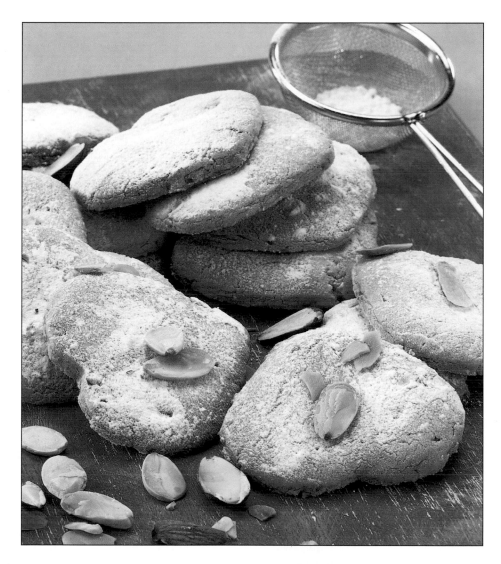

MAKES ABOUT TWENTY-FOUR

INGREDIENTS
    1 cup all-purpose flour
    1½ cups confectioners' sugar
    pinch of salt
    ½ cup chopped almonds
    ½ teaspoon almond extract
    ½ cup unsalted butter, softened
    confrectioners' sugar, for dusting
    halved almonds, to decorate

COOK'S TIPS
Use fancy cutters to make these cookies look even more interesting. Hearts and crescents are two shapes you might like to try.

2 Put the softened butter in the center of the flour mixture and use a knife or your fingertips to draw the dry ingredients into the butter until a dough is formed. Shape the dough into a ball.

3 Place the dough on a lightly floured surface and roll it out to a thickness of about ⅛ inch. Using a 3-inch cookie cutter, cut out about 24 rounds, re-rolling the dough as necessary. Place the rounds on baking sheets, leaving a little space between them. Bake for 25–30 minutes, until pale golden.

1 Preheat the oven to 350ºF. Combine the flour, confectioners' sugar, salt and chopped almonds in a bowl. Add the almond extract.

4 Let sit for 10 minutes, then transfer to wire racks to cool. Dust thickly with confectioners' sugar before serving, decorated with halved almonds.

MEXICAN WEDDING COOKIES

ALMOST HIDDEN BENEATH THEIR VEIL OF CONFECTIONERS' SUGAR, THESE LITTLE SHORTBREAD COOKIES ARE TRADITIONALLY SERVED AT WEDDINGS, AND ARE ABSOLUTELY DELICIOUS. SERVE THEM AFTER DINNER WITH COFFEE AND PERHAPS A GLASS OF THE MEXICAN COFFEE LIQUEUR—KAHLÚA.

MAKES THIRTY

INGREDIENTS
   1 cup butter, softened
   1½ cups confectioners' sugar
   1 teaspoon vanilla extract
   2¾ cups all-purpose flour
   pinch of salt
   1¼ cups pecans,
     finely chopped

1 Preheat the oven to 375°F. Beat the butter in a large bowl until it is light and fluffy, then beat in 1 cup of the confectioners' sugar, with the vanilla.

2 Gradually add the flour and salt to the creamed mixture until it starts to form a dough. Add the finely chopped pecans with the remaining flour. Knead the dough lightly.

3 Divide the dough into 30 equal pieces and roll them into balls. Space about ¼ inch apart on baking sheets. Press each ball lightly with your thumb to flatten it slightly.

4 Bake the cookies for 10–15 minutes, until they are starting to brown. Cool on the baking sheets for 10 minutes, then transfer to wire racks to cool completely.

5 Put the remaining confectioners' sugar in a bowl. Add a few cookies at a time, shaking them in the confectioners' sugar until they are heavily coated. Serve immediately or store in an airtight pan.

ALMOND ORANGE COOKIES

THE COMBINATION OF LARD AND ALMONDS GIVES THESE COOKIES A GREAT TEXTURE, SO THAT THEY MELT IN YOUR MOUTH. THEY ARE PERFECT WITH COFFEE OR HOT CHOCOLATE.

MAKES THIRTY-SIX

INGREDIENTS
   generous 1 cup lard
   generous ½ cup sugar
   2 eggs, beaten
   grated zest and juice of
     1 small orange
   1¾ cups all-purpose flour, sifted with
     1 teaspoon baking powder
   1¾ cups ground almonds
For dusting
   ½ cup confectioners' sugar
   1 teaspoon ground cinnamon

COOK'S TIP
If you can't be bothered to roll out the dough, just divide it into 36 pieces and roll each one into a ball. Place these on baking sheets and flatten each one into a cookie shape with a fork.

1 Preheat the oven to 400°F. Place the lard in a large bowl and beat with an electric beater until light and airy. Gradually beat in the sugar.

2 Continue to whisk the mixture while you add the eggs, orange rind and juice. Whisk for 3–4 more minutes, then stir in the flour mixture and ground almonds to form a dough.

3 Roll out the dough on a lightly floured surface until it is about ½ inch thick. Using cookie cutters, cut out 36 rounds, re-rolling the dough if necessary. Gently lift the rounds onto baking sheets.

4 Bake for about 10 minutes or until the cookies are golden. Let stand on the baking sheets for 10 minutes to cool and firm slightly.

5 Combine the confectioners' sugar and cinnamon. Put the mixture in a small sieve or tea strainer and dust the cookies well. Let cool completely.

FRUIT-FILLED EMPANADAS

*IMAGINE BITING THROUGH CRISP BUTTERY PASTRY TO DISCOVER A RICH FRUITY FILLING FLAVORED
WITH ORANGES AND CINNAMON. THESE ARE THE STUFF THAT DREAMS ARE MADE OF.*

MAKES TWELVE

INGREDIENTS
  2½ cups all-purpose flour
  2 tablespoons sugar
  scant ½ cup chilled butter, cubed
  1 egg yolk
  ice water (see method)
  milk, to glaze
  sugar, for sprinkling
  whole almonds and orange wedges,
    to serve
For the filling
  2 tablespoons butter
  3 ripe plantains, peeled and mashed
  ½ teaspoon ground cloves
  1 teaspoon ground cinnamon
  1⅓ cups raisins
  grated zest and juice of 2 oranges

1 Combine the flour and sugar in a
mixing bowl. Rub in the chilled cubes
of butter until the mixture resembles
fine bread crumbs.

2 Beat the egg yolk and add to the flour
mixture. Add ice water to make a
smooth dough. Shape it into a ball.

3 Melt the butter for the filling in a
saucepan. Add the plantains, cloves
and cinnamon and cook over medium
heat for 2–3 minutes. Stir in the raisins,
with the orange zest and juice. Lower
the heat so that the mixture barely
simmers. Cook for about 15 minutes,
until the raisins are plump and the
juice has evaporated. Set the mixture
aside to cool.

4 Preheat the oven to 400°F. Roll out
the pastry on a lightly floured surface.
Cut it into 4-inch rounds. Place the
rounds on a baking sheet and spoon
on a little of the filling. Dampen the
rim of the pastry rounds with water, fold
the pastry over the filling and crimp the
edges to seal.

5 Brush the empanadas with milk. Bake
them, in batches if necessary, for about
15 minutes or until they are golden.
Let cool a little, sprinkle with sugar and
serve warm, with whole almonds and
orange wedges.

COOK'S TIP
Use a little of the leftover egg white
instead of milk for glazing, if desired.

CHRISTMAS COOKIES <u>WITH</u> WALNUTS

AT CHRISTMAS TIME, THESE ARE INDIVIDUALLY WRAPPED IN SMALL SQUARES OF BRIGHTLY COLORED TISSUE PAPER AND ARRANGED IN LARGE BOWLS. FOLLOW THE MEXICANS' LEAD, AND TRANSFORM THEM INTO GIFTS BY WRAPPING FIVE OR SIX AT A TIME IN CELLOPHANE AND TYING THE PACKAGES WITH COLORED RIBBONS.

MAKES TWENTY-FOUR

INGREDIENTS
½ cup lard
¾ cup confectioners' sugar
1 teaspoon vanilla extract
1¼ cups all-purpose flour
¾ cup broken walnuts,
  finely chopped
½ cup confectioners' sugar
2 teaspoons ground cinnamon

COOK'S TIP
Polvo means "dust," and these cookies should be crumbly and light to eat. Pecans can be used instead of the walnuts, if desired

1 Preheat the oven to 375°F. Place the lard in a large bowl and beat with an electric beater until light and airy.

2 Gradually beat in ¼ cup of the confectioners' sugar, then add the vanilla and beat well.

3 Add the flour by hand, working it gently into the mixture. Do not be tempted to use a spoon or the mixture will be too sticky. Add the walnuts and mix carefully.

4 Divide the dough evenly into 24 small pieces, roll each to a ball, and space well apart on baking sheets. Bake for 10–15 minutes, until golden, switching the baking sheets around halfway through, to ensure even baking. Cool the cookies on wire racks.

5 Put the remaining confectioners' sugar in a bowl and stir in the cinnamon. Add a few cookies at a time, shaking them in the confectioners' sugar until they are heavily coated. Shake off the excess sugar. Serve wrapped in colored paper.

DRINKS

Mexicans have some great means of slaking thirst, from refreshing fruit drinks to rich, satisfying hot chocolate. The traditional drink—pulque—which is made from the pressed juice of the century plant, is very much an acquired taste, but tequila has become popular all over the world, either enjoyed straight, in the traditional way, or as the basis for some wonderful drinks, such as margaritas and bloody Marias.

Fruity agua frescas, sold at stalls by street traders throughout Mexico, are the perfect antidote to hot weather. Like licuados and preparados, they are simple and quick to prepare and make a welcome change from the ultra-sweet sodas that are so popular in Europe.

A jug of Lime Agua Fresca is the perfect way to welcome guests on a warm summer's evening.

Mexican chocolate typically contains almonds and cinnamon, two ingredients that are widely used in Mexican cooking, and the milky hot chocolate drinks are absolutely delicious. Corn-based drinks and coffee laced with cinnamon are enjoyed with meals or served as substitutes for snacks.

Rompope, the thick, creamy Mexican eggnog, tastes much more innocent than it should, and is a wonderful way to unwind at the end of a stressful day.

TEQUILA

THERE ARE SEVERAL DIFFERENT TYPES OF TEQUILA, MEXICO'S NATIONAL SPIRIT. EACH TYPE OF TEQUILA IS AVAILABLE IN SEVERAL DIFFERENT BRANDS, EACH WITH A DISTINCTIVE FLAVOR INFLUENCED BY THE SOIL TYPE, SUGAR CONTENT OF THE AGAVE PLANTS, CLIMATE, COOKING AND FERMENTING PROCESS.

There are many different ways of serving tequila. Perhaps the best known of these is the slammer, when shots of chilled tequila are drunk with salt and lime. *Joven* (young) or *reposada* (rested) tequila is often served at room temperature in small shot glasses called *caballitos*, and sipped slowly so that all the flavors can be savoured. *Anejo* (aged) tequila should be served in a small balloon glass (a large glass would allow too much of the aroma to escape). It can be diluted with a little water, but ice should not be added.

TEQUILA SLAMMERS

Mexicans have long enjoyed the taste of lime and salt with their food and drink. Beer is also drunk with lime and salt.

INGREDIENTS
  chilled tequila
  salt
  wedges of lime

HOW TO SERVE TEQUILA

Pour a shot glass of tequila. Lick the space between the thumb and the index finger on your left hand, then sprinkle this area with salt. Taking care not to spill the salt, hold a lime wedge in the same hand. Pick up the shot glass in your right hand. Lick the salt, down the tequila in one, suck the lime, then slam down your empty glass. Some drinkers manage salt, lime and tequila in the same hand, but this takes practice.

TEQUILA SUNRISE

THIS DRINK TAKES ITS NAME FROM THE WAY THE GRENADINE—A BRIGHT RED CORDIAL MADE FROM POMEGRANATE JUICE—FIRST SINKS IN THE GLASS OF ORANGE JUICE AND THEN RISES TO THE SURFACE.

SERVES ONE

INGREDIENTS
 1½ tablespoons golden tequila
 ¼ cup freshly squeezed
  orange juice
 juice of 1 lime
 1 teaspoon grenadine

1 Half fill a cocktail glass with crushed ice. Pour in the tequila, then the orange and lime juices, which should be freshly squeezed. Don't be tempted to use concentrated orange juice from a carton or bottled lime juice, or the flavor of the finished drink will be spoiled.

2 Quickly add the grenadine, pouring it down the back of a teaspoon held in the glass so that it sinks to the bottom of the drink. Serve immediately.

VARIATION
To make a Pink Cadillac, use Grand Marnier instead of orange juice.

PINEAPPLE TEQUILA

FLAVORS SUCH AS ALMONDS OR QUINCE HAVE BEEN ADDED TO BLANCO OR REPOSADA TEQUILA FOR SOME TIME. MANY BARS HAVE DEVELOPED UNIQUE FLAVORS BY COMBINING INGREDIENTS SUCH AS CHILES WITH BLANCO TEQUILA AND LETTING THEM SIT FOR A PERIOD OF TIME. THE METHOD BELOW WILL MAKE A SMOOTH FRUITY DRINK.

SERVES SIX

INGREDIENTS
- 1 large pineapple
- 2 ounces dark brown sugar
- 1 litre blanco tequila
- 1 vanilla bean

1 Rinse a large (about 3½-pint) wide-necked bottle or demijohn and sterilize by placing it in an oven and then turning on the oven and setting it at 225°F. After 20 minutes remove the bottle from the oven with oven mitts and let cool.

2 Cut the top off the pineapple and then cut off the skin, being careful to get rid of all the scales. Cut in half, remove the hard centre core and discard it. Chop the rest of the pineapple into chunks, ensuring that they are small enough to fit in the bottle neck.

3 When the bottle is completely cold, put the pineapple into the bottle. Combine the sugar and tequila in a pitcher until the sugar dissolves and then pour into the bottle. Split the vanilla bean and add it to the rest of the ingredients.

4 Gently agitate the bottle a few times each day to stir the contents. Let the tequila stand for at least 1 week before drinking. When all the tequila has been drunk, the pineapple can be used in desserts such as ice cream or warmed with butter and cinnamon and served with cream.

VARIATION
If desired, add a piece of fresh pineapple and some ice to each glass before serving.

MARGARITA

THE MOST RENOWNED TEQUILA COCKTAIL, THIS CAN BE SERVED OVER ICE CUBES OR "FROZEN"—
MIXED WITH CRUSHED ICE IN A COCKTAIL SHAKER TO CREATE A LIQUID SORBET EFFECT,
THEN POURED INTO THE GLASS.

SERVES ONE

INGREDIENTS
  3 tablespoons tequila
  1½ tablespoons triple sec
  1½ tablespoons freshly squeezed
    lime juice
crushed ice or ice cubes
lime wedge and salt, for
  frosting glass

COOK'S TIP
White tequila is the traditional spirit to
use, but today many people prefer to
make margaritas with reposada tequila,
which gives a more rounded flavor.

1 Frost a cocktail glass by rubbing the
outer rim with the wedge of lime. Dip
the glass in a saucer of salt so that it is
evenly coated. It is important that there
is no salt inside the glass, so take care
that lime juice is only applied to the
outer rim.

2 Combine the tequila, triple sec and
lime juice in a cocktail shaker, add
crushed ice, if using, and shake to mix.
Carefully pour into the frosted glasses.
If crushed ice is not used, place ice
cubes in the glass and then pour in
the mixture.

MANGO AND PEACH MARGARITA

ADDING PURÉED FRUIT TO THE CLASSIC TEQUILA MIXTURE ALTERS THE CONSISTENCY AND MAKES FOR
A GLORIOUS DRINK THAT RESEMBLES A MILKSHAKE BUT PACKS CONSIDERABLY MORE PUNCH.

SERVES FOUR

INGREDIENTS

   2 mangoes, peeled and sliced
   3 peaches, peeled and sliced
   ½ cup tequila
   ¼ cup triple sec
   ¼ cup freshly squeezed
     lime juice
   10 ice cubes, crushed, if necessary
    (see Cook's Tip)
mango slices, skin on, to decorate

COOK'S TIP
Check that your processor or blender can
be used for crushing ice. If you are not
sure, break ice cubes into smaller pieces
by putting them in a strong plastic bag
and pounding them with a meat mallet.

1 Place the mango and peach slices in
a food processor or blender. Process or
blend until all the fruit is finely chopped,
scrape down the sides of the goblet,
then blend again until the purée is
perfectly smooth.

2 Add the tequila, triple sec and lime
juice, process or blend for a few
seconds, then add the ice. Process or
blend again until the drink has the
consistency of a milkshake.

3 Pour into cocktail glasses, decorate
with the mango slices and serve.

LICUADO DE MELON

AMONG THE MOST REFRESHING DRINKS MEXICANS MAKE ARE FRUIT EXTRACTS MIXED WITH HONEY AND CHILLED WATER.

SERVES FOUR

INGREDIENTS
  1 watermelon
  4 cups chilled water
  juice of 2 limes
  honey (see method)
  ice cubes, to serve

1 Cut the watermelon flesh into chunks, cutting off the skin and discarding the shiny black seeds.

2 Place the chunks in a large bowl, pour in the chilled water and let stand for 10 minutes.

3 Transfer the mixture to a large sieve set over a bowl. Using a wooden spoon, press gently on the fruit to extract all the liquid.

4 Stir in the lime juice and sweeten to taste with honey.

5 Pour into a pitcher, add ice cubes and stir. Serve in glasses.

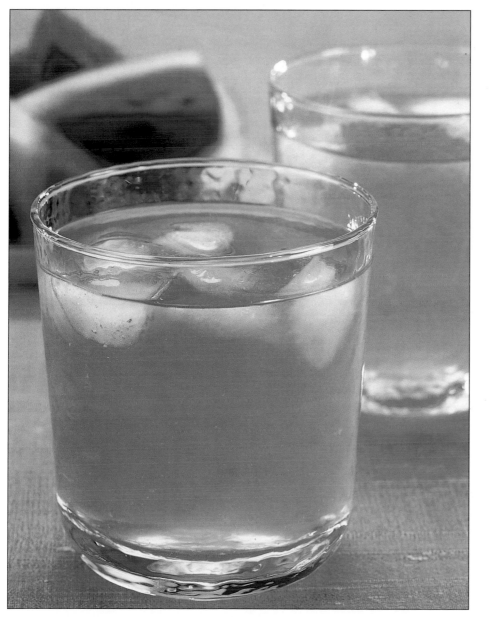

SANGRITA

SIPPING SANGRITA AND TEQUILA ALTERNATELY IS A TASTE SENSATION NOT TO BE MISSED, THE WARM
FLAVORS OF THE FIRST BALANCING THE HARSHNESS OF THE SECOND. THE DRINKS ARE OFTEN SERVED
WITH ANTOJITOS (NIBBLES) AS AN APPETIZER COMBO.

SERVES EIGHT

INGREDIENTS
  1 pound ripe tomatoes
  1 small onion, finely chopped
  2 small fresh green fresno chiles,
    seeded and chopped
  ½ cup juice from freshly
    squeezed oranges
  juice of 3 limes
  ½ teaspoon sugar
  pinch of salt
  1 small shot glass of golden or aged
    tequila per person

1 Cut a cross in the bottom of each
tomato. Place the tomatoes in a
heatproof bowl and pour in boiling water
to cover. Let sit for 3 minutes.

2 Lift the tomatoes out on a slotted
spoon and plunge them into a second
bowl of cold water. The skins will have
begun to peel back from the crosses.
Remove the skins, then cut the
tomatoes in half and scoop out the
seeds with a teaspoon.

3 Chop the tomato flesh and put in a
food processor. Add the onion, chiles,
orange juice, lime juice, sugar and salt.

4 Process until all the mixture is very
smooth, then pour into a pitcher and
chill for at least 1 hour before serving.
Offer each drinker a separate shot
glass of tequila as well. The drinks are
sipped alternately.

COOK'S TIP
This drink can be made with a 14-ounce
can of chopped tomatoes and tastes
almost as good as when made with
fresh tomatoes.

SANGRIA

TESTAMENT TO THE SPANISH INFLUENCE ON MEXICAN COOKING, THIS POPULAR THIRST-QUENCHER IS
OFTEN SERVED IN LARGE PITCHERS, WITH ICE AND CITRUS FRUIT SLICES FLOATING ON TOP.

SERVES SIX

INGREDIENTS
  3 cups dry red wine
  juice of 2 limes
  ½ cup freshly squeezed orange juice
  ½ cup brandy
  ¼ cup sugar
  1 lime, sliced, to decorate
  ice, to serve

VARIATION
In some parts of Mexico a less potent
but equally refreshing version of sangria
is served. Fill tall glasses with ice. Fill
each glass two-thirds full with fresh lime
juice diluted with water and sweetened
with sugar. Fill up with red wine. Tequila
is sometimes added to the lime mixture.

1 Combine the wine, lime juice, orange
juice and brandy in a large glass pitcher.

COOK'S TIP
If no sugar is available, use sugar syrup.
Heat ¼ cup sugar in ¼ cup water. Boil
for 3 minutes, chill and store in a tightly
sealed jar.

2 Stir in the sugar until it has dissolved
completely.

3 Serve in tall glasses with ice. Decorate
each glass with a slice of lime.

CITRUS AGUA FRESCA

THESE REFRESHING FRUIT JUICES ARE SOLD AT STREET STALLS IN TOWNS ALL OVER MEXICO.
THE VARIETIES OF FRUIT USED CHANGE WITH THE SEASONS.

SERVES FOUR

INGREDIENTS
    12 limes
    3 oranges
    2 grapefruit
    2½ cups water
    6 tablespoons sugar
    extra fruit wedges, to decorate
    ice cubes, to serve

1 Squeeze the juice from the limes, oranges and grapefruit. Some fruit pulp may collect along with the juice. This should also be used, once any seeds have been discarded. Pour the mixture into a large pitcher.

2 Add the water and sugar and stir until all the sugar has dissolved.

3 Chill for at least 1 hour before serving with ice and fruit wedges. The drink will keep for up to 1 week in a covered container in the refrigerator.

VARIATION
Use pink or ruby red grapefruit instead of white for a slightly sweeter drink with a deeper color.

TAMARIND AGUA FRESCA

TAMARIND, SOMETIMES REFERRED TO AS THE INDIAN DATE, IS NATIVE TO ASIA AND NORTH AFRICA. SEEDS CAME TO MEXICO VIA INDIA. IT IS USED MEDICINALLY AND AS AN ANTISEPTIC. THE FRUIT HAS A SWEET-SOUR TASTE AND MAKES A DRINK SIMILAR TO LEMONADE.

SERVES FOUR

INGREDIENTS
4 cups water
8 ounces tamarind pods
2 tablespoons sugar
ice cubes, to serve

COOK'S TIP
Jars of tamarind pulp or paste are sold at Indian and Asian food stores. The dried pulp is also sold in solid blocks. All these products need soaking and sieving, but you will be spared the time-consuming task of peeling the pods.

1 Pour the water into a saucepan and heat until warm. Remove from heat and pour into a bowl. Peel the tamarind pods and add the pulp to the warm water. Soak for at least 4 hours.

2 Place a sieve over a clean bowl. Pour the tamarind pulp and water into the sieve, then press the pulp through the sieve with the back of a wooden spoon, leaving the black seeds behind. Discard the seeds.

3 Add the sugar to the tamarind mixture and stir well until dissolved. Pour into a pitcher and chill thoroughly before serving in tumblers filled with ice.

PINEAPPLE ᴬᴺᴰ LIME AGUA FRESCA

THE VIVID COLORS OF THIS FRESH FRUIT DRINK GIVE SOME INDICATION OF ITS WONDERFUL FLAVOR.
IT MAKES A DELICIOUS MIDDAY REFRESHER OR PICK-ME-UP AT THE END OF A HARD DAY.

SERVES FOUR

INGREDIENTS
    2 pineapples
    juice of 2 limes
    2 cups still mineral water
    ¼ cup sugar
    ice cubes, to serve

COOK'S TIP
When peeling a pineapple cut off the top and bottom and remove the skin with a spiral action, cutting deeply enough to remove most of the "eyes." Any remaining "eyes" can be cut out using a small knife.

1 Peel the pineapples and chop the flesh, removing the core and "eyes." You should have about 1 pound flesh. Put this in a food processor or blender and add the lime juice and half the mineral water. Purée into a smooth pulp. Stop the machine and scrape the mixture from the side of the goblet once or twice during processing.

2 Place a sieve over a large bowl. Put the pineapple pulp in the sieve and press it through with a wooden spoon. Pour the sieved mixture into a large pitcher, cover and chill in the refrigerator for about 1 hour.

3 Stir in the remaining mineral water and sugar to taste. Serve with ice.

LIME AGUA FRESCA

THIS IS THE LIME VERSION OF REAL ENGLISH LEMONADE. TRADITIONALLY, LIME PEEL WOULD HAVE BEEN GROUND IN A MOLCAJETE TO EXTRACT THE OIL. MEXICAN LIMES—LIMONES—ARE HARDER AND MORE TART THAN THE SMOOTH-SKINNED VARIETIES MOST OFTEN SOLD AT WESTERN SUPERMARKETS.

SERVES SIX

INGREDIENTS
    7½ cups water
    6 tablespoons sugar
    10 limes, plus slices, to decorate
    ice cubes, to serve

1 Pour the water into a large pitcher, add the sugar and stir until all the sugar has dissolved. Chill for at least 1 hour.

2 Using a zester or grater, remove the zest from the limes, taking care to take only the colored zest, not the pith. Squeeze the juice from the limes and add this to the chilled sugar water, with the lime rind. Stir well and chill again until needed. Serve with ice in tall glasses, decorated with lime slices.

COOK'S TIP
To extract the maximum amount of juice from the limes, roll firmly between your palms for a few moments, or pierce with a skewer, put in a bowl, and microwave on maximum power for 10–15 seconds before juicing. This works with all citrus fruits.

STRAWBERRY <u>AND</u> BANANA PREPARADO

SIMILAR TO A SMOOTHIE, THIS IS A THICK, CREAMY FRUIT DRINK. LEAVE OUT THE ALCOHOL IF DESIRED.

SERVES FOUR

INGREDIENTS
2 cups strawberries, plus extra,
  to decorate
2 bananas
4 ounces coconut milk
½ cup water
¾ cup white rum
¼ cup grenadine
10 ice cubes

1 Hull the strawberries and chop them in halves or quarters if they are large fruits. Peel the bananas and chop them into rough chunks.

2 Put the fruit in a food processor or blender, crumble in the coconut and add the water. Process until smooth, scraping down the sides of the goblet as necessary.

3 Add the rum, grenadine, and ice cubes, crushing the ice first unless you have a heavy-duty processor. Blend until smooth and thick. Serve immediately, decorated with the extra strawberries.

BLOODY MARIA

A NATURAL PROGRESSION FROM SANGRITA, THIS SIMPLE COCKTAIL CONSISTS OF TEQUILA AND TOMATO JUICE COMBINED AND SERVED IN THE SAME GLASS.

SERVES TWO

INGREDIENTS

   1 cup tomato juice, chilled
   1 teaspoon Worcestershire sauce
   4 tablespoons tequila
   few drops of Tabasco sauce
   juice of ½ lemon
   pinch of celery salt
   salt and ground black pepper
   ice cubes and 2 celery stalks, cut
     into sticks, to serve

1 Pour the chilled tomato juice into a large pitcher and stir in the tequila. Add the Worcestershire sauce and stir the mixture well.

2 Add a few drops of Tabasco sauce and the lemon juice. Taste and season with celery salt, salt and pepper. Serve over ice cubes, with celery sticks.

CAFE CON LECHE

*MANY MEXICANS START THE DAY WITH THIS SPICED MILKY COFFEE, AND THOSE WHO HAVE
ENJOYED A HEARTY MIDDAY MEAL WILL OFTEN OPT FOR A CUP OF IT WITH A PASTRY AS THE
AFTERNOON MERIENDA.*

SERVES FOUR

INGREDIENTS
⅔ cup ground coffee
2 cups boiling water
2 cups milk
4 cinnamon sticks, each about
4 inches long
sugar, to taste

1 Put the ground coffee in a cafetière or pitcher, pour on the boiling water and let sit for a few minutes until the coffee grounds settle at the bottom.

2 Push down the plunger of the cafetière or strain the pitcher of coffee to separate the liquid from the grounds. Pour the strained coffee into a clean pitcher.

3 Pour the milk into a heavy pan, add the cinnamon sticks and bring to a boil, stirring occasionally.

4 Using a slotted spoon, lift out the cinnamon sticks and use a smaller spoon to press down on them to release any liquid they have absorbed. Set the cinnamon sticks aside for serving.

5 Add the coffee to the hot milk, then pour into cups. Add a cinnamon stick to each cup. Drinkers should add sugar to taste as needed.

HORCHATA

*THIS DELICIOUS, AROMATIC RICE DRINK TASTES WONDERFULLY CREAMY, YET DOES NOT CONTAIN A
DROP OF MILK. MEXICANS SWEAR BY IT AS A MEANS OF SETTLING UPSET STOMACHS OR CURING
HANGOVERS, AND IT IS OFTEN SERVED AT BREAKFAST.*

SERVES FOUR

INGREDIENTS
2¼ cups long-grain rice
3 cups water
1¼ cups blanched whole almonds
2 teaspoons ground cinnamon
finely grated zest of 1 lime, plus
strips of zest, to decorate
¼ cup sugar
ice cubes, to serve

1 Put the rice in a sieve and rinse thoroughly under cold running water. Drain, transfer to a large bowl and pour in the water. Cover and soak for at least 2 hours, preferably overnight.

2 Drain the rice, reserving 2½ cups of the soaking liquid. Spoon the rice into a food processor or blender and grind as finely as possible.

3 Add the almonds to the processor or blender and continue to grind in the same way until finely ground.

4 Add the cinnamon, grated lime zest and sugar to the ground rice and ground almonds. Add the reserved soaking water from the rice and mix until all the sugar has dissolved.

5 Serve in tall glasses with ice cubes. Decorate with strips of lime rind.

CAFE DE OLLA

THIS IS ONE OF THE MOST POPULAR DRINKS IN MEXICO. THE NAME MEANS "OUT OF THE POT," WHICH REFERS TO THE CONTAINER IN WHICH THE COFFEE IS MADE. TRADITIONALLY, THE SWEETENER IS PILONCILLO, THE LOCAL UNREFINED BROWN SUGAR, BUT ANY DARK BROWN SUGAR CAN BE USED. THIS COFFEE IS ALWAYS DRUNK BLACK.

SERVES FOUR

INGREDIENTS
   4 cups water
   ½ cup *piloncillo* or dark brown sugar
   4 cinnamon sticks, each about
     6 inches long
   ⅔ cup freshly ground coffee, from
     dark-roast coffee beans

COOK'S TIP
If you do not have a fine sieve, improvise with a regular sieve lined with coffee filter paper. For a special occasion serve the coffee with chocolate-dipped cinnamon sticks, which can be used to stir with.

1 Place the water, sugar and cinnamon sticks in a saucepan. Heat gently, stirring occasionally to make sure that the sugar dissolves, then bring to a boil. Boil rapidly for about 20 minutes, until the syrup has reduced by a quarter.

2 Add the ground coffee to the syrup and stir well, then bring the liquid back to the boil. Remove from the heat, cover the pan and let stand for around 5 minutes.

3 Strain the coffee through a fine sieve, pour into cups and serve immediately.

ATOLE

THIS DRINK, WHICH IS MADE FROM WHITE CORN MASA, IS TRADITIONALLY FLAVORED WITH PILONCILLO (MEXICAN UNREFINED BROWN SUGAR) AND GROUND CINNAMON. IT HAS THE CONSISTENCY OF A THICK MILKSHAKE. FRESH FRUIT PURÉES ARE OFTEN ADDED BEFORE SERVING, AND SOME RECIPES INTRODUCE GROUND ALMONDS OR MILK.

SERVES SIX

INGREDIENTS
   1¾ cups white *masa harina*
   5 cups water
   1 vanilla bean
   ¼ cup *piloncillo* or dark
     brown sugar
   ½ teaspoon ground cinnamon
   1 cup fresh strawberries, chopped
     pineapple or orange segments
     (optional)

1 Put the *masa harina* in a heavy saucepan and gradually beat in the water to make a smooth paste.

2 Place the pan over medium heat add the vanilla bean and bring the mixture to a boil, stirring constantly until it thickens. Beat in the sugar and ground cinnamon and continue to beat until the sugar has dissolved. Remove from heat.

3 If adding the fruit, purée it in a food processor or blender until smooth, then press the purée through a sieve.

4 Stir the purée into the corn mixture and return to the heat until warmed through. Remove the vanilla bean. Serve.

AFTER-DINNER COFFEE

A SUPERB END TO A MEAL. KAHLÚA, THE MEXICAN COFFEE LIQUEUR USED IN THIS DRINK, IS ALSO DELICIOUS SERVED IN A LIQUEUR GLASS AND TOPPED WITH A THIN LAYER OF CREAM.

1 Put the ground coffee in a heatproof pitcher or cafetière, pour on the boiling water and let sit until the coffee grounds settle at the bottom.

2 Strain the coffee through a sieve or push down the plunger in the lid of the cafetière to separate the liquid from the grounds. Pour the strained coffee into a clean heatproof pitcher.

3 Add the tequila, Kahlúa and vanilla to the coffee and stir well to mix. Add the sugar and continue to stir until it has dissolved completely.

4 Pour the mixture into small coffee cups, liqueur coffee glasses or tall glasses that will withstand the heat of the coffee.

SERVES FOUR

INGREDIENTS
⅓ cup dark-roast ground coffee
2 cups boiling water
½ cup tequila
½ cup Kahlúa liqueur
1 teaspoon vanilla extract
2 tablespoons dark brown sugar
⅔ cup heavy cream

VARIATIONS
If you prefer, you can use Tia Maria instead of Kahlúa, or even a chocolate liqueur.

5 Hold a teaspoon just above the surface of one of the coffees. Pour the cream very slowly down the back of the spoon so that it forms a pool on top of the coffee. Repeat with the remaining coffees. Serve immediately.

ROMPOPE

LEGEND HAS IT THAT THIS RICH EGGNOG WAS FIRST MADE IN THE KITCHENS OF A CONVENT IN PUEBLA. SOME VERSIONS ARE THICKENED WITH GROUND ALMONDS OR SERVED WITH FRESH BERRIES SUCH AS RASPBERRIES. IT IS TRADITIONAL TO SEAL BOTTLES OF ROMPOPE WITH ROLLED CORN HUSKS OR STRIPPED EARS OF CORN.

MAKES 6¼ CUPS

INGREDIENTS
- 4 cups milk
- 1½ cups sugar
- ½ teaspoon baking soda
- 1 cinnamon stick, about 6 inches
- 12 large egg yolks
- 1¼ cups dark rum

4 Return the mixture to a clean pan, place over low heat and cook until the mixture thickens and the back of the spoon is visible when a finger is drawn along it.

5 Stir in the rum, pour into sterilized bottles and seal tightly with stoppers or plastic wrap. Chill until needed. Serve *rompope* very cold. It will keep for up to 1 week in the refrigerator.

1 Pour the milk into a saucepan and stir in the sugar and baking soda. Add the cinnamon stick. Place the pan over medium heat and bring the mixture to a boil, stirring constantly. Immediately pour the mixture into a bowl and cool to room temperature. Remove the cinnamon stick, squeezing it gently to release any liquid.

2 Put the egg yolks in a heatproof bowl over a pan of simmering water and whisk until the mixture is very thick and pale.

3 Add the whisked yolks to the milk mixture a little at a time, beating after each addition.

CHAMPURRADA

THIS POPULAR VERSION OF ATOLE IS MADE WITH MEXICAN CHOCOLATE. A SPECIAL WOODEN WHISK CALLED A MOLINOLLO IS TRADITIONALLY USED WHEN MAKING THIS FROTHY DRINK.

SERVES SIX

INGREDIENTS
  4 ounces Mexican chocolate, about
    2 discs
  5 cups water or milk, or a mixture
  7 ounces white *masa harina*
  2 tablespoons dark brown sugar

COOK'S TIP
If you can't find Mexican chocolate, improvise by mixing 4 ounces dark bitter chocolate (minimum 70 percent cocoa solids) with ¼ cup ground almonds, ¼ cup sugar and 2 teaspoons ground cinnamon in a food processor. Process until a fine powder is obtained.

1 Put the chocolate in a mortar and grind with a pestle until it becomes a fine powder. Alternatively, grind the chocolate in a food processor.

2 Put the liquid in a heavy saucepan and gradually stir in all the *masa harina* until a smooth paste is formed. Use a traditional wooden *molinollo*, if you have one, or a wire whisk for a frothier drink.

3 Place the pan over medium heat and bring the mixture to a boil, stirring constantly until the frothy drink thickens.

4 Stir in the ground chocolate, then add the sugar. Serve immediately.

MEXICAN HOT CHOCOLATE

MEXICAN CHOCOLATE IS FLAVORED WITH ALMONDS, CINNAMON AND VANILLA, AND IS SWEETENED WITH SUGAR. ALL THE INGREDIENTS ARE CRUSHED TOGETHER IN A SPECIAL MORTAR, AND HEATED OVER COALS. THE POWDERED MIXTURE IS THEN SHAPED INTO DISKS. MAKING THE CHOCOLATE IS DIFFICULT BUT FORTUNATELY THE DISKS CAN BE BOUGHT AT SPECIALTY STORES.

SERVES FOUR

INGREDIENTS
  4 cups milk
  2–4 ounces Mexican chocolate
    (1–2 disks)
  1 vanilla bean

VARIATION
If you prefer, you can use dark bitter chocolate instead of Mexican chocolate. You will need slightly less, as the flavor will be more intense.

1 Pour the milk into a saucepan and add the chocolate. Precisely how much to use will depend on personal taste. Start with one disk and use more next time if necessary.

2 Split the vanilla bean lengthwise using a sharp knife, and add it to the milk.

3 Heat the chocolate milk gently, stirring until all the chocolate has dissolved, then whisking with a wire whisk or a *molinollo* until the mixture boils. Remove the vanilla bean and divide the drink among four mugs or heatproof glasses. Serve immediately.

INDEX